Finance Markets, the New Economy and Growth

Edited by
LUIGI PAGANETTO
University of Rome 'Tor Vergata', Italy

ASHGATE

Published by
Ashgate Publishing Limited
Gower House
Croft Road
Aldershot
Hants GU11 3HR
England

Ashgate Publishing Company
Suite 420
101 Cherry Street
Burlington, VT 05401-4405
USA

Ashgate website: http://www.ashgate.com

British Library Cataloguing in Publication Data
Finance markets, the new economy and growth
1. Finance 2.Economic development
I. Paganetto, Luigi
332'.09051

Library of Congress Control Number: 2005929794

ISBN-10: 0 7546 4236 4

Printed and bound in Great Britain by MPG Books Ltd, Bodmin, Cornwall

FINANCE MARKETS, THE NEW ECONOMY AND GROWTH

Contents

List of Figures

List of Tables

List of Contributors

Fabrizio ADRIANI has a PhD in Economics from the University of Rome, Tor Vergata. Recent publications include: 'Do High-Tech Stock Prices Revert to Their Fundamental Value?' with L. Becchetti in *Applied Financial Economics*, 2004; and 'Fair Trade: a third generation welfare mechanism to make globalisation sustainable', with L. Becchetti, in *Dissecting Globalisation*, 2004.

Leonardo BECCHETTI has a PhD in Economics from the University of Oxford and an MSc in Economics from The London School of Economics. He is currently Professor in the Faculty of Economics at the University of Rome, Tor Vergata. Recent publications include: 'The determinants of suboptimal technological development in the System Company-Component Producers relationship', with L. Paganetto, in *International Journal of Industrial Organisation*, 2001; 'The positive effect of industrial district on export performance of Italian firms', with L. Rossi, in *The Review of Industrial Organisation*, 2000; 'The First Shall Be Last', with M. Bagella and A. Carpentieri, in *Journal of Banking and Finance*, 2000; and 'Finance, Investment and Innovation: a Three Pillars Approach based on *a priori* identification, direct revelation and econometric estimation', with M. Bagella and C. Caggese, in *Research in Economics*, 2000.

Michele BOLDRIN is Professor of de America Latina at the *Fundacion BBVA* in Madrid and Professor of Economics in the Department of Economics at the University of Minnesota. He has served as an advisor to various international agencies and governments. Recent publications include: the ER Lawrence Klein Lecture 'The Case Against Intellectual Monopoly', with D.K. Levine, in *International Economic Review*, 2004; and *Against Intellectual Monopoly*, with D.K. Levine, forthcoming.

Robert E. CARPENTER is Professor of courses in Industrial Organization, Corporate Finance, International Corporate Finance, Intermediate Macroeconomics, and Principles of Microeconomics, at the University of Maryland, Baltimore County. Recent publications include: 'Is the Growth of Small Firms Constrained by Internal Finance?' with Bruce Petersen, in *Review of Economics and Statistics*, 2002; and 'Seasonal Cycles, Business Cycles, and the Comovement of Inventory Investment and Output', with Daniel Levy, in the *Journal of Money, Credit, and Banking*, 1998.

Giovanni FERRI is Professor of Economics at the University of Bari. Recent publications include: 'More Analysts, Better Ratings: Do Rating Agencies Invest Enough in Less Developed Countries?', in the *Journal of Applied Economics*, 2004; 'How Do Global Credit-Rating Agencies Rate Firms from Developing Countries?', with L. Liu, in *Asian Economic Papers*, 2003; and 'The Macroeconomic Impact of Bank Capital Requirements in Emerging Economies: Past Evidence to Assess the Future', with M.C. Chiuri and G. Majnoni, in the *Journal of Banking and Finance*, 2002.

Jean-Paul FITOUSSI is Professor at the Universités à l'Institut d'Etudes Politiques in Paris. He has been President of the Conseil Scientifique de l'IEP de Paris since 1997 and is President of l'OFCE, Observatoire Français des Conjonctures Economiques. Recent publications include: 'La democrazia e il mercato, Feltrinelli', 2004; 'Ségregation urbaine et integration sociale', with Eloi Laurent and Joel Maurice, Les rapports du Conseil d'Analyses Economique, La Documentation Francaise, 2004; 'Rapport sur l'Etat de l'Union Européenne', 2004, dir. J.P. Fitoussi and J. Le Cacheux, 2003.

Jean-Luc GAFFARD is Professor of Economics at the University of Nice-Sophia Antipolis and at the Institut Universitaire de France. Recent publications include: 'Technological Shocks and the Conduct of Monetary Policy', with M. Amendola and F. Saraceno, in *Revue Economique*, 2004; 'Wage Flexibility and Unemployment: the Keynesian Perspective Revisited', with M. Amendola and F. Saraceno, in the *Scottish Journal of Political Economy*, 2004; 'Persistent Unemployment and Co-ordination Issues: an evolutionary perspective', with M. Amendola, in the *Journal of Evolutionary Economics*, 2003; and 'Out of Equilibrium', with Mario Amendola, 1998.

Marzio GALEOTTI is Professor of Economics at the University of Milan. Recent publications include: 'Learning by Doing vs. Learning by Researching in a Model for Climate Policy Analysis', with E.Castelnuovo, G. Gambarelli and S. Vergalli, Fondazione Eni Enrico Mattei Working Paper, *Ecological Economics*, 2003; 'Productivity and Structural Reforms: Evidence on the Italian Economy', with Lidia Bagnoli, Francesco Nucci and Ottavio Ricchi, Treasury Ministry, *Rivista Internazionale di Scienze Economiche e Commerciali*, 2003; 'Inventories, Employment, and Hours', with Louis J. Maccini and Fabio Schiantarelli, Boston College, Economics Department Working Paper in the *Journal of Monetary Economics*, 2002; and 'Trade Links with the SEEC's: Trade Specialization and Industrial Structure', with Giuseppe De Arcangelis, Giovanni Ferri and Giorgia Giovannetti, Treasury Ministry, *Journal of Southern Europe and the Balkans*, 2001.

David K. LEVINE is Professor of Economics in the Department of Economics at the University of California, Los Angeles. Recent publications include: 'The Economics of Ideas and Intellectual Property', with M. Boldrin, at the *Proceedings of the National Academy of Sciences*, 2004; 'Modeling Altruism and Spitefulness in Experiments', in *Critical Studies in Economic Institutions: Trust*, edited by G. M. Hodgson and E. L. Khalil, 2002, reprinted from *Review of Economic Dynamics*; 'Information Aggregation, Currency Swaps, and the Design of Derivative Securities', with B. Chowdhry and M. Grinblatt, in the *Journal of Political Economy*, 2002; and 'Dynamic Games', edited with Aldo Rustichini, a special issue of *Review of Economic Dynamics* (2000).

Luigi PAGANETTO is Dean of the Faculty of Economics and Business Administration, Full Professor of International Economics and President of the Center for International Studies on Economic Growth at the University of Rome, Tor Vergata. He is editor of the 'CEIS-Il Mulino' series and a member of the editorial boards of 'Sviluppo economico'. He is also a member of the ENEA technical scientific committee, the Council of the Ministry for Foreign Affairs Institute, the Council of Ente Cassa di Risparmio of Rome, the Board of Directors of Poligrafico dello Stato, a member of the Italian private employers' association Confindustria's Technical-Scientific Committee, an adviser to the Italian Prime Minister's Office and Chairman of the Committee of the Information Society, and a member of the Italian export credit agency (SACE) board of experts. He is the author of several articles and books in Macroeconomic Theory, International Economics and Italian and European Industrial Economics. Recent publications include: 'Finance, Research, Education and Growth', edited with E.S. Phelps, (forthcoming); 'Crescita endogena ed economia aperta', with L.P. Scandizzo, 2001; 'Scienza, tecnologia e innovazione: quali politiche', edited with C. Pietrobelli, 2001; 'Borsa, investimenti e crescita', 2000; 'La Banca Mondiale e l'Italia: dalla ricostruzione allo sviluppo', with L.P. Scandizzo, 2000; and 'Istituzioni e governo dell'economia', edited with G. Tria, 1999.

Bruce C. PETERSEN is Professor of Economics at Washington University. Recent publications include: 'Is the Growth of Small Firms Constrained by Internal Finance?' with R. Carpenter, 2002; 'Investment-Cash Flow Sensitivities Are Useful: A Comment on Kaplan and Zingales', with S. Fazzari and R.G. Hubbard; 2000; and 'Financing Constraints and Inventory Investment: A Comparative Study with High-Frequency Panel Data', with R. Carpenter and S. Fazzari, 1998.

Ottavio RICCHI is senior advisor at Consiglio Tecnico-Scientifico degli Esperti, Ministero dell'Economia e delle Finanze, where he manages the Italian Treasury Econometric Model and provides consultancy on quantitative studies related to the Italian Economy. He worked as Italian Economist for DRI (currently Global Insight) and previously he was Research Fellow at the University of Strathclyde.

Dominick SALVATORE Recent publications include: 'International Economics', 8th edition, 2004; 'Managerial Economics in a Global Economy', 5th edition, 2004; 'The Euro, the European Central Bank, and the International Monetary System', 2003; 'Globalization, Comparative Advantage and Europe's Double Competitive Squeeze', 2004.

Pasquale Lucio SCANDIZZO is Professor of Political Economy, at the University of Rome, Tor Vergata. Recent publications include: 'Valutare l'Incertezza, L'Analisi Costi Benefici nel XXI Secolo', with G. Pennisi, and P.L. Scandizzo, 2003; 'Financing Technology: An Assessment of Theory and Practice', with P.L. Scandizzo, 2003; 'L'Impresa e il Mercato, Le Teorie e i Fatti', with P.L. Scandizzo, 2002; and 'La Banca Mondiale e l'Italia: dalla ricostruzione allo sviluppo', with L. Paganetto and P.L. Scandizzo, 2000.

Paul WACHTEL is Professor of Economics in Stern School of Business at New York University. Recent publications include: 'Financial Sector Development in Transition Economies: Lessons from the First Decade', with John Bonin, 2003; 'Inflation Thresholds and the Finance-Growth Nexus', with Peter L. Rousseau, 2002; and 'How Much Do We Know About Growth and Finance?', 2002.

PART ONE

Chapter 1

Asset Valuation, Liquidity Issues and Growth Regimes

Jean-Paul Fitoussi and Jean-Luc Gaffard

The development of a child is normally accompanied by some growth in height, weight, physical power, etc. A simple recognition such as this could not possibly contribute anything substantial toward our understanding of the biological development of a human individual. This understanding has increased only with the discoveries of the physiological interrelations between phenomena that are not all as conspicuous as the outward manifestations of growth. Similarly, the understanding of the ways followed by economic change can come only from a physiological picture of that process (N. Georgescu-Roegen, 1976, pp. 42-43).

1. Introduction

The 'New Economy' proponents pointing to the recent and exceptional performance of the US economy are talking about a new golden age. This new age of the economy would be the result of a combination between the implementation of new information and communication technologies, a neutral monetary policy and a market-oriented finance mechanism. The 2001 report of the US council of economic advisers is more impressionist when it points out that 'extraordinary gains in performances ... have resulted from this combination of mutually reinforcing advances in technologies, business practices, and economic policies' (Economic Report of the President, 2001, p. 23). Beyond the semantic differences, a real debate about the nature of growth should be brought back to the surface. The problem is to know whether a change in 'fundamentals' – technology, tastes, institutions – has the effect of shifting upwards the productivity trend and making obsolete the business cycle, or whether a better co-ordination of economic activity has been obtained, independently of the nature of the 'fundamentals'.

Some growth accounting analyses (Jorgenson and Stiroh, 2000; Oliner and Sichel, 2000) seem to confirm the existence of a change in the trend of productivity whose dynamics would look similar to that of the 1960s. They attribute it to the investment boom in the information and communication technologies in the 1990s. However, Gordon (2000a) claims that the recent increase in productivity (1995-98) is in fact due to a huge increase in the productivity of the computer industry, while for the rest of the economy the productivity slowdown is still alive and kicking.

Here two questions come to the surface: one concerns the trend and the other the level of output, which the economy is capable of realizing. In the standard analysis of growth the second question is considered as a particular aspect of the first one. Thus Solow distinguishes 'between the potential output of an economy and its actual output' whereby 'the business cycle consists in fluctuations of actual output around a given trend of potential output' (1997, p. 73). Recent empirical contributions just mentioned (Jorgenson and Stiroh, 2000; Gordon, 2000a) maintain the focus on the trend of potential output, taking up the same issue of the slowdown of productivity in the last 20 years and of its recent revival in the United States. However, the very definition of a potential trend of output is only possible in equilibrium where it can be univocally associated to a technology which only in this state can be fully specified in terms of given input-output relations. On the other hand, 'if one looks at substantial more-than-quarterly departures from equilibrium growth, as suggested, for instance, by the history of the large European economies since 1979, it is impossible to believe that the equilibrium growth path itself is unaffected by the short-to-medium-run experience. In particular, the amount and direction of capital formation are bound to be affected by the business cycle, whether through gross investment in new equipment or through the accelerated scrapping of old equipment' (Solow, 1970 (2000), p. xvii). In other words, short-run forces govern the growth performance of the economy. This appears as the result of an evolution path sketched out step by step, with respect to which the standard distinction between short and long run fades away. Among these forces, the financial ones have a strong impact. They cannot be reduced to saving incentives associated with specific institutional frameworks, as is the case when we keep making reference to an equilibrium path that they would determine, as suggested in recent developments of growth analysis (see Levine, 1997). Rather finance has to be considered as an essential element of co-ordination mechanisms, which determine the actual evolution path followed by the economy.

The chapter is aimed at investigating the financial problems which characterize growth processes and influence the global performance of the economy. Section 2, taking advantage of Solow's reflections in his Nobel lecture, will be devoted to reminding us to what extent asset pricing matters in the growth process. Section 3 will present the *structuralist* view developed by Phelps, within an equilibrium analytical framework, whose main advance consists in taking into account asset pricing and the associated wealth effects perceived by firms' managers. Then, the question of business assets valuation will be revisited from an out-of-equilibrium perspective. This will lead us to consider the way in which intertemporal co-ordination failures determine the evolution path actually followed by the economy. Section 4 will develop a *sequential* approach of innovation and growth, and will present liquidity constraints as an essential determinant of the actual profile of the economy. Finally, in Section 5, we shall go back to the interpretation of contrasted situations of the United States, Japan and the largest European economies.

2. The Financial Dimension of Growth

Traditional equilibrium growth models (*à la* Solow) describe characteristics and properties of constant and uniform growth paths and 'work out the price and interest-rate dynamics that would support an equilibrium path' (Solow, 1970 (2000), p. xii). In fact, one of the main achievements of these models is precisely to relate the stability property of the steady state to the competitive pricing. In this analytical framework, equilibrium investment as well as the value of capital only depends on exogenous variables, i.e. the rate of productivity growth and the saving rate.

Things become much more complex when we try to combine short-run and long-run macroeconomics. As underlined by Solow himself, 'the hard part of disequilibrium growth is that we do not have – and it may be impossible to have – a really good theory of asset valuation under turbulent conditions' (ibid., p. xv), and hence a really good theory of investment.

As a matter of fact, economies are not generally in a steady state in the sense that they do not follow a path characterized by a constant growth rate. The actual wage, interest and price dynamics do not support a steady state. As a consequence, the rate of accumulation is no longer determined only by the exogenous variables previously mentioned. It also depends on the sequence of prices, which interact along the way with the actual dynamics of productivity and saving rate. Therefore, asset valuation comes to the fore as an argument of the investment function, but in a complex way. As we shall see below, the reason is that this asset valuation does not express 'fundamental' values, but reflects co-ordination difficulties. It is well documented in the empirical literature that investment is inelastic with respect to changes in relative factor price, and is no more determined by the ratio between the market value of capital and its replacement cost (the Tobin's q). As a matter of fact, price disequilibria (including discrepancies between the price of assets and their fundamental values) result in unexpected changes in profits, which makes it difficult to predict investment.

The modern way to escape from these difficulties consists in imagining an economy the evolution of which is strictly guided by the behaviour of an immortal consumer (or a dynasty) which is supposed to maximize an intertemporal utility function. Within this kind of model, fluctuations are interpreted as optimal paths followed in response to random (real or financial) shocks. Changes in wage and interest and associated changes in asset valuation support an equilibrium, which is no longer a position of the rest of the economy, and becomes an assumption 'included in the way the theory is set up' (Hicks, 1965, p. 17). Within this framework, 'every firm is just a transparent instrumentality, an intermediary, a device for carrying out intertemporal optimization subject only to technological constraints and initial endowments. Thus any kind of market failure is ruled out from the beginning by assumption. There are no strategic complementarities, no co-ordination failures, no prisoners' dilemma' (Solow, ibid.). In sophisticated versions of these optimal growth models, an essential reference to firms' strategic behaviours and co-ordination failures can be introduced. Anyway, shocks of different nature determine the actual evolution of the key variables (investment, output, employment ...). Asset valuation does not create a problem insofar as different intertemporal equilibria correspond to different and alternative sequences of prices. The actual price dynamic does not support any longer a steady state, but it supports an intertemporal equilibrium path, and in particular equilibrium business cycles.

Another way to deal with the problem of asset valuation and investment behaviour under turbulent conditions is to really pay attention to price disequilibria. As Solow reminds us, this is the way suggested by Malinvaud (1983). The analysis is based on two key ideas, 'namely, that some disequilibria may be sustained over rather long periods, and that the existence of these disequilibria significantly reacts on the growth process, to speed it up, slow it down or change its course' (ibid., p. 95). In the model, prices – the real wage rate and the real interest rate – are sticky so that their incomplete adjustment results in persistent market disequilibria. The key relation is an investment function, the arguments of which are excess capacity and profitability. However, the determination of profitability as a measure of the disequilibrium in prices (wage, interest and price of final output) is problematic for two reasons. Firstly, there is no clear understanding of the way prices are adjusted from time to time. Secondly, in the absence of money and financial assets, the determination of the interest rate is itself problematic. In fact the puzzle of investment behaviour remains unsolved.

Clearly, in standard equilibrium growth models asset valuation does not really matter in the sense that the competitive pricing insulates investment from any endogenous influence. So, in order to make clear the nature of the transmission mechanism through which financial variables can affect the growth process, one can develop a general equilibrium model which makes an explicit reference to the way asset valuation really influences output and labour demand decisions. Alternatively one can try to build a disequilibrium model, which requires the specification of an investment function.

3. Asset Valuation, Wealth Effects, and Growth: The *Structuralist* View Revisited

Decline in world rate of interest and quickening of productivity growth provide a partial explanation of US employment and output recovery in the 1990s. But they do not fully explain the degree of this recovery. A better explanation is obtained when adding a stock market indicator as explanatory variable in the unemployment equations (Fitoussi, Jestaz, Phelps and Zoega, 2000). This empirical result seems to give consistency to a thesis that focuses on the role of business assets valuation

Phelps' *structuralist* theory of slumps and recoveries brings into light the essential influence of assets pricing (Phelps, 1994). According to this theory, recent developments in information and communication technologies would have stimulated expectations of a large set-up in productivity, and hence changes in the valuation of business assets, both tangibles and intangibles, physical and human assets. These changes in turn would have an impact on the rate of investment in these assets, and on the equilibrium growth path.

In this analytical framework, the sharp slowdown of productivity growth from the 1970s onwards and its recent revival in the US are purely exogenous phenomena. Interpreted as definitive changes in the rate of change of productivity, they result in definitive changes in asset valuation, and hence in the bargaining conditions on the labour market, which involve changes in the demand for labour, and hence in the natural rate of unemployment. Changes in asset valuation and real or expected changes in productivity trend are the two faces of the same exogenous phenomenon.

In other words, only changes in 'fundamentals', including new expectations by firms' managers, are considered here. Then changes in managers' expectations and in their asset valuation would be at the origin of fluctuations actually interpreted as reflecting changes in the trend. On the other hand, as in all optimal growth models, the production side of the economy exactly performs what the maximizing economic agents require. As a consequence, no co-ordination failures occur which would involve unexpected outcomes. Investment and asset valuation remain determined by the fundamentals

Within the logic of models that describe intertemporal growth equilibria, it does not matter whether stock market prices express managers' valuation of business assets (based on their profit expectations) or whether they result from the valuation by independent stockholders (or speculators). The full co-ordination assumption makes them quite similar.

This can no longer be the case when intertemporal co-ordination failures of the kind analysed by Leijonhufvud (1968) occur. These failures are apparent in asset valuation by the market, and they result from stockholders' behaviour and/or from monetary and fiscal policy. They create unexpected constraints, and hence a break in the equilibrium, which induce firms to react in a way which does not ensure that the economy will move back to the previous full employment equilibrium.

The transmission mechanism through which the real interest rate affects the demand for labour is added to a standard macroeconomic model, as a core building block. A basic sequence of events is the following. Too high real interest rates, for example, reveal the existence of intertemporal co-ordination failures. They result in a bias against consumption and in favour of savings, but also in a bias against shares and in favour of more liquid reserves. These different facets of the intertemporal co-ordination problem all contribute to reduce employment and output. Quite importantly, this mechanism can be activated by the structure of the policy mix at work, i.e. as the joint effect of an expansive budgetary policy and a tight monetary policy. While increasing budget deficit tends to raise nominal interest rates, monetary tightening keeps prices down. As a result real interest rates rise (Fitoussi and Phelps, 1988, p. 60). Firms' time preference changes, and as a result these decide to raise prices and to reduce output and employment, in order to increase their current profits. Within this kind of analytical framework, different short-term equilibria are defined, which correspond to different and successive asset valuations which do not correspond to the fundamentals.

However, the sole consideration of the impact of asset valuation on equilibrium values of key variables leads us to ignore the problem of equilibration, that is how the economy gets from the old equilibrium to the new one. A more comprehensive view of what happens along the way requires another modelling that focuses on out-of-equilibrium processes of change.

4. Innovation, Out-of-Equilibrium Growth and Finance

As a 'gale of creative destruction', innovation is essentially a disequilibrium phenomenon. The length of the construction period (i.e. the delay between the moment of the investment decision and the moment when the corresponding final output will be delivered) makes firms vulnerable to liquidity problems, that is, to the availability and the distribution of loanable funds. Then, a breaking-up in the temporal production structure, that is, in the balance between investment and final output, is likely to happen (Hicks, 1973; Amendola and Gaffard, 1988, 1998). The structure of productive capacity inherited from the past can no longer sustain a steady state. This involves specific co-ordination problems, which cannot be reduced only to the information issues. The point is not merely that the market information is incomplete or ill-formed. Co-ordination failures are an intrinsic feature of a decentralized market economy in which investment decisions are not reversible and production takes time. These co-ordination failures result in discrepancies between costs and proceeds over time, and in market disequilibria on the final output market, the labour market and the credit or the financial market.

The Nature of Disturbances

The introduction of a new and superior technology implies an immediate increase in the pseudo-natural rate of interest.[1] As a consequence, the capital value of production processes, which embody the old technology, will be reduced, their economic life will be shortened, and hence proceeds from sales will diminish for a while (Amendola, 1972). More generally, any human or financial resource constraint, which prevents investment from being at the level required by the construction of the new technology, will result in a fall in the wage fund, and hence in excess capacity on the market for final good which implies less proceeds at a given moment of time (Amendola and Gaffard, 1998). On the other hand, insofar as innovation requires more resources to be invested in new processes, for the acquisition of new technology to be effective, there must be real reserves. 'Failing this possibility, the only way to make things work is to transmute the capital that was embodied in the late stages of old production processes into capital embodied in the early stages of new processes, that is a disruption of other activities which is "bound to be a strain"' (Hicks, 1990, p. 535). Then inflationary pressures (and/or deficits in the trade balance in open economies) necessarily appear 'because the goods in which the wages (...) will be spent (...) cannot be provided out of the product of the labour which is newly employed, for that is not yet ready' (ibid.).

All these disturbances create liquidity problems, which to some extent express the existence of disequilibria both on the credit market and on the financial one. Any supplementary pressure on real interest rates for monetary or fiscal reasons will aggravate them.

One can do the conjecture that a price dynamic exists, which supports the transition towards a new steady state associated with the new technology. In this

1 The pseudo-natural interest rate takes account of the movement of prices (Hicks, 1977).

case, asset valuation will coincide with fundamental values and will be in harmony with investment decisions. Required liquidity should be obtained. But there is no reason for this dynamic to prevail and expected value of business assets corresponds to their fundamental values. Such an expected value depends on what happens along the way, that is on the actual – out-of-equilibrium – price dynamics. Then, investment cannot be explained by the day-to-day changes in asset valuation, and liquidity issues become of real importance.

The Investment Puzzle

As a matter of fact, the profitability of each investment (at each moment of time) depends on the undertaking of other investments in time. Each investment belongs to a bundle of complementary investments over time, and it would not be rational for a firm to drop it only because the interest rate increases at a given moment of time (Hicks, 1989, p. 119). As a consequence, investment, at each moment, should be determined so as to maintain in equilibrium the temporal structure of productive capacity, i.e. so as to preserve the complementarity over time of successive investments. This behaviour could appear as a routine. Anyway it respects an intertemporal profitability condition. In that sense, it requires a quasi-equilibrium prices dynamic. However, investment can deviate from this equilibrium path for liquidity reasons. Either liquidity constraints prevent firms from carrying out the required investment, or excess loanable funds make possible a strong competition between firms in each sector that results in an excess capacity. What happens to investment finally depends on liquidity decisions taken by both non-financial and financial agents. Any liquidity difficulty, which would result in a breaking up in the linked chain of investments, would provoke strong disturbances in the growth process, and in fact lower growth performances in the medium run.

Then banking policy as well as asset valuation by capital markets must be considered in relation to the necessity for an economy facing technological changes to have the right amount of liquidity and the right distribution of this liquidity at the right moment. Using an account inspired by Hicks (1977), it is possible to give a more precise content to these liquidity issues.

	Liabilities	*Assets*
Core (central bank)	Money (M+m)	Financial securities (F)
Mantle (banks and stockholders)	Financial securities (F+f)	Industrial securities (I) + Money (m)
Industry (firms, households, and government)	Industrial securities (I)	Real assets (R) + Financial securities (f) + Money (M)

As a consequence of their innovative choice, firms have to invest and hold more real assets (R). However, 'an increase in real investment, with constant money supply (M+m), must reduce liquidity somewhere. If the investment is financed by borrowing, the main loss in liquidity falls on the mantle; if by drawing on reserves, the main loss falls on industry itself. If either has ample reserves, the loss of liquidity can be borne' (ibid., p. 79). Otherwise, liquidity difficulties emerge, which take the form of credit rationing or debt deflation. This makes critical the role of banking policy and/or stockholders' behaviours for maintaining the economy near steady state growth equilibrium (within the limits of a stability corridor). What happens to investment, and hence to growth and unemployment, strongly depends on the way liquidity issues are dealt with, that is on the joint influence of banking policy and stockholders' behaviours. Too less or too much liquidity, we maintain, is equally damaging. In the first case the required investments cannot be carried out, in the second a too strong capacity competition can result in an excess capacity and negative current profits, which may induce both decreasing share prices and debt deflation.

Therefore, financial institutions are important, not so much because they are associated with incentive schemes more or less appropriate in the sense that they determine a higher or a lower saving rate, or a better or a worse resource allocation, but as concerns their capacity to smooth the evolution of the economy. In this perspective, neither market-oriented nor bank-oriented financial institutions can be considered as optimal ones *per se*. As it is well documented (see Levine, 1997), a large and liquid stock market, for example, may stimulate the acquisition of information, and hence improve the resource allocation. Its way of functioning may also deprive agents from any incentives to spend resources in this acquisition of information. In fact, the existence of a large and liquid stock market may result in strong (and inappropriate) fluctuations in asset valuation. What actually happens is determined by the interaction between banking policy and the liquidity of stock markets.

5. Financial Conditions of Well-Managed Innovation Processes

Let us start from the observation of the different performances of the US on the one hand, and European countries on the other hand. It is well documented that both have been confronted by successive positive supply shocks – e.g. the introduction of new and superior technologies – most of them involving a higher investment at cost.[2] But available data reveal that there are strong differences among the countries over time. The persistence of high and rising unemployment is becoming a sort of permanent character of the main European countries (France, Germany, Italy, Spain) in contrast to the United States where unemployment levels are much lower and relatively more stable. Different stylized facts, besides different institutional characteristics of the labour markets, match this variety of

2 In Hicks' (1973) parlance, gross investment in terms of cost is not the same as gross investment in terms of output capacity.

employment trends. Mainly, a substantially stable investment rate, and a relatively constant share of wages in the United States; high fluctuations in the rate of investment and in the share of wages in the economies of continental Europe.

These facts reveal that the dynamic of productivity is not exogenous. It is the expression of a process of transformation of the productive structure and of the ability of the agents to organize and carry out this process within the constraints posed by the institutional features of the economy. Productivity gains associated with the introduction of a new technology will be effective and unemployment will be reabsorbed only if co-ordination problems, in particular those associated with finance mechanisms of the growth process, are correctly dealt with. Productivity in other words, rather than the expression of specific technical conditions, is the outcome of the way in which the economy involved is able to deal with the co-ordination problems which emerge as the result of the breaking of the equilibrium (Amendola and Gaffard, 1998, pp. 220-22).

Understanding the productivity (and the investment) puzzle requires acknowledging the existence of the diversity of growth regimes, instead of concentrating the attention on convergence issues. A growth regime is defined as a set of rules and institutions which govern expectations and behaviours of economic agents, and hence investment and productivity dynamics. Then, each regime is identified to a different region in the investment – productivity space (Böhm and Punzo, 2001). Changes of regime are the result of alterations in expectations and behaviours. They are associated with shifts in the partitioned investment – productivity space (ibid.). The mechanism causing regime switches is both exogenous and endogenous (Brida, Bimonte and Punzo, 2001) in the sense that change occurs when key variables reach certain thresholds, that is when the growth mechanism itself generates an alteration in the behaviour, which, nevertheless, obeys to exogenous rules.

In this analytical context, the rate at which an economy grows without inflation pressures certainly depends on the sustainable productivity growth. But given the intertemporal complementarity of production processes, productivity is no longer independent of investment dynamics. Growth regimes and changes in growth regime determine the growth performance. When the economy oscillates between two unstable regimes, one characterized by an excessive investment growth with respect to the growth of final output, and the other, on the contrary by a too low investment growth, the growth rate that corresponds to zero inflation is lower and lower. This growth rate can be the threshold at which there is a turning point. As turning point, it depends, among other things, as we shall see, on the monetary policy and its articulation with the asset valuation on the stock market.

Out of equilibrium, that is along the process of restructuring of productive capacity stirred by innovation, actual output and productivity levels cannot be interpreted as deviations from a potential trend which is no longer in the background. So the main question to be addressed is not whether a new technology (e.g. information and communication technologies) generates a sustainable increase in the productivity growth rate. Rather, the focus must be on the conditions in which the economy can really take advantage of a new technology step by step. In fact, we consider that an economy does not *automatically* capture the gains associated with the implementation of a new technology. The object of the analysis becomes in other words the level of output and productivity which the economy is actually capable of realizing, that is, the effective evolution of the innovation process interpreted as a process of restructuring of productive capacity. The viability and the effective outcome of this process are the relevant issues in this light, and the conditions under which viability is assured the target of policy interventions and institutional devices (Amendola and Gaffard, 1998, pp. 245-50). In this perspective, changes in liquidity constraints modify the short-run equilibrium of the economy, and hence the level of employment. The articulation over time between decisions and constraints determines the sequence of short-run equilibria, i.e. what happens to employment and output in the medium run. Thus, 'monetary policy cannot be expected to lift the long term sustainable growth rate (but) the Fed's role is to make sure that any productivity gains that occur spontaneously or as a result of supply-side policies are realized in jobs and output and do not go to waste in recessions and unemployment' (Tobin, 1997).

Policy Dilemma

A first policy dilemma occurs as the time of reaching the growth rate, that corresponds to zero inflation, is accomplished, and the required accumulation of capital not yet completed. The choice lies between maintaining a loose monetary policy in the perspective of allowing the accumulation of capital to be completed, or adopting a tight monetary policy in the perspective of fighting any inflation pressures. If the latter alternative is chosen, it will determine a turning point in the business cycle and results in recession and losses of jobs. In the medium run, the growth-supply curve (the curve that links the real growth rate to the inflation rate) shifts upwards. The growth rate of the economy that corresponds to zero inflation becomes lower and lower (and the Non-Accelerating-Inflation Rate of Unemployment (NAIRU) higher and higher) as observed in most of the European countries. If the former alternative is chosen, productivity gains will be obtained, and hence inflation pressures will be temporary, and structural unemployment will be eliminated. The growth-supply curve will shift downwards as observed in the US.

As a matter of fact, business cycle peaks are endogenous. However, there is a real difficulty in identifying what the limits that the economy hits are and why they change. 'To understand the potential difficulty, suppose that erring policy makers have in the past reacted imprudently to "supply shocks" in ways that prematurely and systematically curtailed economic expansion. In that case, the business cycle peak is endogenous to policy. Suppose they did this because of the rise of a false doctrine of limits – such as the natural rate hypothesis. It is then possible that if growth policies had been more sustained, disciplined and aggressive, then the perceived decline in the trend productivity growth rate would have been smaller than it was, and the estimated natural rate would also have been lower than it has appeared to be' (Galbraith, 1997, p. 99).

When a positive supply shock occurs that results in the need for more investment, and hence in inflationary pressures, central banks can try to bring inflation back to the target level as soon as possible, with the consequence of exacerbating the initial negative impact of the shock on output and employment. They can, alternatively, decide an accommodating monetary policy bringing inflation back to the target more slowly with the consequence of simultaneously reducing inflation and unemployment. The latter policy consists in accepting a transitory inflation in the perspective of reducing unemployment.

Then the problem that central banks are facing is no longer a problem of credibility of the commitment to price stability. It is a problem of dealing with real constraints, which are in the nature of innovation processes. Asset valuation, of course, depends on monetary policy.

The second policy dilemma is about the relation of monetary policy to the financial assets pricing. Tight monetary policy may be coupled with restricted new investment market financing. Loose monetary policy goes hand-in-hand with stock market bubbles, which make it easier for firms to realize their capital accumulation objectives. Asset prices bubbles create distortions in the structure of productive capacity, leading to a rise and then fall in investment with respect to final output. So raising or lowering interest rates as asset prices rise and fall above and below what are estimated to be required levels is supposed to help to smooth these fluctuations. In particular, central banks should prevent asset price movements if these movements originate in the asset markets themselves and result in an excess of investment with respect to the future final output. However, there is a difficulty both in evaluating the nature of the asset price movements and in reconciling the latter objective with considerations about the output gap.

Comparative Analysis of Growth Processes: US and European Countries in the 1980s and 1990s

The question to be addressed does not concern the convergence towards a given equilibrium growth path. It is about the nature of growth regimes and stability conditions. What international comparisons reveal is, on the one hand, the diversity of evolution among countries that have faced the same kind of shocks and have access to the same technologies, and, on the other hand, the essential role of monetary and financial behaviours.

Out of equilibrium, capital accumulation conditions generate a multiphase or multi-regime dynamic in which changes of phase or of regime are determined by the impact of resource constraints and changes in economic policy. This is a conception of dynamic economics which consists in considering an unstable (dynamically) system, 'which, however, as it expands, contains a term which grows dynamically and eventually stabilizes the system' (Goodwin, 1990, p. 63). In our perspective, such a term, the financial term, may stabilize the system and end by dampening structural fluctuations, or, on the contrary, it may generate structural fluctuations strong enough but not explosive. In other words, there would be a self-regulation feedback mechanism, which would prevent, more or less efficiently, persistent misalignment between key variables (i.e. investment and consumption).

In the case of the US economy, there is no clear trace of significant changes in growth regime during the last two decades. Quite the opposite, most of the European countries as well as Japan exhibit wild and recurrent changes in growth regimes (Böhm, Gaffard and Punzo, 2001). One is naturally driven to the twofold conjecture: that the higher degree of structural instability seen in the latter countries may account for their poorer employment and productivity performance *vis-à-vis* the US, and this may also be explained by central and commercial banks' as well as stockholders' behaviours. Some crucial episodes in the growth process of the different countries lend support to such conjecture.

Most of the European countries (France, Germany, Italy) experienced an irregular growth from the late 1970s. In these countries, as a consequence of previous co-ordination failures, including economic policy failures during the 1970s, too stringent real constraints have emerged, which have implied that any recovery has raised inflation pressures, inflation expectations, and hence maintained a restrictive monetary policy. As a matter of fact, the lack of productive resources that has followed first negative (oil prices) then positive (technological) supply shocks has been responsible for a stagflation phenomenon. Then, restrictive monetary policies carried out in the perspective of dramatically reducing a too high rate of inflation have made the productive resource constraints more and more stringent. Severe changes in growth regimes, as shown in the investment-productivity framework space, have been experienced (Böhm, Gaffard and Punzo, 2001). They have resulted both in a productivity slowdown and in an increasing NAIRU.[3] Later on, attention has been maintained on inflation. A stable price level and above all a strong exchange rate (particularly in France) were the objectives pursued through a restrictive monetary policy. Low inflation eventually prevailed. During the 1990s, share prices normalized by productivity more or less held their ground in Germany, France, Italy, and Spain, while they have strongly increased in the US (Fitoussi, Jestaz, Phelps and Zoega, 2000). This confirms that liquidity constraints remained high on one side while being relaxed on the other.[4] Despite the need for a more intense accumulation of capital, investment was sacrificed, the consequence of which was a lower and lower non accelerating inflation growth rate. Inappropriate economic policies were responsible for irregular and low growth.

The Netherlands experienced convergence towards a quasi steady state from the mid 1980s to late 1990s. The crucial episode has been a long expansion starting in the mid 1980s. Trend inflation rose from 1987 to 1991. But rising inflation did not provoke an immediate policy response. Thus steady growth continued through 1992 whereas most of the European countries were in recession. Inflation run-up was not permanent. This episode was significant insofar as it revealed a better co-ordination, whose main aspects were, on the one hand, loose banking policy with respect to the price level, and on the other hand, regulated wages movement. As is well documented, the point of departure of the new way was the Wassenaar agreement, a 1982 agreement on wage restraints accepted by the Dutch unions. This agreement introduced an income policy, which dampened the inflationary effects of final demand pressures, and allowed the central bank to carry out a less

---

3 L. Ball (1997, 1999), who pointed out the influence of aggregate demand on long-run movements of unemployment, confirms this point.

4 Liquidity constraints do not necessarily take the form of rationing. They can be stringent only because firms decide to privilege the reduction of their indebtedness.

restrictive monetary policy. This policy mix was clearly aimed at boosting investment spending in a moment where it was necessary. Besides, from the early 1980s onwards, the Netherlands have had a rising rate of employment, which has clearly followed rising share prices (normalized by productivity) (see Fitoussi, Jestaz, Phelps and Zoega, 2000). That supports the hypothesis about the role of asset prices in employment determination, which is the proper of equilibrium models, but also the conjecture according to which releasing liquidity constraints – here thanks to stock market bubbles that push capital costs down – allows firms to manage transition to the new technologies and capture productivity gains associated with them.

The United Kingdom also appears as an economy having managed to escape from unstable growth regimes. After experiencing a strong growth cycle between 1978 and 1994, similar to those experienced by France, Germany and Italy, it seems to have re-integrated a stability corridor (Böhm, Gaffard and Punzo, 2001). The crucial moment in the UK evolution could be the late 1980s and the early 1990s. The UK experienced a strong expansion in the late 1980s. The boom in borrowing commonly explains this expansion. Due to the combination of financial liberalization, high confidence and high asset prices, it generated a boom in investment and in consumption as well. At the same time, the Bank of England did not tighten policy immediately after inflation had started to rise. Moreover, the experience of the UK in the early 1990s was like that of the US in the early 1980s: policy easing in response to the recession.

The truly important difference between most of the European countries and the US is likely to be that in the US the rate of investment has remained constant and investment has always augmented in response to supply shocks. This is due to the fact that 'policy has not generated bouts of severe inflation and so has not had to generate bouts of recession to control it' (Romer, 1999, p. 32). On the other hand, at the same time, the stock market bubble pushed capital costs down and allowed firms to carry out desired investments. As a consequence, the rate of growth consistent with price stability has risen, and correlatively the NAIRU has decreased. The US economy did not experience structural fluctuations (Böhm, Gaffard and Punzo, 2001). However, the US investment boom during the late 1990s was probably unsustainable. A rise in productivity growth encouraged firms to become over-optimistic about future returns. The inevitable result was an over-investment in new technologies with regards to the actual perspectives of profit.[5] Too much liquidity would have favoured excessive investments in the new sectors. Now as profits plunge, share price evolution is going to reverse, and firms are being forced to cut their investment plans.

Recent evolution and policy issues, which characterize the Japanese economy, can be interpreted within the same analytical framework. From 1991 onwards, the Japanese economy has gone through an extended period of slow growth. This growth slowdown has been viewed as a correction of an

---

[5] Quoted by *The Economist* (12 May 2001), Credit Suisse First Boston estimates that American firms have overspent on IT equipment to the tune of US$190 billion over the past two years.

unsustainable boom, which meant that the actual growth rate was for a while above the potential one. Similar explanations attributed the bulk of the slowdown to a reduction in the rate of potential output due to a change in the demographic trend and in the Total Factor Productivity trend as well. However, estimations of the gap between actual and potential output conclude that it exceeds four or five per cent, so that not only demand policies but, to a larger extent, these growth policies aimed at promoting a better intertemporal co-ordination should be of real importance. At the beginning of the 1990s there was a break in the intertemporal co-ordination, the main aspect of which was a too low consumption ratio and the inability to transform savings in productive investments. This resulted in changes in growth regimes and structural fluctuations. Until 1985 the Japanese economy was near a steady state. Then the Japanese economy clearly exited from the stability corridor and started to experience a growth cycle, i.e. the alternation of unstable growth regimes (Böhm, Gaffard and Punzo, 2001). Here it is worth mentioning that one of the main features of the Japanese economy, in the last period, is the low interest rates. Co-ordination failures lead this economy into a liquidity trap. Moreover, as is well documented, Japan faced a huge problem of bad bank loans which was both the legacy of the burst of the assets bubbles in the 1980s and the consequence of the subsequent slow growth. Now cleaning up banks is essentially a microeconomic problem, the solution of which does not necessarily result in bad macroeconomic performances. As a matter of fact, on the one hand, a write-off of banks' bad loans will intensify deflationary pressures. On the other hand, this makes it all the more essential to conduct a loose monetary policy, precisely in order to disconnect micro and macroeconomic problems. In this perspective, it has been proposed that the Bank of Japan should try to bring inflation and inflation expectations up to four per cent for 15 years (Krugman, 1998). Insofar as it cannot cut short-term interest rates, which are equal to zero, the Bank of Japan, by purchasing long-term government bonds, could affect the economy through inflation expectations, a fall in the exchange rate and a rise in equity price. Japanese evolution is a good example of the narrow connection between monetary policy, asset valuation and the growth process.

6. Concluding Comment

Financial institutions and rules clearly affect the steady state growth rate, as other 'fundamentals' – technology, preferences – do. But, on the other hand, financial and monetary behaviours have an essential influence on the profile of the growth path actually followed by the economy, and hence on its medium-run performance. This has strong consequences on the architecture of monetary and financial policies, which cannot be reduced to the definition of rules to be strictly applied.

References

Amendola, M. (1972), 'Modello neo-Austriaco e Transizione fra Equilibri Dinamici', *Note Economiche* 4, 53-74.

Amendola, M. and J.-L. Gaffard (1988), *The Innovative Choice*, Oxford: Basil Blackwell.

Amendola, M. and J.-L. Gaffard (1998), *Out of Equilibrium*, Oxford: Clarendon Press.

Ball, L. (1997), 'Disinflation and the NAIRU', in C.D. Romer and D.H. Romer (eds), *Reducing Inflation, Motivation and Strategy*, National Bureau of Economic Research Studies in Business Cycle, Chicago: University of Chicago Press.

Ball, L. (1999), 'Aggregate Demand and Long Run Unemployment', *Brookings Papers on Economic Activity* (2), 189-236.

Böhm, B. and L.F. Punzo (2001), 'Investment-Productivity Fluctuations and Structural Change', in L.F. Punzo (ed.), *Cycles, Growth, and Structural Change*, London: Routledge.

Böhm, B., J.-L. Gaffard and L.F. Punzo (2001), 'Industrial Dynamics and Employment in Europe', Research Report, European Commission, Targeted Socio-Economic Research program.

Brida, G., S. Bimonte and L.F. Punzo (2001), 'Notions of Regime: a review', working paper, University of Siena.

Economic Report of the President (2001), Washington: United States Government Printing Office.

Fitoussi, J.-P. and E.S. Phelps (1988), *The Slump in Europe*, Oxford: Basil Blackwell.

Fitoussi, J.-P., D. Jestaz, E.S. Phelps and G. Zoega (2000), 'Roots of the Recent Recoveries: Labor Reforms or Private Sector Forces', *Brookings Papers on Economic Activity* (1), 237-311.

Galbraith, J.K. (1997), 'Time to Ditch the NAIRU', *Journal of Economic Perspectives*, 11, 11-32.

Georgescu-Roegen, N. (1976), 'Dynamic Models and Economic Growth', in *Energy and Economic Myths*, New York: Pergamon Press.

Goodwin, R.M. (1990), *Chaotic Economic Dynamics*, Oxford: Clarendon Press.

Gordon, R.J. (2000a), 'Does the "New Economy" Measure up to the Great Inventions of the Past?', *Journal of Economic Perspectives*, forthcoming.

Gordon, R.J. (2000b), 'Interpreting the "One Big Wave" in U.S. Long Term Productivity Growth', in *Productivity, Technology, and Economic Growth*, Bart van Ark, Simon Kuipers and Gerard Kuper (eds), Amsterdam: Kluwer Publishers, forthcoming.

Gordon, R.J. (2000c), 'Comments on Jorgenson and Stiroh', *Brookings Papers on Economic Activity* (I), 125-235.

Hicks, J.R. (1965), *Capital and Growth*, Oxford: Clarendon Press.

Hicks, J.R. (1973), *Capital and Time*, Oxford: Clarendon Press.

Hicks, J.R. (1977), *Economic Perspectives*, Oxford: Clarendon Press.

Hicks, J.R. (1989), *A Market Theory of Money*, Oxford: Clarendon Press.

Hicks, J.R. (1990), 'The Unification of Macroeconomics', *Economic Journal* 100, 528-38.

Jorgenson, D.W. and K.J. Stiroh (2000), 'Raising the Speed Limit: U.S. Economic Growth in the Information Age', *Brookings Papers on Economic Activity* (1), 125-235.

Krugman, P. (1998), 'It's baaack: Japan's Slump and the Return of the Liquidity Trap', *Brookings Papers on Economic Activity* (2), 137-205.

Leijonhufvud, A. (1968), *On Keynesian Economics and the Economics of Keynes*, Oxford: Oxford University Press.

Levine, R. (1997), 'Financial Development and Economic Growth: Views and Agenda', *Journal of Economic Literature* XXXV, 688-726.

Malinvaud, E. (1983), 'Notes on Growth Theory with Imperfectly Flexible Prices', in J.-P. Fitoussi (ed.), *Modern Macroeconomic Theory*, Oxford: Basil Blackwell.

Oliner, S.D. and D.E. Sichel (2000), 'The Resurgence of Growth in the Late 1990s, Is Information Technology the Story?', *Journal of Economic Perspective*.

Phelps, E.S. (1994), *Structural Slumps: The Modern Equilibrium Theory of Unemployment, Interest, and Assets*, Cambridge Mass.: Harvard University Press.
Phelps, E.S. (1995), 'The Origins and Further Development of the Natural Rate of Unemployment', in *The Natural Rate of Unemployment*, R. Cross (ed.), Cambridge: Cambridge University Press.
Phelps, E.S. and G. Zoega (1998), 'Natural-Rate Theory and OECD Unemployment', *Economic Journal*, 108, 782-801.
Romer, C.D. (1999), 'Changes in Business Cycles: Evidences and Explanations', mimeo, February, NBER Working Paper No 6948.
Solow, R.M. (1970), *Growth Theory*, Oxford: Oxford University Press (new edition 2000).
Solow, R.M. (1997), *Learning from 'Learning by Doing': Lessons for Economic Growth*, Stanford: Stanford University Press.
Tobin, J. (1997), 'Can We Grow Faster?', NAM Symposium on Growth Policy.

Chapter 2

Factor Saving Innovation

Michele Boldrin and David K. Levine

1. Introduction

A variety of arguments have been advanced as to why growth models with increasing returns are superior to those with diminishing or constant returns. From a theoretical stand point, the endogenous versus exogenous nature of economic growth is the principal one. Romer (1994), for example, says that the fact that 'technical advance comes from things that people do' and is not merely 'a function of elapsed calendar time', argues against concave models of 'exogenous' technological change. In this interpretation, endogeneity means that technological innovations should come from 'things people do'. In this chapter we focus on the issue of 'endogeneity' of growth in a concave setting. We distinguish between growth due to the accumulation of factors, and growth in the total productivity of such factors, which we refer to as technological advance. To be concrete, we will propose that the growth rate or the rate of technological advance are endogenous if they are affected in a non-trivial way by changes in the rate of intertemporal substitution in consumption. Notice that in the Solow growth model, neither the growth rate nor the rate of technological advance are endogenous in this sense. In Rebelo's (1991) AK model, the growth rate is endogenous, but the rate of technological advance is not. On the other hand, in models with increasing returns such as those of Lucas (1988) or Romer (1990), not only is the growth rate endogenous, but so is the growth of total factor productivity.

In this chapter we examine a stylized concave model in which there are infinitely many different qualities of capital. In this world, higher levels of total factor productivity are naturally associated with higher qualities of capital. There is a fixed and potentially binding labor (or natural resource) constraint. Improvement in the quality of capital is labor-saving, in the sense that better qualities of capital require less labor input to produce a given amount of output. In addition to producing consumption, and reproducing capital of the same quality, capital can also be used to produce capital of a higher quality. This leads to a model in which investment provokes both *capital widening*, meaning the total stock of capital grows larger, and *capital deepening*, meaning that the quality of the capital stock is improved. In fact, because of the fixed labor supply, capital deepening is necessary for capital widening. Without moving to higher qualities of capital that use less labor per unit of output, there is no reason to build more capital.

The endogeneity of growth in this model depends on how rapidly it is possible to produce higher quality capital. If capital of higher quality can be produced quickly, we get a model identical in essence to the 'exogenous growth' model of Solow: a new quality of capital is introduced every period, and the economy grows at a fixed rate independent of the subjective discount factor and other preference or technology parameters.

If new quality capital can only be produced slowly, the situation changes drastically. Both the growth rate and the rate of technological advance are fully endogenous and depend on the subjective discount factor and other parameters of preferences. The greater the degree of patience, the more rapidly new qualities of capital are introduced, and the faster the economy grows. In this model, technical advances clearly come from things that people do. In fact, contrary to models where externalities carry the day, technological improvements here come from things that people consciously choose to do. They introduce new technologies in those periods when they are needed to relax the labor constraint, and they do not introduce new technologies in periods in which such need is absent. Another striking feature of this model is that it does not exhibit a smooth growth path. Growth follows a natural cycle in which gradual upward increases in consumption are interrupted by periodic 'recessions' in which consumption growth remains flat. These periods of 'creative destruction' are those in which a shift to a new technological paradigm first takes place.

The existence of growth cycles in the rate at which technological advances take place can be extended to models with many goods, sectors and inputs, as long as natural resources are essential in production. This rather straightforward extension implies our result has general relevance. In a world in which natural resources are scarce, natural resource-saving technological advances are needed to increase per capita consumption. Then, either the technology introducing the new machine is extremely productive, or growth must take place through cycles. Said differently, balanced growth is feasible only in the highly uninteresting situation in which either the economy is already very rich or the innovation technology is unusually productive. In all other circumstances, cyclical growth is the only equilibrium outcome. We submit this as a testable 'theory of Total Factor Productivity', as advocated in Prescott (1998).

In addition to endogenous growth and a natural 'business cycle', our economy exhibits several other striking features. It exhibits 'path dependence' meaning that the long-run growth rate of the economy can depend on the initial stock of capital. Indeed, a small change in initial capital can make the difference between long-run innovation and growth, and long run stagnation and decline. Finally, it is possible for the economy to grow in the short run, introducing new technologies and with consumption increasing, yet in the long run fall back into stagnation with declining consumption, unemployment and only the worst possible technology employed.

2. The Model

We consider an infinite horizon economy, t=0,1,2,... with a continuum of homogeneous consumers. Consumers value consumption $c_t \in \Re_+$. The *period utility* function $u(c_t)$ is bounded below, continuously differentiable, strictly increasing, and strictly concave. It satisfies the Inada conditions $\lim_{t\to 0} u'(c_t) = +\infty$ and $\lim_{t\to +\infty} u'(c_t) = 0$.

Total *lifetime utility* is given by $U(c) = \sum_{t=0}^{\infty} \delta^t u(c_t)$ here $0 \le \delta < 1$ is the common subjective discount factor.

Let $\mu = \sup\left\{ \tilde{\mu} \,\|\, \sum_{t=0}^{\infty} \delta^t u\left(\tilde{\mu}^t\right) < \infty \right\}$. Notice that $\mu > 1/\delta$.

Consumption is produced by *activities* that use labor and capital as inputs. In addition, capital is produced from capital, and labor reproduces itself. Capital comes in an infinite sequence of different qualities, indexed by *i*=0,1,...

Write the vector $z = (\kappa, \ell)$ where κ, is an infinite vector of capital stocks of different qualities, and Q is a scalar denoting labor. The period commodity space consists of the set $Z \subseteq \ell_+^\infty$ composed of sequences $(z_1, z_2, ..., z_n, ...) \ge 0$ for which $z_n = 0$ for all but finitely many n. We let the symbol χ_i denote the vector consisting of one unit of capital *i* and zero units of all other capitals. So, for example, $(\chi_2, 0)$ is an input vector with 1 unit of quality 2 capital and zero units of everything else.

The set of all activities *a* is denoted by A. An activity $a \in$ A may be written as a vector consisting of a triplet $[z(a); z^+(a); c(a)]$, where $z(a), z^+ \in Z, c(a) \in \Re_+$. Here $z(a) = [\kappa(a), \ell(a)]$ represents the input requirement for activity *a* in period *t*, $z^+(a) = [\kappa^+(a), \ell^+(a)]$ represents the output of period t+1 inputs produced by activity a, and c(a) represents consumption produced by activity *a* for period t.

Our basic assumption is that capital of quality i can be used to produce consumption, capital of the same quality or capital of the next highest quality. We assume that labor is an input (and also an output) in the production of consumption, but not into the production of capital. As we discuss in the conclusion, this is consistent with the idea that there is little labor mobility between the consumption and investment sectors, and even if we were to allow labor mobility, the general nature of our results do not change.

Specifically, there is a sequence of activities for producing consumption, one for each quality of capital *i*. For quality *i* capital, the activity is $[\chi_i, 1/\gamma^i; 0, 1/\gamma^i; 1], \gamma > 1$. In other words, to produce a unit of consumption requires a unit of capital (of any quality) and a number of units of labor that is smaller, the higher is the quality of the capital. Notice that labor appears both as an input and as an output: in words, it reproduces itself.

Two sequences of activities can produce capital. They are $[\chi_i,0;\beta\chi_i,0;0], \beta>1$ and $[\chi_i,0;\rho\chi_{i+1},0;0], \rho>0$. This means that the current quality of capital may be used either to produce β units of the same quality of capital, or ρ units of the next quality of capital. We set $\beta>\rho$, so that introducing the next quality of capital goods instead of widening the current one requires a sacrifice of current consumption. We assume that $\mu>\min\{\beta,\gamma\}$ so maximum utility over feasible consumption paths is finite. We also assume that there is free disposal, and an activity that produces next period labor by means of current period labor $[0,1;0,1;0]$.

The endowment z_0 is the initial amount of quality 0 capital, κ_0^0 and one unit of labor.

2.1 Equilibrium

A $\lambda\in\left(\times_{t=0}^{\infty}\Re_+^A\right)$ is called a *production plan*, a $c\in\left(\times_{t=0}^{\infty}\Re_+\right)$ is called a *consumption plan*. Together they determine an (intertemporal) *allocation*.

Definition 1 *The allocation* λ, c *is a* feasible *allocation for the* initial condition z_0 *if for all* $t\geq 0$

$$1\geq\sum_{a\in A}\lambda_t(a)\ell(a)$$

$$\kappa_0^0\geq\sum_{a\in A}\lambda_0(a)\kappa(a)$$

$$\sum_{a\in A}\lambda_t(a)z^+(a)\geq\sum_{a\in A}\lambda_{t+1}(a)z(a)$$

Definition 2 *The allocation* λ^*,c^* *solves the social planner problem for initial condition* z_0 *if it solves*

$$\max_{\lambda,c}U(c)$$

subject to feasibility of the allocation.

Notice that in a feasible production plan $\lambda_t(a)=0$ if a uses as input any quality of capital greater than *t*. Denote by A_t the set of *viable activities* which use as input qualities of capital no greater than *t*.

Let q_t^i denote the price of quality *i* capital at time *t*, let q_t^ℓ denote the price of labor at time *t*, and let p_t denote the price of consumption at time *t*. We denote by q_t the vector of all input prices at time *t*, and let q,p respectively denote the infinite sequence of prices of the two inputs and consumption starting in period 0. Prices q,p and a feasible allocation λ,c are a *competitive equilibrium* if c maximizes $U(c)$ subject to the budget constraint

$$\sum_{t=0}^{\infty} p_t c_t \leq q_0^0 p_0^0 + q_0^\ell,$$

and activities satisfy the *zero profit condition*

$$q_{t+1}\cdot\left[\kappa^+(a),\ell^+(a)\right]+p_t c(a)-q_t\cdot\left[\kappa(a),\ell(a)\right]\leq 0, \forall a\in A_t, t=0,1,...$$

with equality if $\lambda_t(a)>0$.

In the appendix we prove the relevant version of the First and Second Welfare Theorems:

Theorem 1 *Suppose that λ^*,c^* is a feasible allocation for the initial condition zo. Then λ^*,c^* solves the social planner problem if and only if we can find prices q,p such that q,p , λ^*,c^* are a competitive equilibrium.*

The following existence and uniqueness result is also proved in the appendix.

Theorem 2 *For given z_0, a competitive equilibrium exists, and there is a unique competitive equilibrium consumption plan c^*.*

For any given value of c_t observe that either $c_t \leq 1$ or for some $i>0, \gamma^{i-1}<c_t<\gamma^i$. In the former case define $\eta(c_t)=0$, in the latter $\eta(c_t)=1$. Define

$$\kappa_0^0(c_t)=\begin{cases} \beta^{-t}c_t & \eta(c_t)=0 \\ \beta^{-t}\left(\dfrac{\beta}{\rho}\right)^{\eta(c_t)}\dfrac{\gamma c_t-\gamma^{\eta(c_t)}}{\gamma-1}+\beta^{-t}\left(\dfrac{\beta}{\rho}\right)^{\eta(c_t)-1}\dfrac{\gamma^{\eta(c_t)}-c_t}{\gamma-1} & \eta(c_t)>0 \end{cases}$$

The latter expression represents 'the amount of initial capital required to produce c_t when it is produced using only qualities $\eta(c_t)$ and $\eta(c_t)-1$ capital'. Define also the 'initial capital requirement to produce c'

$$\kappa_0^0(c) = \sum_{t=0}^{\infty} \kappa_0^0(c_t).$$

Finally, define the constants

$$\zeta_0 = 1$$
$$\zeta_i = (\beta / \rho)^{i-1}[(\beta\gamma / \rho) - 1]/(\gamma - 1).$$

For $q_0^0 \geq 0$ and $t = 0,1,...$, we use these constants to define the following correspondence $c'_t \in C_t(c_t, q_0^0)$ from $c_t \in [0, \gamma^t]$ into $\Re_+$

$$\begin{array}{ll} u'(c'_t) = (\beta\delta)^{-t} q_0^0 \zeta_{\eta(c_t)} & \text{if } c_t < \gamma^{\eta(c_t)}, \eta(c_t) \leq t \\ (\beta\delta)^{-t} q_0^0 \zeta_{\eta(c_t)} \leq u'(c'_t) \leq (\beta\delta)^{-t} q_0^0 \zeta_{\eta(c_t)+1} & \text{if } c_t = \gamma^{\eta(c_t)}, \eta(c_t) < t \\ (\beta\delta)^{-t} q_0^0 \zeta_{\eta(c_t)} \leq u'(c'_t) & \text{if } c_t = \gamma^{\eta(c_t)}, \eta(c_t) = t \end{array}$$

This correspondence consists of horizontal and vertical line segments forming the steps of a 'descending' stair. It is upper-hemi-continuous, convex valued and non-increasing. It is immediate to see that, for given q_0^0 and t, it has only one fixed point $c_t^* \in (0, \gamma^t]$. The key property of this correspondence is that its fixed points capture the first order conditions for an optimal path. In the appendix we prove the following.

Theorem 3 *For given z_0 the feasible consumption plan c^* is an optimum if and only if there exists a q_0^0 such that*

$$\kappa_0^0 \geq \kappa_0^0(c^*) \text{ with equality unless } q_0^0 = 0$$

$$c_t^* \in C_t(c_t^*, q_0^0)$$

Moreover, equilibrium prices are given by the following

$$q_t^i = \beta^{-t} \left(\frac{\beta}{\rho} \right)^i q_0^0,$$

$$w_t = \gamma^{\eta(c_t^*)} \left[\delta^t u'(c_t^*) - \beta^t (\beta / \rho)^{\eta_t} q_0^0 \right]$$

and

$$q_T^t = \sum_{t=T}^{\infty} w_t$$

The equilibrium production plan is any feasible plan that produces c_t^* using only quality $\eta(c_t^*)$ and $\eta(c_t^*)-1$ quality capital, and has full employment whenever $\eta(c_t^*)>0$.

3. Solow, Growth Cycles and Stagnation

Here we focus on the long-run behavior of the economy. We show that there are three possible outcomes. In the first, a new technology is introduced every period and the economy grows at the rate γ. We refer to this as the *Solow* growth path. For the technology which is being considered here, the Solow path provides the highest attainable level of consumption in each single period; hence our reference to this as 'nirvana' or 'golden age' path. At the opposite extreme, it may be the case that no new technologies are ever introduced after a finite number of new qualities of capital have been adopted, and the capital stock either declines or remains the same over time. We refer to this as the *stagnation* steady state. While possible in principle, golden age and stagnation are very unlikely outcomes requiring extreme configurations of the parameter values. Finally, the economy may enter an irregular growth cycle, in which two different qualities of capital are used for a period of time, then the lower quality capital is dropped and a new quality of capital is introduced for the first time, and so on. We refer to this as the *growth cycle.* This is the main focus of our interest.

We first study the Solow balanced growth path, which is the easiest, and next the growth cycle, which is the most interesting. We conclude with the special case of stagnation.

3.1 The Solow Balanced Growth Path

Improving the quality of capital does not change the amount of output that can be produced from that capital, but it does reduce the labor requirement for one unit of output. Since there is a fixed supply of labor, the economy can grow, but only by continually moving to more advanced qualities of capital that make it possible to produce increased amounts of output from the existing stock of labor. When the innovation occurrs, ρ units of new capital are produced for each unit of old capital invested, generating an additional demand of $\rho/\gamma-1$ units of labor input. If $\rho>\gamma$ the latter quantity is positive and, in each period, it is possible to shift the entire stock of capital from one quality to the next without causing labor to be unemployed. If a new quality of capital is introduced each period, the capital stock can grow fast enough that all labor is employed on capital of the newest quality.

In this case the rate of technological progress is independent of preferences, and also independent of preferences, consumption grows at the fixed rate γ. We refer to this as the Solow growth path, since this is the same result as in the Solow growth model with exogenous technological progress.

If the initial capital stock is large enough, then the unique equilibrium is this Solow growth path beginning with consuming a unit in period one. Notice that if this path is feasible it must be optimal, since it is not possible by any plan to have higher consumption in any period.

Recall that κ_0^0 is the initial stock and κ_t^i denotes the capital stock of quality i at time t. Along a Solow growth path, at t only κ_t^t is positive. Suppose that κ_0^0 is the least capital stock needed for the Solow growth path. Then we must have $\kappa_1^1 = \gamma\kappa_0^0$. In addition a unit of capital must be used to produce consumption of 1 in period 0, so $\kappa_1^1 = \rho(\kappa_0^0 - 1)$. Solving, we find that

$$\kappa_0^0 = \frac{\rho}{\rho - \gamma}$$

We summarize by

Theorem 4 *If* $\rho > \gamma$ *and* $\kappa_0^0 \geq \rho/(\rho - \gamma)$, *the unique equilibrium is a balanced growth path in which a new technology is introduced every period, consumption in period* t *is* γ^t, *capital also grows at the rate* γ *and there is full employment in all periods.*

Next we look at the behavior of prices, factor shares and observable TFP along the Solow path. Notice first that $v_t = 1$ and $\eta_y = t$ all t. Further, $\kappa_0^0(\gamma^t) = \rho/(\rho - \gamma)$. Hence $q_0^0 = 0$ if $\kappa_0^0 > \rho/(\rho - \gamma)$. In fact, in this Solow case, we may take the initial price *of* capital $q_0^0 = 0$, also for $\kappa_0^0 = \rho/(\rho - \gamma)$ since utility does not increase with increases in the capital stock. This implies also that the price of all qualities of capital in all periods is zero. Normalizing the marginal utility of income $\psi = 1$, the consumption prices are

$$p_t = \delta^t u'(\gamma^t).$$

Wages are

$$w_t = \gamma^t p_t$$

and the real wage $\tilde{w}_t = w_t / p_t = \gamma^t$, so real wages grow exponentially over time.

Notice that, independently from our normalization of the initial price of capital, output grows at a constant and exogenous rate γ and factor shares are constant at the level determined in the first period. The capital/labor ratio is also growing at the constant rate γ. Similarly for 'effective' or, as we call it here, enhanced labor with the productivity of physical labor growing at the exogenous rate γ. Hence our golden age is observationally equivalent to the traditional Solow growth model, with a Cobb–Douglas production function and exogenous technological progress.

3.2 The Growth Cycle

When circumstances are not so lucky, that is when either $\gamma < \rho$ or the initial stock of capital $\kappa_0^0 < \rho/(\rho - \gamma)$ is too low to make the Solow path immediately accessible, the long-run behavior of both consumption and the introduction of new technologies will generally depend upon preferences, and in particular on the subjective discount factor δ. There are two cases, depending on whether $\delta\beta > 1$, or $\delta\beta \leq 1$. If there was no labor constraint, this would correspond to the case in which the equilibrium exhibits sustained growth through capital accumulation, or stagnation, with consumption eventually bounded or decreasing. As we shall see, this remains the case with a labor constraint. We take the case of a growing economy, that is $\delta\beta > 1$, first.

3.2.1 The General Case We begin by establishing that $\delta\beta > 1$ does correspond to sustained growth. First we observe that consumption is non-decreasing:

Lemma 1 *Suppose that* $\delta\beta > 1$. *Then* $c_{t+1}^* \geq c_t^*$.

Proof. The correspondence C is a stairstep with vertices

$$\left(\gamma^i, [u']^{-1}\left((\beta\delta)^{-t} q_0^0 (\beta\delta)^{i-1}[(\beta\gamma/\rho) - 1](\gamma - 1)\right)\right)$$

Increasing $\delta\beta$ increases the height of the vertex for each γ^i. In addition, the upper bound on the domain of the correspondence, γ^t, grows larger with t as well. It follows that the fixed point c_t^* must be non-decreasing.

An immediate implication is that the technologies used to produce consumption must be improving over time, for with full employment, consumption would otherwise have to decrease. It is also the case that asymptotically, there is no upper bound on the quality of capital used to produce consumption.

Lemma 2 *Suppose that* $\delta\beta > 1$. *Then there is no upper bound on the qualities of capital used to produce consumption.*

Proof. Observe that for fixed i as $t \to \infty$,

$$\frac{(\beta\delta)^{-t} q_0^0 (\beta/\rho)^{i-1}[(\beta\gamma/\rho) - 1]}{(\gamma - 1)} \to 0$$

Hence, for any given i, for large enough t the fixed point of C must lie to the right of γ^i, meaning that a better quality capital than i is used to produce consumption.

The general picture is this. As t grows larger, the correspondence C moves up and to the right. Observe that C has only horizontal and vertical segments. If the correspondence moves upwards sufficiently slowly ($\delta\beta$ near 1) then the fixed point will generally lie on the same segment for several consecutive periods. This length of time will determine the rate at which new technologies are introduced. In addition, the system behaves differently on horizontal and vertical segments. On horizontal segments, two types of capital are used to produce consumption, and consumption grows as the correspondence C shifts upwards. We refer to this as a boom. On vertical segments, only one type of capital is used to produce consumption, and consumption remains constant as the correspondence C shifts upwards. We refer to this as a recession (strictly speaking, a growth recession). In other words the economy exhibits an endogenous cycle in technological innovation and, therefore, in the growth rate of Total Factor Productivity.

One striking fact is that during a recession, the real wage increases. Specifically, during a recession, consumption is constant, so the present value price of consumption declines by a factor δ. On the other hand, the present value price of each quality of capital declines at $1/\beta < \delta$, and in particular the real price of capital falls. Since only one activity is used to produce consumption, zero profits for this activity imply the real wage must increase. During a recession, the real price of 'higher' quality capital declines, and the real wage increases, until it become profitable to introduce the next higher quality of capital into producing consumption to save on labor. In this sense, technological progress is 'biased' in this model as it takes place to conserve a particular factor when its relative price is high enough to make the innovation profitable.

3.3 The Continuous Time Limit

We can get a more accurate picture of the cycle by studying a special case. Suppose the time Δ between periods is small. So that the cycle does not depend on time, assume that, at least for consumption exceeding a minimum amount, preferences have the CES form

$$u(c_t) = -(1/\theta)[c_t]^{-\theta}.$$

In addition, take $\delta = e^{-r\Delta}, \beta = e^{b\Delta}$, the assumption $\delta\beta > 1$ corresponds to $b > r$. We also assume that innovations are discrete, so that the extent to which machine i saves on labor relative to machine $i-1$ is independent of time. Hence $\gamma > 1$ independently of Δ. We also have $\rho = \tilde{\rho}e^{d\Delta}$. Since innovations are costly, we assume that $\tilde{\rho} < 1$. As we are interested only in small values of Δ, we may also assume that $\rho = \tilde{\rho}e^{d\Delta} < \gamma$. We also denote calendar time by $\tau = t\Delta$.

Suppose at some particular time that $c_t^* = \gamma^{i-1}$. Then

$$u'(c_t^*) = (\beta\delta)^{-t} q_0^0 (\beta/\rho)^{i-1}[(\beta\gamma/\rho)-1]/(\gamma-1).$$

This corresponds to the beginning of a horizontal segment or a boom. In our special case, we may write this as

$$c_t^* = \left\{ \left(e^{(b-r)\Delta}\right)^{-\tau/\Delta} q_0^0 \left[\left(\frac{e^{(b-d)\Delta}}{\tilde{\rho}} \right)^{i-1} \frac{\gamma e^{(b-d)\Delta} - \tilde{\rho}}{\tilde{\rho}(\gamma-1)} \right] \right\}^{-1/(\theta+1)}$$

As τ increases, so does c_t^* until eventually $c_t^* = y^i$, at which point the recession occurs. We can calculate a good approximation to this length of time by taking the continuous time limit when $\Delta \to 0$

$$c_t^* = \left[e^{(r-b)\tau} q_0^0 \left(\gamma/\tilde{\rho}\right)^{i-1} \left(\frac{\gamma/\tilde{\rho} - 1}{\gamma - 1} \right) \right]^{-1/\theta+1}$$

In other words, consumption is simply growing at the rate $(b-r)/(\theta+1)$. The length of the boom τ_b is determined by the amount of time required for consumption to grow by a factor of γ or

$$\tau_b = \frac{\theta+1}{b-r} \ln \gamma$$

The recession, on the other hand, lasts from t to $t+\tau_r/\Delta$ where

$$(\beta\delta)^{-t} q_0^0 (\beta/\rho)^{i-1} [(\beta\gamma/\rho)-1]/(\gamma-1) = (\beta\delta)^{-(t+\tau_r/\Delta)} q_0^0 (\beta/\rho)^i [(\beta\gamma/\rho)-1]/(\gamma-1)$$

The continuous time approximation gives

$$e^{(r-b)\tau_r} \frac{e^{(b-d)\Delta}}{\tilde{\rho}} = 1$$

Taking the limit for $\Delta \to 0$ and solving for τ_r

$$\tau_r = -\frac{\ln \tilde{\rho}}{b-r}$$

Consider first the length $\tau_c = \tau_b + \tau_r$ of the whole cycle. This is

$$\tau_c = \frac{1}{b-r} \left[\ln \left(\frac{\gamma^{1+\theta}}{\tilde{\rho}} \right) \right]$$

which is increasing in γ, θ and r and decreasing in b and ρ. The shorter the cycle, the more quickly new technologies are introduced, so we find that innovation responds negatively to the quality of the innovation γ, the preference parameter θ, and the subjective degree of impatience θ. The most interesting of these is the quality of the innovation γ. Higher quality innovations in this model lead to less innovation, because they make it possible to grow for a longer period of time without hitting the labor constraint. On the other hand, we find that there is more innovation if the cost of producing capital, as measured by the inverse of either b or $\tilde{\rho}$, goes down.

The relative length of the two phases, booms and recessions, is

$$\frac{\tau_b}{\tau_r} = -(1+\theta)\frac{\ln\gamma}{\ln\tilde{\rho}}$$

Interestingly enough, neither the productivity of the capital widening technology, nor the degree of impatience affects the relative length of booms and recessions. Economies where people exhibit low willingness to substitute consumption over time (high values of B) have longer (but 'less rampant') booms for a given recession length.

As we noted above, improved quality of innovation (high γ) makes it possible to grow for a longer period of time without hitting the labor constraint. This increases the length of booms, but not of recessions. Finally, a large cost of innovation is bound to increase the relative amount of time spent in recession.

The average growth rate of consumption over an entire cycle is the value of g solving

$$\gamma = \exp\left[\frac{g}{b-r}\ln\left(\frac{\gamma^{1+\theta}}{\tilde{\rho}}\right)\right]$$

which is

$$g = \frac{b-r}{1+\theta-\ln\tilde{\rho}/\ln\gamma}$$

Hence, economies where people are more willing to substitute consumption over time grow faster on average, as do economies able to implement more substantial innovations.

We already noted above that the real wage grows during recession. As there is always full employment, this implies a counter-cyclical movement in the labor share of national income. Over the entire cycle, productivity of labor grows by a factor γ, the same for the real wage. As consumption is constant during recessions, its price relative to both old and new capital must be increasing then. Overall, the price of a machine of quality i decreases over time relative to that of consumption and the rate of decrease is uniform across qualities.

3.4 Stagnation

Finally we turn to the case in which $\delta\beta < 1$. In the absence of a labor constraint, this would imply that the economy remains stagnant, either with constant consumption if $\delta\beta = 1$, or declining consumption if $\delta\beta < 1$. With the labor constraint, if $\rho > \gamma$ and $\kappa_0^0 \geq \rho/(\rho - \gamma)$ we have already indicated that the equilibrium is the Solow path of exogenous sustained growth regardless of whether $\delta\beta \leq 1$. In this case, introducing a labor constraint and the possibility of factor saving technological progress changes a stagnant economy in which consumption never grows into an expanding economy in which consumption grows forever, and new technologies are introduced every period. In the long run, the additional constraint can be seen as the incentive toward adopting technological innovations that lead to higher consumption.

On the other hand, the next theorem shows that if either the Solow path does not exist because $\rho < \gamma$, or there is insufficient initial capital, then the picture is indeed one of a stagnant economy in the long run. There is an upper limit on the highest quality of capital ever produced, and ultimately consumption either stops growing ($\delta\beta = 1$) or declines ($\delta\beta < 1$).

Theorem 5 *Suppose either $\rho < \gamma$ or $\kappa_0^0 \geq \rho/(\rho - \gamma)$. If $\delta\beta < 1$ there exists a technology I such that no quality of capital greater than I is ever produced, and a period T such that for all $t \geq T$*

If $\delta\beta = 1, c_t^* = c_T^*$
If $\delta\beta < 1, c_{t+1}^* < c_t^* < 1$

Proof. Under the conditions given, it follows that $q_0^0 > 0$. As $i \to \infty$, the Inada condition for $c \to \infty$ implies

$$[u']^{-1}(\delta\beta)^{-1} q_0^0 (\beta/\rho)^{i-1}\left[\frac{(\beta\gamma/\rho)-1}{(\gamma-1)}\right] \leq [u']\left(q_0^0(\beta/\rho)^{i-1}\left[\frac{(\beta\gamma/\rho)-1}{(\gamma-1)}\right]\right) \to 0$$

It follows that there is some technology I for which, for all t,

$$[u']^{-1}\left((\delta\beta)^{-1} q_0^0 (\beta/\rho)^{I-1}\left[(\beta\gamma/\rho)-1\right]/(\gamma-1)\right) < \gamma^I$$

Consequently, no technology $i \geq I$ is used to produce consumption. It follows that the optimal consumption plan does not ever produce any capital of quality $i \geq I$.

For $\delta\beta = 1$ the correspondence C does not either increase or decrease, it simply shifts to the right; once $t \geq I$ it follows that there is a unique and time independent fixed point of C.

For $\delta\beta < 1$, as $t \to \infty$ we have $[u']^{-1}((\delta\beta)q_0^0) \to 0$, so eventually the fixed point of C must lie below 1. Since $[u']^{-1}((\delta\beta)q_0^0)$ is also strictly decreasing, so is c_t^*.

This theorem also demonstrates another important possibility in this economy: path dependence. That is, suppose that $\delta\beta < 1$ and $\rho > \gamma$. Then if initial capital exceeds the level $\kappa_0^0 \geq \rho/(\rho-\gamma)$ needed for the Solow path, the long run is one of technological innovation and sustained growth. On the other hand, if initial capital falls a bit short of the threshold, so that $\kappa_0^0 < \rho/(\rho-\gamma)$ in the long run, only the lowest possible quality capital is produced, there is unemployment, and consumption continually falls. In particular, if we were to compare two economies with different initial capital endowments, one above and one below the threshold, we would discover that they do not 'converge' to the same long-run growth path.

Finally, we point out a further interesting property of our economy: consumption and growth paths that, depending upon initial conditions, may be strictly non monotone. More precisely, even when $\kappa_0^0 < \rho/(\rho-\gamma)$ the economy may innovate and grow for some period of time, before falling back into stagnation. For economies of this kind, relatively rich at the beginning but highly impatient or not very efficient at reproducing already existing capital, consumption will grow at a rate $\gamma > 1$ for a while and then rapidly decrease at a rate $(\delta\beta)^{1/(1+\theta)}$ forever. It is as if the airplane gets off the runway, then falls back to the ground.

To see, this consider an economy in which $\rho > \gamma$, $\delta\beta < 1$ and $\beta/(\beta-1) < \kappa_0^0 < \rho/(\rho-\gamma)$. In the competitive equilibrium, for $T \geq 1$ periods consumption grows at a rate y, starting at $c_0 = 1$, and falls at a rate $(\delta\beta)^{1/(1+\theta)}$ for $t > \overline{T}$. The length $\overline{T}$ of the 'temporary golden age' can be computed as the higher integer for which

$$\sum_{t=0}^{T}\left(\frac{\gamma}{\rho}\right)^t < \kappa_0^0$$

One can check that, for $T \to \infty$ the left hand side of the last expression converges to $\rho/(\rho-\gamma)$, the minimum initial condition to achieve eternal nirvana.

4. Conclusion

We examine a model in which an essential input cannot be increased at the same speed as the others. Hence, growth in per capita consumption needs factor saving innovations to take place. An innovation, new machine, is factor saving when it reduces the input requirement of some factor per unit of output. Machines that need less of a certain factor than other machines must be more expensive. Hence, factor saving innovations necessarily induce a non-trivial trade-off between capital widening and capital deepening. Capital widening is less costly, but eventually hits a factor constraint (labor in our example) forcing growth through capital deepening. Consequently, the rate at which new technologies are introduced becomes endogenous, depending among other things on the rate of intertemporal substitution in consumption, on the technology and on the economy's initial conditions. As in other models of endogenous growth, the rate of growth of consumption is also endogenous in the same sense.

At least since Hicks' (1932) seminal writings, economists have been debating about factor saving innovations that are 'biased'. The latter term indicates that technological progress augments productivity for some factor(s) more than for others and it does so because of relative price incentives. We have built a general equilibrium model in which these circumstances are realized and looked at their implications. Our main finding is that, under these circumstances, technological adoption is likely to be endogenous and, indeed, affected by relative prices and initial conditions. Further, we have proved that when technological progress is factor saving it must come in cycles unless special circumstances occur.

We have chosen to model the factor constraint as binding in the consumption sector only, and to concentrate on the case of just one fixed factor. However, the basic message remains the same regardless of such simplifying restrictions. Obviously, when the scarce factor can grow at a rate n, the whole analysis can be replicated for $\beta > n$. When more than one scarce factor exists, factor saving innovations can take place along different directions. While this may complicate the model and its equilibrium dynamics, providing an interesting topic of future extensions, the basic message about the oscillatory nature of factor saving technological innovation would only be strengthened. Finally, the basic message does not depend upon the sector in which the constraint binds, or whether labor is perfectly mobile between the two sectors. Indeed, we worked out preliminary versions of the case of perfect labor mobility between the two sectors, without qualitatively different results. Notice, incidentally, that our example does not require that there be no labor used in the production of capital, just that there is labor immobility between the two sectors, and that the labor constraint binds first in the consumption sector. This particular example is a useful starting point because of its simplicity and the stark results it delivers. In addition we do not think the assumption of perfect labor mobility between the two sectors is especially more plausible than complete immobility between the two sectors.

Appendix

Lemma 1 *A consumption plan c, with $c_t > 0$ for all t, maximizes $U(c)$ subject to the budget constraint if and only if for some $\psi \geq 0$*

$$p_t = \psi \delta^t u'(c_t)$$

$$\sum_{t=0}^{\infty} p_t c_t = q_0^0 \kappa_0^0 + q_0^\ell$$

Proof. This is standard.

Theorem 2 *Suppose that* λ^*, c^* *is a feasible allocation for the initial condition* z_0. *Then* λ^*, c^* *solves the social planner problem if and only if we can find prices* q, p *such that* q, p, λ^*, c^* *are a competitive equilibrium.*

Proof. That a competitive equilibrium solves the social planner problem is a standard first welfare theorem proof. To prove the second, we need to show that we can find prices that support a solution to the social planner problem.

Suppose that λ, c^* is a solution to the planner problem for the initial condition z_0. Let z^* be the corresponding inputs. Let z_{T+1} denote a vector of labor and capital of quality $i \le T+1$. Let $V^{T+1}(z_{T+1})$ denote the maximum utility, discounted at $t=0$, of beginning with the endowment z_{T+1} in period $T+1$ and continuing forward. Let $U^T(c)=\sum_{t=0}^{T}\delta^t u(c_t)$.

Observe that λ^*, c^* solves the problems of maximizing $U^T(c)+V^{T+1}(z_{T+1})$ subject to social feasibility. This is a finite dimensional problem. By standard finite dimensional arguments, we can find finite dimensional price vectors $\overline{q}^T$, $\overline{p}^t$ so that the zero profit conditions are satisfied for viable activities up to $T+1$. By the same standard arguments, the vector $c_t^*, t=0,...,T$ and the scalar z_{T+1}^* are optimal for the consumer under the budget constraint, $\sum \overline{p}_t^T c_t + \overline{q}_{T+1}^T z_{T+1} = \left(\overline{q}_0^\kappa\right)^T \kappa_0^0 + \left(\overline{q}_0^\ell\right)^T$. We may also normalize prices so that $\overline{p} = \delta^t u'(c_t^*)$. Let Q_T denote the set of all (non-negative) infinite dimensional price sequences for which the projection on $\Re_+^T \times \Re_+^{2\times(T+1)}$ is a supporting price vector for the finite dimensional problem above. Observe that $Q^T \supseteq Q^{T+1}$ and that these are closed spaces. It follows that $Q=\bigcap_{T\to\infty} Q^T$ is closed, although possibly empty. Next observe that $\overline{\overline{q}}_t^{T+1}$ is a supergradient of $V^{t+1}(z_{t+1})$ at z_{t+1}^*. Notice that $\overline{q}_{t+1}^T$ is bounded below by zero and above by some finite two dimensional vector $\overline{q}_{t+1}^T z_{t+1}^* + V^{t+1}(0) \le V^{t+1}(z_{t+1}^*)$ and the latter is finite. It follows that the intersection Q is non-empty. Let q be in Q. By construction q and p (which is uniquely defined from the first order condition) satisfy zero profits. From the consumer budget constraint in the truncated problems, we have $\sum_{t=0}^{T} p_t c_t^* + q_{T+1} z_{T+1}^* = q_0^k \kappa_0^0 + q_0^\ell$. Since $\overline{q}_{t+1}$ is a gradient of $V^{t+1}(z_{t+1})$ at z_{t+1}^*, we have $q_{T+1} z_{T+1}^* + V^{T+1}(0) \le V^{T+1}(z_{t+1}^*)$. Also $V^{T+1}(0)=\delta^{T+1}u(0)/(1-\delta)$ and

$V^{T+1}(z^*_{T+1}) = \sum_{t=T+2}^{\infty} \delta^t u(c^*_t)$. Since $\sum \delta^t u(c^*_t) < \infty$ it follows that $\lim_{T\to\infty} V^{T+1}(z^*_{T+1}) \to 0$,

and so $q_{T+1} z^*_{T+1} \to 0$, which gives $\sum_{t=0}^{\infty} p_t c^*_t = q^0_0 \kappa^0_0 + q^\ell_0$

Theorem 3 *For given* z_0 *, a competitive equilibrium exists, and there is a unique competitive equilibrium consumption plan* c^* .

Proof. Since $U(c)$ is bounded above on the feasible set of feasible consumption paths, it is continuous in the product topology. Since this set is compact in the product topology, an optimum exists; it is unique since U is strictly concave.

Define a simple plan to be a pair of sequences of integers $(\nu,\eta) = (\nu_0, \eta_0, \nu_1, \eta_1, \ldots)$ where $\nu_t \in \{1,2\}$, $\nu_0 = 1$; $t \geq \eta_t \geq 0$, and $\eta_t > 0$ if $\nu_t = 2$. A production plan (λ, k) is consistent with the simple plan (ν,η) if

1. exactly ν_t different qualities of capital are employed in period t to produce consumption
2. when $\nu_t = 1$ the quality of capital employed to produce consumption is η_t , and
3. when $\nu_t = 2$ the two qualities of capital used to produce consumption are η_t, η_{t-1} .

We say that a production plan exhibits full employment if there is unemployment only in periods where no quality of capital other than 0 is used to produce consumption. We say that a simple plan (ν,η) and a consumption stream c are consistent if there is a full employment production plan (λ,k) consistent with the simple plan that yields the output c . If $\nu_t = 1$ and $\eta_t = 0$ then (λ,k) uses exactly $\kappa^{\eta_t}_t = c_t \leq 1$ units of quality 0 capital. If $\nu_t = 1$ and $\eta_t > 0$ then it uses $\kappa^{\eta_t}_t = \gamma^{\eta_t}$ units of quality η_t capital for full employment, so $c_t = \gamma^{\eta_t}$. If $\nu_t = 2$ then it uses exactly $\kappa^{\eta_t}_t$ units of quality η_t capital and exactly $\kappa^{\eta_t - 1}_t$ units of quality $\eta_t - 1$ capital, where these are the unique solution of $\kappa^{\eta_t}_t / \gamma^{\eta_t} + \kappa^{\eta_t - 1}_t / \gamma^{\eta_t - 1} = 1$, and $\kappa^{\eta_t}_t + \kappa^{\eta_t - 1}_t = c_t$.

For convenience, we now replicate the definitions from the text. For any given value of c_t observe that either $c_t < 1$ or for some $i > 0, \gamma^{i-1} < c_t \leq \gamma^i$. In the former case define $\eta(c_t) = 0$, in the latter $\eta(c_t) = i$. Let

$$\kappa_0^0(c_t) = \begin{cases} \beta^{-t}c_t & \eta(c_t) = 0 \\ \beta^{-t}\left(\frac{\beta}{\rho}\right)^{\eta(c_t)} \frac{\gamma c_t - \gamma^{\eta(c_t)}}{\gamma - 1} + \beta^{-t}\left(\frac{\beta}{\rho}\right)^{\eta(c_t)-1} \frac{\gamma^{\eta(c_t)} - c_t}{\gamma - 1} & \eta(c_t) > 0 \end{cases}$$

and

$$\kappa_0^0(c) = \sum_{t=0}^{\infty} \kappa_0^0(c_t).$$

Set

$$\zeta_0 = 1$$
$$\zeta_i = (\beta / \rho)^{i-1}[(\beta\gamma / \rho) - 1]/(\gamma - 1).$$

Define the correspondence $c'_t \in C_t(c_t, q_0^0)$ by

$$\begin{array}{ll} u'(c'_t) = (\beta\delta)^{-t} q_0^0 \zeta_{\eta(c_t)} & \text{if } c_t < \gamma^{\eta(c_t)}, \eta(c_t) \le t \\ (\beta\delta)^{-t} q_0^0 \zeta_{\eta(c_t)} \le u'(c'_t) \le (\beta\delta)^{-t} q_0^0 \zeta_{\eta(c_t)+1} & \text{if } c_t = \gamma^{\eta(c_t)}, \eta(c_t) < t \\ (\beta\delta)^{-t} q_0^0 \zeta_{\eta(c_t)} \le u'(c'_t) & \text{if } c_t = \gamma^{\eta(c_t)}, \eta(c_t) = t \end{array}$$

This correspondence is upper-hemi-continuous, convex valued and non-increasing.

Theorem 4 *For given z_0 the feasible consumption plan c^* is an optimum if and only if there exists a q_0^0 such that*

$$\kappa_0^0 \ge \kappa_0^0(c^*) \text{ with equality unless } q_0^0,$$

and

$$c^* \in C_t(c^*, q_0^0)$$

Moreover, equilibrium prices are given by

$$q_t^i = \beta^{-t}\left(\frac{\beta}{\rho}\right)^i q_0^0$$
$$w_t = \gamma^{\eta(c_t^*)}\left[\delta^t u'(c_t^*) - \beta^t (\beta/\rho)^{\eta_t} q_0^0\right]$$

and

$$q_T^t = \sum_{t=T}^{\infty} w_t$$

The equilibrium production plan is any feasible plan that produces c_t^* using only quality $\eta(c_t^*)$ and $\eta(c_t^*)-1$ quality capital, and has full *employment whenever* $\eta(c_t^*)>0$.

Proof. For given z_0 suppose the feasible consumption plan c^* is an optimum.

We first claim that there is an initial price *of* capital q_0^0, a non-negative sequence of wages $w=(w_0,w_1,\ldots)$ and a simple plan (v,η) consistent with c^* such that the following conditions hold

1. $\delta^t u'(c_t^*)-\beta^{-t}(\beta/\rho)^{\eta_t}q_0^0-w_t/\gamma^{\eta_t}=0$
2. if $v_t=2$ then $\delta^t u'(c_t^*)-\beta^{-t}(\beta/\rho)^{\eta_t-1}q_0^0-w_t/\gamma^{\eta_t-1}=0$
3. if $v_t=1$ and $\eta_t<t$ then $\delta^t u'(c_t^*)-\beta^{-t}(\beta/\rho)^{\eta_t+1}q_0^0-w_t/\gamma^{\eta_t+1}\le 0$
4. if $v_t=1$ and $\eta_t>0$ then $\delta^t u'(c_t^*)-\beta^{-t}(\beta/\rho)^{\eta_t-1}q_0^0-w_t/\gamma^{\eta_t-1}\le 0$
5. $w_{t=0}$ if there is unemployment at t.

First observe that if capital of quality $i>0$ is used to produce consumption for period t and there is unemployment, strictly greater consumption in that period can be had by replacing quality i capital in period t with quality 0. The full employment condition is consequently necessary for an optimum along any path that uses capital of quality other than $i=0$.

We now apply the zero profit conditions for competitive equilibrium. Let q_t^i denote the price of quality i capital in period t, and let q_t^ℓ denote the price of labor. Beginning with one unit of quality 0 capital in period 0, i quality upgrades producing ρ units of capital each and $t-i$ periods producing β units of capital are required to get from quality 0 at time 0 to quality i at time t, for all possible $i\le t$. The order in which the ρ and β phases come does not matter. It follows then, from the zero profit condition applied to the capital producing activities only, that if $i\le t$ then

$$q_t^i=\frac{q_0^0}{\rho^i\beta^{t-i}}=\beta^{-t}\left(\frac{\beta}{\rho}\right)^i q_0^0$$

From the fact that labor can always reproduce itself, we have

$$q_t^\ell\ge q_{t+1}^\ell$$

with equality if there is unemployment in period t. So we may define the wage rate

$$w_t = q_t^{\wp} - q_{t+1}^{\wp} \geq 0$$

We may then write the profits from the activity that at time t produces consumption c_{t+1} from quality i capital as

$$\pi_t^i = \delta^t u'(c_t) - \beta^{-t}(\beta/\rho)^i q_0^0 - w_t/\gamma^i$$

Recall that in equilibrium profits must be non-positive. Observe that this function is strictly concave as a function of i for fixed values of c_t, q_0^0, w_t. It follows that if this is non-positive for all $i \leq t$ it is zero for at most two activities, in which case it is strictly negative for all other activities, or if it is zero for one activity, it is sufficient that it be non-positive for the next highest and next lowest ones to be non-positive for all activities. So since in equilibrium $p_t = \delta^t u'(c_t^*)$ conditions 1–5 are indeed necessary.

Next we observe that $c_t^* \in C_t(c_t^*, q_0^0)$ if and only if 1–4 hold. In case $c_t < \gamma^{\eta(c_t^*)}$ full employment requires that c_t be produced using qualities $\gamma^{\eta(c^8)}, \gamma^{\eta(c^8)-1}$ of capital. Then $v_t = 2$ and 1) and 2) must hold. Solving yields $u'(c_t^*) = (\beta\delta)^{-t} q_o^o \zeta_{\eta(c_t^*)}$ and

$$w_t = \frac{\beta^{-t}\left|(\beta/\rho)^{\eta(c_t^*)} - (\beta/\rho)^{\eta(c_t^*)-1}\right| q_0^0}{1/\gamma^{\eta(c_t^*)-1} - 1/\gamma^{\eta(c_t^*)}}$$

which is non-negative since $\beta/\rho \geq 1$ and $1/\gamma < 1$.

Turning to $c_t = \gamma^{\eta(c_t)}$ we have 1, 3 and 4

$$\delta^t u'(c_t^*) - \beta^{-t}(\beta/\rho)^{\eta(c_t^*)} q_0^0 - w_t/\gamma^{\eta(c_t^*)} = 0$$

$$\delta^t u'(c_t^*) - \beta^{-t}(\beta/\rho)^{\eta(c_t^*)+1} q_0^0 - w_t/\gamma^{\eta(c_t^*)+1} \leq 0$$

$$\delta^t u'(c_t^*) - \beta^{-t}(\beta/\rho)^{\eta(c_t^*)-1} q_0^0 - w_t/\gamma^{\eta(c_t^*)-1} \leq 0$$

We can solve the first equation for w_t. Substituting into the second inequality, we see that it is satisfied if and only if $u'(c^*) \leq (\beta\delta)^{-t} q_0^0 \zeta_{\eta(c_t)}$ and the first if and only if $(\beta\delta)^{-t} q_0^0 \zeta_{\eta(c_t)-1} \leq u'(c^*)$. It is easy to check that these two inequalities also imply that $w_t \geq 0$.

Finally observe that $\kappa_0^0 \geq \kappa_0^0(c^*)$ with equality unless $q_0^0 = 0$ since otherwise it would be possible to produce c^* with less than the initial capital stock.

This proves that the conditions of the Theorem are necessary for an equilibrium. To show that they are also sufficient, observe that the Inada conditions imply that $u'(\cdot)$ maps $[0,\infty)$ onto itself, hence, for every $q_0^0 > 0$, there is a κ_0^0 for which q_0^0 is the equilibrium price of capital. Let c^* be the corresponding optimal consumption. This satisfies the necessary condition $c_t^* \in C_t(c_t^*, q_0^0)$ and $\kappa_0^0 = \kappa_0^0(c^*)$. Since $c_t^* \in C_t(c_t^*, q_0^0)$ has a unique solution, it follows that these conditions are sufficient as well.

References

Hicks, J.R. (1932), *The Theory of Wages*, London: Macmillan, 1963 (1st edition, 1932).

Lucas, R.E. Jr. (1988), 'On the Mechanics of Economic Development', *Journal of Monetary Economics*, 24, 1-55.

Prescott, E. (1998), 'Needed: A Theory of Total Factor Productivity', *International Economic Review*, 39, 525-551.

Rebelo, S. (1991), 'Long Run Policy Analysis and Long Run Growth', *Journal of Political Economy*, 99, 500-521.

Romer, P. (1990), 'Endogenous Technological Change', *Journal of Political Economy*, 98, S-S.

Romer, P. (1994), 'Che Origins of Endogenous Growth', *Journal of Economic Perspectives*, 8, 3-22.

Chapter 3

ICT 'Bottlenecks' and the Wealth of Nations: A Contribution to the Empirics of Economic Growth

Leonardo Becchetti and Fabrizio Adriani

1. Introduction

The empirical literature on the determinants of economic growth has progressively tested the significance of factors which were expected to contribute to growth in addition to the traditional labour and capital inputs. In this framework valuable contributions have assessed, among others,[1] the role of: human capital (Mankiw, Romer and Weil, 1992) (from now on MRW), the government sector (Hall and Jones, 1997), social and political stability (Alesina and Perotti, 1994), corruption (Mauro, 1995), social capital (Knack and Keefer, 1997), financial institutions (Pagano, 1993; King and Levine, 1992) and income inequality (Persson and Tabellini, 1994; Perotti, 1996).

The paradox of this literature, though, is that it has left the labour augmenting factor of the aggregate production function unspecified. The impact of technological progress on the differences between rich and poor countries has therefore been neglected by implicitly assuming that knowledge and its incorporation into productive technology is a public good, freely available to individuals in all countries (Temple, 1999).

This approach does not consider properly the nature of ICT and its role on growth. It neglects the fact that the core of ICT is made by weightless, expansible and infinitely reproducible *knowledge products* (software, databases) which create value, by increasing productivity of labour or by adding value to traditional physical products or traditional services. Knowledge products are almost public goods. Expansibility and infinite reproducibility make then non-rivalrous, and copyright (instead of patent) protection make them much less excludable than other types of innovation such as new drugs (Quah, 1999).

[1] Durlauf and Quah (1998) survey the empirical literature on growth and list something like 87 different proxies adopted to test the significance of additional factors in standard growth models. None of them is even akin to proxies adopted in this chapter to measure factors crucially affecting ICT diffusion.

Hence, if ICT consisted only of knowledge products, it would be almost immediately available everywhere no matter the country in which it was created. This does not occur though as the immediate diffusion and availability of knowledge products is prevented by some 'bottlenecks'. In our opinion these 'bottlenecks' are: i) the capacity of the network to carry the largest amount of knowledge products in the shortest time; ii) the access of individuals to the network in which knowledge products are immaterially transported; and iii) the power and availability of terminals which process, implement and exchange knowledge products which flow through the network.

In this framework, economic freedom and the development of financial markets may affect both ICT diffusion and its impact on growth. Insufficient access provision and excess taxation limit the diffusion of personal computers and Internet accesses (Quah, 1999). Liberalisation in the telecommunication sector reduces the costs of accessing the network and well-developed financial markets make it easier to finance projects which aim to implement the capacity of the network and the quality of 'terminals'.[2]

The omitted consideration of 'bottleneck-reducing' Information and Communication Technology (from now on BR-ICT) is partially justified so far by the scarcity of data,[3] but has relevant consequences on the accuracy of growth estimates. First (*omitted variable critique*), if BR-ICT variables which proxies for the diffusion of technology are significant and omitted, parameters of the other MRW regressors (labour and investment in physical and human capital) are biased as far as they are correlated with it. Second (*cross-sectional constant critique*), the omitted specification of the labour augmenting technological progress biases regressions on the determinants of levels of per capita income as the difference in technological progress across countries cannot be treated as a cross-sectional constant, implicitly attributing the same level of technology to every observation (Islam, 1995; Temple, 1999).[4] The solution of fixed effect panel data (Islam, 1995) is a partial remedy to it as it takes into account unobservable individual country effects.

In addition to reducing most of these problems, the inclusion of BR-ICT variables in the estimate may also avoid that uncontrolled heterogeneity in levels of

---

[2] The relationship between information and communication technology and productivity has long been debated over the past three decades. In the 1980s and in the early 1990s, empirical research generally did not find relevant productivity improvements associated with ICT investments (Bender, 1986; Loveman, 1988; Roach, 1989; Strassmann, 1990). This research showed that there was no statistically significant, or even measurable, association between ICT investments and productivity at any level of analysis chosen. More recently, as new data were made available and new methodologies were applied, empirical investigations have found evidence that ICT is associated with improvements in productivity, in intermediate measures and in economic growth (Oliner and Sichel, 1994; Brynjolfsson and Hitt, 1996; Sichel, 1997; Lehr and Lichtenberg, 1999).

[3] Quah writes in 1999 that 'the latest technologies have not been around for very long. Thus, convincing empirical time-series evidence on their impact will be difficult to obtain'.

[4] The only relevant exception may be when regressions are run on regions with a certain degree of technological homogeneity such as the US regions in the Barro and Sala-i-Martin (1992) paper on convergence.

per capita income lead to a significant correlation between the lagged level of per capita income and the error term in the convergence regressions, thereby violating one of the required assumptions for consistency of OLS estimates (*cross-country heterogeneity critique*).[5]

In this paper we show that the introduction of BR-ICT variables, by allowing us to model the unknown country differences in the diffusion of technology, generates a sharp increase in the explanatory power of cross-sectional estimates of the determinants of levels of income per worker and significantly reduces the effects of the *cross-sectional constant* and *omitted variable critiques*. The increased significance in the GDP per worker level regression reduces in turn the effects of the *cross-country heterogeneity critique* making possible a cross-sectional estimate of convergence in growth rates.

The robustness of the main result of the chapter (significance of the initial level and the rate of growth of BR-ICT technology in the cross-section and growth regressions) is accurately tested. With bootstrap estimates we find that it is not affected by departures from the normality assumption for the distribution of the dependent variable. A sensitivity analysis which follows the Levine and Renelt (1992) approach shows that the introduction of measures of macroeconomic policy performance and of economic, civil and political freedom does not substantially weaken the significance of BR-ICT variables. Generalised 2-Stage Least Squares (G2SLS) panel estimates evidence that the ICT-growth relationship is not affected by endogeneity and exogenous subsample splits demonstrate that our evidence is robust to the issue of parameters heterogeneity.

The chapter documents all these findings and is divided into four sections (including introduction and conclusions). In the second section we outline our theoretical hypotheses on the role of BR-ICT variables on aggregate growth. In the third section we present and comment empirical tests on our hypotheses.

2. The Determinants of Differences

2.1 Levels of Per Capita Growth

The considerations developed in the introduction on the role of ICT on growth lead us to formulate the following hypothesis:

Hypothesis 1: factors affecting ICT 'bottlenecks' are a good proxy for measuring the amount technological progress augments labour productivity in an MRW human capital growth model.

Consider the standard MRW (1992) production function taking into account the role of human capital:

---

[5] According to Evans (1997) this problem can be neglected only when at least 90-95 per cent of heterogeneity is accounted for.

$$Y_t = F(K, H, AL) = K_t^{\alpha} H^{\beta} (A_t L_t)^{1-\alpha-\beta} \text{ with } \alpha + \beta < 1 \tag{1}$$

where H is the stock of human capital, while L and K are the two traditional labour and physical capital inputs.

Physical capital and human capital follow the standard laws of motion.

$$\begin{aligned} \dot{K} &= s_K Y - \delta K \\ &= s_K F(K, AL) - \delta K \end{aligned} \tag{2}$$

$$\begin{aligned} \dot{H} &= s_H Y - \delta H \\ &= s_H F(K, AL) - \delta H \end{aligned} \tag{3}$$

where s_k and s_h are the fractions of income respectively invested in physical and human capital.

The exogenous growth of the labour input is expressed as:

$$L_t = L_0 e^{nt}. \tag{4}$$

Differently from MRW (1992), we model labour augmenting technological progress by assuming that most of it is proxied by weightless, infinitely reproducible, knowledge products (software, databases) which are conveyed to labour through crucial bottlenecks represented by the access to the network, the capacity of the network and the availability of terminals which process and exchange knowledge products.

We accordingly specify its dynamics as:

$$A_{(t)} = A_{KP(t)} A_{BR\text{-}ICT(t)} \tag{5}$$

with $A_{BR\text{-}ICT(t)} = A_{BR\text{-}ICT(0)}\, e^{gBR\text{-}ICT(t)}$ and $A_{KP(t)} = A_{KP(0)}\, e^{gKP(t)}$

$A_{BR\text{-}ICT}$ is a measure of the stock of ICT factors reducing the above-mentioned bottlenecks and $g_{BR\text{-}ICT}$ its rate of growth, while $A_{KP(t)}$ is the contribution to technological progress of the stock of weightless infinitely reproducible knowledge products and g_{KP} is its rate of growth.

By rewriting the production function in terms of output per efficiency units as $y=k\ h$ we can obtain the two standard growth equations.

$$\dot{k}_t = s_k y_t - (n + g + \delta) k_t \tag{6}$$

$$\dot{h}_t = s_h y_t - (n + g + \delta) h_t \tag{7}$$

where $g = g_{BR\text{-}ICT} + g_{KP}$.

If we set the growth of physical and human capital equal to zero in the steady state we get:

$$k^* = \left(\frac{s_k^{1-\beta} \cdot s_h^{\beta}}{n+g+\delta} \right)^{\frac{1}{1-\alpha-\beta}} \tag{8}$$

$$h^* = \left(\frac{s_k^{\alpha} \cdot s_h^{1-\alpha}}{n+g+\delta} \right)^{\frac{1}{1-\alpha-\beta}}. \tag{9}$$

Substituting h^* and k^* into the production function and taking logs we obtain:

$$\frac{Y}{L} = Af(k^*, h^*) = Ak^{*\alpha} h^{*\beta} = A_{KP(0)} e^{g_{KP}t} A_{BR-ICT(0)} e^{g_{BR-ICT}t} k^{*\alpha} h^{*\beta} \tag{10}$$

and:

$$\ln\left(\frac{Y_t}{L_t}\right) = c + \ln\left(A_{BR-ICT(0)}\right) + g_{BR-ICT}t + \frac{\alpha}{1-\alpha-\beta}\ln(s_k) + \frac{\beta}{1-\alpha-\beta}\ln(s_h) - \frac{\alpha+\beta}{1-\alpha-\beta}\ln(n+g+\delta) \tag{10'}$$

or

$$\ln\left(\frac{Y_t}{L_t}\right) = c + \ln\left(A_{BR-ICT(0)}\right) + g_{BR-ICT}t + \frac{\alpha}{1-\alpha-\beta}\left[\ln(s_k) - \ln(n+g+\delta)\right] + \frac{\beta}{1-\alpha-\beta}\left[\ln(s_h) - \ln(n+g+\delta)\right] \tag{10''}$$

where $c = ln(A_{KP(0)}) + g_{KP}t$ is the quasi-public good component of knowledge products and is therefore assumed constant across countries. The difference with the traditional MRW (1992) specification is that we reinterpret the intercept and we add to it two additional terms respectively measuring the log of the stock of BR-ICT at the initial period and its rate of growth per time units. Therefore, the possibility that all countries have the same steady state level of per capita income depends not only on the levelling of their rate of population growth and of their physical and human capital investment rates, but also on their initial stocks and on their rates of growth of BR-ICT. The model therefore introduces an additional factor affecting per capita income levels. A second important difference in this equation is that the country-specific rate of growth of technology plus depreciation

($g+\delta$ in all previous models) is no more treated as fixed and equal to 0.05 for all countries[6] (an heroic assumption) but it varies and is crucially influenced by the measured country-specific growth rates of BR-ICT technology.

2.2 Convergence of Per Capita Growth

Under hypothesis 1 it is possible to show that, in the proximity of the balanced growth path, y converges to y^* at the rate $(1 - \alpha - \beta)(n+g) \equiv \lambda$ since the solution of the differential equation[7]

$$dln(y)/dt = -\lambda[ln(y) - ln(y^*)] \tag{11}$$

is:

$$ln(y_t) - ln(y^*) = e^{-\lambda t}[ln(y_0) - ln(y^*)]. \tag{12}$$

If we add $ln(y^*) - ln(y_0)$ to both sides we get an equation explaining the rate of growth:

$$ln(y_t) - ln(y_0) = -(1 - e^{-\lambda t})[ln(y_0) - ln(y^*)].$$

Replacing $ln(y^*)$ with our solution we get:

$$\begin{aligned} &\ln(y_t) - \ln(y_0) = (1 - e^{-\lambda t})\frac{\alpha}{1-\alpha-\beta}\ln(s_k) + \\ &(1 - e^{-\lambda t})\frac{\beta}{1-\alpha-\beta}\ln(s_h) - (1 - e^{-\lambda t})\frac{\alpha+\beta}{1-\alpha-\beta}\ln(n+g+\delta) - \\ &(1 - e^{-\lambda t})\ln(y_0) \end{aligned} \tag{13}$$

or:

$$\begin{aligned} &\ln((Y/L)(t) - \ln((Y/L)(0)) = c' + g_{BR-ICT}t + (1 - e^{-\lambda t})\frac{\alpha}{1-\alpha-\beta}\ln(s_k) + \\ &(1 - e^{-\lambda t})\frac{\beta}{1-\alpha-\beta}\ln(s_h) - (1 - e^{-\lambda t})\frac{\alpha+\beta}{1-\alpha-\beta}\ln(n+g+\delta) - \\ &(1 - e^{-\lambda t})\ln((Y/L)(0)) + (1 - e^{-\lambda t})\ln(A_{BR-ICT(0)}) \end{aligned} \tag{13'}$$

where $c' = g_{KP}t + (1 - e^{-\lambda t})\ln(A_{KP(0)})$.

---

[6] This is the approach followed by Solow (1956), Mankiw, Romer and Weil (1992) and Islam (1995) among many others.

[7] This obviously implies that the speed of convergence differs across countries and is crucially influenced by the pace of BR-ICT growth.

Table 3.1 Shapiro-Wilks Normality Tests on Selected Regressors

Years	1985		1986		1987		1988		1989		1990		1991	
Variable	z	Prob>z	z	Prob>z	z	Prob>z	z	Prob>z	z	Prob>z	z	Prob>z	z	Prob>z
gdp	2.720	0.003	no obs.	no obs.	no obs.	no obs.	no obs.	no obs.	no obs.	no obs.	3.083	0.001	3.106	0.001
ICT1	3.663	0.000	3.713	0.000	3.806	0.000	3.945	0.000	3.992	0.000	4.066	0.000	4.127	0.000
ICT2	no obs.	no obs.	no obs.	no obs.	no obs.	no obs.	no obs.	no obs.	no obs.	no obs.	no obs.	no obs.	no obs.	no obs.
ICT3	-0.480	0.684	0.287	0.387	1.280	0.100	1.767	0.039	1.527	0.063	1.888	0.029	2.029	0.021
ICT4	1.288	0.099	1.272	0.102	0.770	0.221	1.876	0.030	2.132	0.017	2.568	0.005	2.689	0.004
ICT	7.366	0.000	7.470	0.000	7.573	0.000	3.768	0.000	3.748	0.000	3.916	0.000	3.792	0.000
S_k - n+g+d	4.419	0.000	3.849	0.000	6.571	0.000	6.178	0.000	5.799	0.000	8.273	0.000	1.379	0.084
S_H- n+g+d	4.098	0.000	4.295	0.000	4.356	0.000	4.333	0.000	4.304	0.000	4.236	0.000	4.273	0.000
Years	**1992**		**1993**		**1994**		**1995**		**1996**		**1997**		**1993-1997**	
Variable	**z**	**Prob>z**	**z**	**Prob>z**	**z**	**Prob>z**	**z**	**Prob>z**	**z**	**Prob>z**	**z**	**Prob>z**	**z**	**Prob>z**
gdp	2.988	0.001	3.119	0.001	2.957	0.002	2.974	0.001	3.064	0.001	2.864	0.002	11597	0.000
ICT1	4.163	0.000	4.151	0.000	4.228	0.000	4.337	0.000	4.450	0.000	4.485	0.000	7052.0	0.000
ICT2	no obs.	no obs.	no obs.	no obs.	2.119	0.017	1.503	0.066	1.810	0.035	1.756	0.040	2119.0	0.017
ICT3	1.954	0.025	2.172	0.015	2.467	0.007	3.021	0.001	3.471	0.000	3.446	0.000	5063.0	0.000
ICT4	2.761	0.003	2.748	0.003	2.675	0.004	2.818	0.002	2.835	0.002	2.857	0.002	7426.0	0.000
ICT	3.632	0.000	3.524	0.000	3.346	0.000	3.418	0.000	3.466	0.000	3.469	0.000	6474.0	0.000
S_k - n+g+d	4.519	0.000	3.136	0.001	4.277	0.000	3.046	0.001	3.458	0.000	1.063	0.144	5243.0	0.000
S_H- n+g+d	4.294	0.000	3.801	0.000	3.942	0.000	4.240	0.000	2.711	0.003	5.362	0.000	10233.0	0.000

Note: ICT1: main telephone lines per 1,000 people; ICT2: Internet hosts (or the number of computers with active Internet Protocol (IP) addresses connected to the Internet) per 10,000 people; ICT3: Mobile phones (per 1,000 people); ICT4: Personal computers (per 1,000 people); ICT (COMPOSITE INDEX): unweighted average of ICT1, ICT2, ICT3 and ICT4.

The difference with respect to the traditional MRW approach is in the interpretation of the common intercept (which now incorporates the worldwide diffusion of quasi-public knowledge products) and in the fact that convergence may be prevented by differences in the stock of initial BR-ICT factors or in their rates of growth.

3. Empirical Analysis

3.1 The Database and Descriptive Statistics

Variables for our empirical analysis are taken from the World Bank database.[8] The dependent variable *Y/L* is the gross domestic product per working-age person converted to international dollars using purchasing power parity rates,[9] *L* is the number of people who could potentially be economically active (population aged between 15-64). s_k is gross domestic investment over GDP, s_h is the (secondary education) ratio of total enrolment, regardless of age, to the population of the age group that officially corresponds to the level of education shown (generally the 14-18 age cohort).[10] To measure factors reducing ICT bottlenecks we consider four different proxies: i) the number of main telephone lines per 1,000 inhabitants;[11] ii) Internet hosts (per 10,000 people) or the number of computers with active Internet Protocol (IP) addresses connected to the Internet, per 10,000 people; iii) mobile phones (per 1,000 people); iv) personal computers (per 1,000 people).[12]

Table 3.1 provides some descriptive statistics on the above-mentioned variables and shows that the dependent variable is not normally distributed when we both consider individual year and overall sample datasets. This fact, neglected by the existing literature, should be taken into account when running regressions in levels and rates of growth. Furthermore, simple statistics of sigma convergence clearly confirm that BR-ICT indicators are far from being freely available public goods as the variability in the diffusion of BR-ICT across countries is extremely high and persistent (Figure 3.1). On average, for the entire observation period, it is higher when we consider the latest ICT innovation (the standard deviation of the

---

[8] We cannot use the Penn World Tables as the time period for which we dispose of BR-ICT data does not significantly overlap with that of the Summers and Heston database.

[9] An international dollar has the same purchasing power over GDP as the US dollar in the United States.

[10] It is also defined as the gross enrolment ratio to compare it with the ratio (net enrolment ratio) in which the denominator is the enrolment ratio only of the age cohort officially corresponding to the given level of education.

[11] Telephone mainlines are telephone lines connecting a customer's equipment to the public switched telephone network. Data are presented per 1,000 people for the entire country.

[12] Since all these factors are expected to ease the diffusion and processing of knowledge products on the Internet a qualitative measure of their 'power' (i.e. the processing capacity of PCs) would improve the accuracy of our proxies. Such information though is not available for long time periods and across the countries observed in our sample.

diffusion of Internet hosts across countries is two and a half its mean while the standard deviation of the diffusion of main telephone lines is almost equal to its mean).

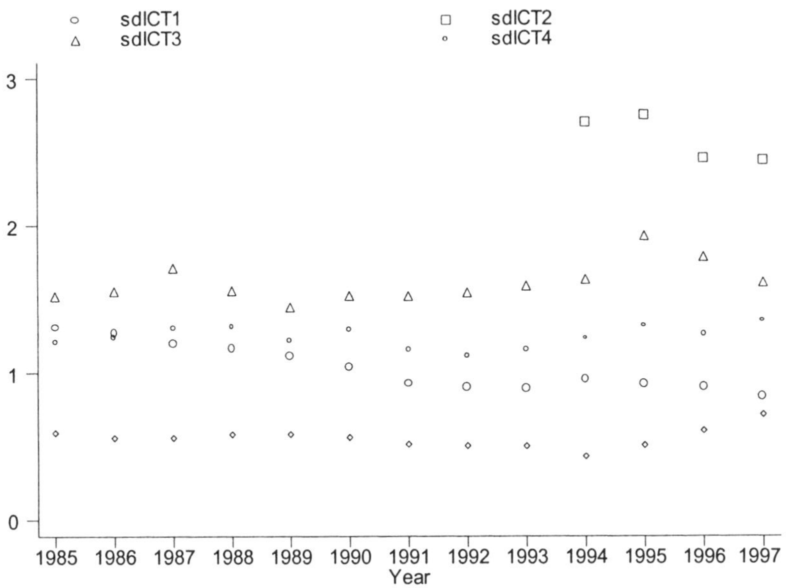

Figure 3.1 Sigma Convergence of BR-ICT Indicators (standard deviation to mean ratios)

Note: sdICT1: standard deviation/mean ratio of main telephone lines per 1,000 people; sdICT2: standard deviation/mean ratio of Internet hosts (or the number of computers with active Internet Protocol (IP) addresses connected to the Internet) per 10,000 people; sdICT3: standard deviation/mean ratio of mobile phones (per 1,000 people); sdICT4: standard deviation/mean ratio of personal computers (per 1,000 people). The last symbol represents sdICT (COMPOSITE INDEX): unweighted average of ICT1, ICT2, ICT3 and ICT4.

Table A.1 in the Appendix provides the list of countries included in the estimates. For each country we display the level of the BR-ICT variable in the first and in the last available year. This table documents that we have data for 115 countries from 1983 if we just consider the diffusion of telephone lines, while for much fewer countries and more limited time, if we consider the other three BR-ICT indicators.

For this reason we define a composed indicator which is an unweighted average of each of the four normalised BR-ICT indicators (when available). We then perform our estimates alternatively with the composed and with each of the individual BR-ICT indicators.

Table 3.2 Cross-section Regressions with and without BR-ICT Indicators

	(1991-1997)					(1983-1997)	
	MRW-TYPE ESTIMATE	EQUATION (1) WITH ICT1	EQUATION (1) WITH ICT3	EQUATION (1) WITH ICT4	EQUATION (1) WITH THE COMPOSITE INDEX	MRW	EQUATION (1) WITH THE COMPOSITE INDEX
$ln(S_k)-ln(n+g+d)$	0.017	-0.003	-0.008	0.008	0.003	0.363	0.086
	[2.280]**	[-0.430]	[-1.260]	[1.610]*	[0.540]	[2.060]	[0.63]
$ln(S_h)-ln(n+g+d)$	0.025	0.004	0.004	0.002	0.007	0.895	0.322
	[18.240] **	[1.820] **	[1.750]*	[0.880]	[3.380] **	[12.560]**	[3.69]**
$g_{BR\text{-}ICT}t$		0.240	0.118	0.230	0.174		0.299
		[2.080] *	[3.000] **	[2.220] *	[4.550] **		[8.03] **
$ln(A_{BR\text{-}ICT(0)})$		0.451	0.301	0.438	0.388		0.302
		[10.180] *	[10.050] **	[12.690] **	[9.970] **		[8.48] **
CONSTANT	6.982	7.066	9.000	7.779	8.905	1.171	6.733
	[35.920] **	[51.590] **	[31.940] **	[31.180] **	[38.780] **	[1.480]	[7.76] **
R^2	0.799	0.9127	0.877	0.939	0.9127	0.772	0.874
Implied α						0.160	--
Implied β						0.395	0.242
Countries	94	88	47	47	94	100	99

Note: the table reports results on the estimation of equation (1). In the second to fourth column the traditional MRW approach is augmented with ICT variables. ICT1: main telephone lines (per 1,000 people); ICT3: Mobile phones (per 1,000 people); ICT4: Personal computers (per 1,000 people); ICT COMPOSITE INDEX: unweighted average of ICT1, ICT2, ICT3 and ICT4 where ICT2 is the number of computers with active Internet Protocol (IP) addresses connected to the Internet per 10,000 people. g is $g_{BR\text{-}ICT}+g_{KP}$, where $g_{BR\text{-}ICT}$ is the growth rate of the selected ICT variable, and g_{KP} is assumed constant across countries. S_h, S_k and $g_{BR\text{-}ICT}t$ are calculated as estimation period averages, while the dependent variable has the end of period value. T-stats are reported in square brackets. ** 95 per cent significance with bootstrap standard errors, * 90 per cent significance with bootstrap standard errors. We use the percentile and bias corrected approach with 2000 replications.

3.2 Econometric Estimates of the Determinants of Levels of Income Per Worker

As a first step we regress equation (1) in levels.[13] Our time span is quite limited when we consider a common starting year for the individual BR-ICT indicators (1991-97), while it becomes much wider when we use the composite indicator. Table 3.2 compares results from the standard MRW model with the model specified in (1) with the different BR-ICT indicators.[14]

A first thing to be noted is that elasticities of investment in physical and human capital are, as expected, also much smaller on such a limited time span (1991-97) in the traditional MRW estimate, even though both factors significantly affect levels of income per worker. The introduction of starting year levels ($A_{BR\text{-}ICT(0)}$) and rates of growth of BR-ICT variables ($g_{BR\text{-}ICT}$) significantly improves the overall goodness of fit and explains almost 94 per cent of the cross-sectional heterogeneity in the specification in which BR-ICT is proxied by the diffusion of personal computers. $A_{BR\text{-}ICT(0)}$ and $g_{BR\text{-}ICT}$ variables are always strongly significant and with the expected sign. On the other hand, the fact that their slopes are smaller than one, the value implicitly assumed by the econometric specification, supports the intuition that ICT is bottleneck-reducing. In fact, roughly speaking, one can assume that the coefficients of these two variables[15] are the returns of BR-ICT in spreading knowledge. It is, therefore, rather intuitive that widening a bottleneck has decreasing returns as it progressively reduces pressure. The strong significance of the constant term also confirms the hypothesis that BR-ICT factors do not exhaust the contribution of technology to growth and that a common (quasi) public technological factor exists to which (in our opinion) knowledge products contribute. While for the second variable an instrumental variable test is needed to check whether our results are affected by endogeneity (see the generalised 2-stage least square specification explained further), this is certainly not the case for the lagged BR-ICT level ($A_{BR\text{-}ICT(0)}$).

---

13 We perform the estimate with four different specifications which alternatively consider the ILO labour force and population in working age as labour inputs and observed income or trend income as a dependent variable. The ILO labour force includes the armed forces, the unemployed, and first-time job-seekers, but excludes homemakers and other unpaid caregivers and workers in the informal sector. We use trend income alternatively to observed income to avoid our results being influenced by cyclical effects on output (Temple, 1999). Estimates with the alternative proxies for the labour input and the dependent variable do not differ substantially and are available from the authors upon request.

14 By estimating (10'') we implicitly impose the restriction of equality between the coefficient of $log(n+g+\delta)$ and the sum of coefficients of logs of s_k and s_h. Estimates in which the assumption is removed do not provide substantially different results and are available from the authors upon request.

15 Consistently with our hypothesis, tests on the equality of $A_{BR\text{-}ICT}$ and $g_{BR\text{-}ICT}$ coefficients in Table 3.2 show that these coefficients are not significantly different from each other and almost identical in the 1983-1997 sample (respectively 0.302 and 0.299).

Furthermore, the four regressors included in (10'') are all significant only when we use the composite index, while in almost all other cases the introduction of the BR-ICT variables seems to cast doubts on the significance of the short-term elasticity of the investment in physical capital and also on that of human capital when we specify the BR-ICT variable with mobile phones or personal computers.[16] The reestimation of the model with bootstrap standard errors shows that the significance of the BR-ICT variables remains strong for all the considered indicators.

A final estimate done by using the composite index on the 1983-1997 time range gives us the idea of what happens when we extend the estimation period and when regression coefficients measure medium and not short-term elasticities. Magnitudes of physical and human capital investment coefficients are now higher and closer to those found in MRW. A striking result is that s_k is no more significant when BR-ICT variables are included in the estimate, while s_h is significant with an implied β of *23.*[17] This number is below the range calculated by MRW for the USA.[18] The first result seems to suggest that, apart from the difference in estimation periods, the physical capital contribution falls when we properly consider the role of BR-ICT technological factors (which, in a late sense, are part of physical capital). In the same originary MRW (1992) estimate the physical capital factor share drops to 0.14 in the OECD sample from 0.41 in the overall sample and this change may be explained in the light of our results given the higher contribution of BR-ICT technology to output in the first group of countries.

Further support for this hypothesis comes from the Jorgenson and Stiroh (1999) empirical paper showing the dramatic decrease in the selling and rental price of computers in the USA, paralleled by an increase in the same prices for physical capital between 1990 and 1996. Since the decline in computer prices depends on liberalisation and competition on domestic ICT markets it is reasonable to assume that there has been much more substitution between BR-ICT and physical capital in the most advanced OECD countries and therefore that cross country higher levels and growth rates of income per worker are associated with higher level and growth rates of BR-ICT diffusion, but not necessarily with higher rates of investment in physical capital.[19]

---

16 The weakness of the human capital variable when we introduce personal computers is consistent with the hypothesis that the productive contribution of skilled workers passes through (or is enhanced by) the technological factor. For evidence on this point see Roach (1991), Berndt et al. (1992) and Stiroh (1998).

17 The lack of cross-sectional significance of s_k can be anticipated even by the simple inspection of descriptive statistics. If we divide our sample into three equal subgroups of countries according to levels of income per worker (high, medium and low income) we find that values of s_h are respectively 83.60, 58.92 and 50.46, while values of s_k are much more equal across subgroups (23.57, 23.18 and 23.00).

18 According to MRW which compare minimum wage to average manufacturing wage in the US, the human capital factor share should be between 1/2 and 1/3.

19 The same shift in technological patterns induced by the ICT revolution seems to be an autonomous cause of substitution between ICT and physical capital since ICT investment modifies the trade-off between scale and scope economies. The ICT literature finds that, while software investment increases the scale of firm operations, telecommunications

Output elasticities of the two BR-ICT variables, when included in our estimate, seem therefore to reduce the output elasticity of human capital and to obscure the cross-sectional contribution of physical capital. They significantly contribute, though, to explain large differences in income per capita which would remain partially unexplained were the role of BR-ICT technology to be neglected. A plausible rationale for this finding is that part of the contribution of human capital to output depends on BR-ICT technology.[20] The former is overstated if the latter is not accounted for.

Table 3.3 Sensitivity Analysis on Cross-section Regressions (1985-1997 estimates with the composite BR-ICT index)

Regressors		Coefficient	T-stat.	R^2	Obs	Additional variables		
$ln(S_k)$-$ln(n+g+d)$	*High*	0.064	1.290	0.685	74	GOV	EXP	INTSPREAD
	Base	0.000	-0.010	0.535	94			
	Low	-0.006	-0.110	0.662	84	EXP	SD_INFL	ECONFREE
$ln(S_h)$-$ln(n+g+d)$	*High*	0.425	5.860	0.660	74	GOV	INTSPREAD	CIVFREE
	Base	0.312	4.370	0.535	94			
	Low	0.254	3.500	0.671	83	EXP	SD_GDC	ECONFREE
$ln(A_{BR\text{-}ICT(0)})$	*High*	0.094	4.060	0.553	91	EXP	GDC	CIVFREE
	Base	0.102	4.500	0.535	94			
	Low	0.070	3.260	0.685	74	GOV	EXP	INTSPREAD
$g_{BR\text{-}ICT}t$	*High*	0.115	5.060	0.553	91	EXP	GDC	CIVFREE
	Base	0.124	5.500	0.535	94			
	Low	0.093	4.220	0.660	74	GOV	INTSPREAD	POLFREE

Note: the sensitivity analysis is run by adding to the benchmark model all three by three combinations of the following variables; GOV: average government consumption to GDP; EXP: export to GDP; INFL: inflation, standard deviation of inflation; GDC: average growth rate of domestic credit; SD_GDC: standard deviation of domestic credit; ECONFREE: economic freedom; CIVFREE: civil freedom; INTSPREAD: average difference between lending and borrowing rate in the domestic banking system. In the table we select for each regressor of the base model only the benchmark estimate and the two replications in which the coefficient has the highest and the lowest significance.

investment creates a 'flexibility option' easing the switch from a Fordist to a flexible network productive model (Milgrom and Roberts, 1988) in which products and processes are more frequently adapted to satisfy consumers' taste for variety (Barua, Kriebel and Mukhopadhyay, 1991; Becchetti, Londono Bedoya and Paganetto, 2000).

[20] It is reasonable to figure out, for instance, that higher world processing capacity or the possibility of exchanging information on the Internet increases the productivity of high-skilled more than that of low-skilled workers.

Table 3.4 The Determinants of Levels of Income Per Working-age Person when Indexes of Economic Freedom are Included

Variable	ECFREE COMPOSITE	ECFREE (I)	ECFREE (II)	ECFREE (III)	ECFREE (IV)	ECFREE (V)	ECFREE (VI)	ECFREE (VII)
$ln(S_k)-ln(n+g+d)$	0.010	0.064	0.073	0.001	0.060	-0.225	0.022	0.111
	[0.080]	[0.450]	[0.530]	[0.010]	[0.460]	[-1.890]*	[0.160]	[0.860]
$ln(S_h)-ln(n+g+d)$	0.288	0.269	0.308	0.315	0.314	0.147	0.252	0.294
	[3.480] **	[2.670]	[3.250] **	[3.240]*	[3.510]*	[1.840]*	[2.720]*	[3.370]*
$g_{BR-ICT}t$	0.219	0.310	0.291	0.311	0.249	0.373	0.246	0.253
	[5.980] **	[8.140] **	[7.600] **	[8.160] **	[6.460] **	[9.290] **	[6.020] **	[6.940] **
$ln(A_{BR-ICT(0)})$	0.225	0.306	0.285	0.311	0.253	0.354	0.266	0.248
	[6.530] **	[8.390] **	[7.720] **	[8.660] **	[6.950] **	[9.640] **	[7.260] **	[7.060] **
ECFREE	0.217	-0.055	0.065	0.030	0.083	0.109	0.121	0.097
	[5.820] **	[-1.540]	[2.590]*	[1.560]	[4.170] **	[3.540]*	[3.620]	[4.800] **
CONSTANT	5.978	7.613	6.604	7.044	6.345	8.972	6.766	6.172
	[3.050] **	[8.280] **	[7.850] **	[8.350] **	[7.980] **	[12.49] **	[8.470] **	[7.940] **
Countries	86	87	87	87	87	84	87	87
R^2	0.917	0.885	0.891	0.886	0.903	0.929	0.899	0.908

Note: the index of economic freedom published in the *Economic Freedom of the World: 2000 Annual Report* (ECFREE COMPOSITE) is a weigthed average of the seven following composed indicators designed to identify the consistency of institutional arrangements and policies with economic freedom in seven major areas: ECFREE(I) Size of Government: Consumption, Transfers, and Subsidies [11.0%], i) General Government Consumption Expenditures as a per cent of Total Consumption (50%); ii) Transfers and Subsidies as a per cent of GDP (50%).

ECFREE(II) Structure of the Economy and Use of Markets *(Production and allocation via governmental* [14.2%] *and political mandates rather than private enterprises and markets*) i) Government Enterprises and Investment as a Share of the Economy (32.7%); ii) Price Controls: Extent to which Businesses Are Free to Set Their Own Prices (33.5%); iii) Top Marginal Tax Rate *(and income threshold at which it applies*) (25.0%); iv) The Use of Conscripts to Obtain Military Personnel (8.8%). ECFREE(III) Monetary Policy and Price Stability *(Protection of money as a store of value and medium of exchange*)[9.2%], i) Average Annual Growth Rate of the Money Supply during the Last Five Years (34.9%) minus the Growth Rate of Real GDP during the Last Ten Years; ii) Standard Deviation of the Annual Inflation Rate during the Last Five Years (32.6%); iii) Annual Inflation Rate during the Most Recent Year (32.5%). ECFREE(IV) Freedom to Use Alternative Currencies *(Freedom of access to alternative currencies*) [14.6%] i) Freedom of Citizens to Own Foreign Currency Bank Accounts Domestically and Abroad (50%); ii) Difference between the Official Exchange Rate and the Black Market Rate (50%). ECFREE(V): Legal Structure and Property Rights *(Security of property rights and viability of contracts*) [16.6%] i) Legal Security of Private Ownership Rights *(Risk of confiscation*) (34.5%); ii) Viability of Contracts *(Risk of contract repudiation by the government*) (33.9%); iii) Rule of Law: Legal Institutions Supportive of the Principles of Rule of Law (31.7%) and Access to a Non-discriminatory Judiciary. ECFREE(VI) International Exchange: Freedom to Trade with Foreigners [17.1%] i) Taxes on International Trade, ia Revenue from Taxes on International Trade as a per cent of Exports plus Imports (23.3%), ib Mean Tariff Rate (24.6%), ic Standard Deviation of Tariff Rates (23.6%); ii) Non-tariff Regulatory Trade Barriers, iia) Per cent of International Trade Covered by Non-tariff Trade Restraints (19.4%), iic Actual Size of Trade Sector Compared to the Expected Size (9.1%). ECFREE(VII) Freedom of Exchange in Capital and Financial Markets [17.2%], i) Ownership of Banks: Per cent of Deposits Held in Privately Owned Banks (27.1%); ii) Extension of Credit: Per cent of Credit Extended to Private Sector (21.2%); iii) Interest Rate Controls and Regulations that Lead to Negative Interest Rates (24.7%); iv) Restrictions on the Freedom of Citizens to Engage in Capital Transactions with Foreigners (27.1%). *Any of the considered freedom indicators has a 0-10 value range. A higher value means a higher level in the item considered by the indicator.*

T-stats are reported in square brackets.
** 95 per cent significance with bootstrap standard errors, * 90 per cent significance with bootstrap standard errors. We use the percentile and bias corrected approach with 2000 replications.

The use of a cross-sectional regression for estimating the determinants of levels of per capita income has been strongly criticised by Islam (1995). His argument is that the labour augmenting A-factor in the aggregate production function represents country-specific preferences and technological factors. It is therefore not possible to assume that it is absorbed in the intercept and therefore constant across countries (*cross-sectional constant critique).* Our estimate overcomes the problem by specifying the technological variable, but what if some additional country-specific variables (deep fundamentals such as *ethos* or governance parameters such as economic freedom) are omitted? We have two solutions here: i) a reestimation of (1) as a cross-section with the introduction of variables which may proxy for those omitted; ii) a panel estimate of the same equation in which fixed effects capture all additional country-specific variables.[21]

With respect to the first approach we propose a sensitivity analysis in which we subsequently introduce three by three combinations of the following additional explanatory variables: i) average government consumption to GDP; ii) export to GDP; iii) inflation; iv) standard deviation of inflation; v) average rate of government consumption expenditures; vi) average growth rate of domestic credit; vii) standard deviation of domestic credit and, finally, three indexes of economic, civil and legal freedom.[22] All these variables, with the exception of indexes of economic, civil and legal freedom are also used by Levine and Renelt (1992) in their sensitivity analysis on the determinants of growth.

Results of sensitivity analysis run on the 1985-1997 period with the BR-ICT composite index show that all regressors of specification (1) are substantially robust (no change in significance and limited change in magnitude) to the inclusion of any combination of the above-mentioned additional explanatory variables (Table 3.3).[23]

Since the sensitivity analysis emphasises the strong significance of economic freedom we reestimate the model by adding this variable and by decomposing it into its seven attributes (Table 3.4). In this way we find that five of the seven attributes are significant (legal structure and property rights, structure of the economy and use of markets, freedom in financial markets, in foreign trade and in exchange markets) while only government size and macroeconomic stability do not directly affect growth in the cross-sectional estimate in levels.

With respect to the second approach suggested to overcome the *cross-sectional constant critique*, fixed effect panel results confirm the robustness of the significance of the technological variable (Table 3.5). The ICT significance in fixed effect panel estimates is also robust to the inclusion of any combination of

21 The fixed effect is preferred to the random effect approach as the second retains the strong assumption of independence between regressors and the disturbance term.

22 The role of inflation on growth is examined, among others, by Easterly and Rebelo (1993). For a survey on the role of financial variables on growth see Pagano (1993). The impact of political variables including political freedom has been analysed by Brunetti (1997). The relationship between economic freedom and growth has been investigated, among others, by Dawson (1998) and by Easton and Walker (1997).

23 The different estimation period with respect to Table 3.2 is necessary for the reduced availablity of data on civil, legal and economic freedom.

Table 3.5 The Determinants of Levels of Income Per Worker Estimated with Panel Data Fixed Effects and G2SLS Fixed Effects

	PANEL FIXED EFFECTS					G2SLS (FIXED EFFECTS)			
	MRW-type estimate	ICT1	ICT3	ICT4	C. index	ICT1	ICT3	ICT4	C. index
$ln(S_k)-ln(n+g+d)$	0.155	0.111	0.137	0.155	0.166	0.103	0.177	0.140	0.205
	[5.760]	[5.200]	[3.850]	[4.060]	[6.090]	[4.760]	[4.330]	[3.200]	[5.280]
$ln(S_h)-ln(n+g+d)$	0.434	0.184	0.252	0.298	0.434	0.138	0.119	0.126	0.436
	[10.530]	[5.020]	[5.240]	[6.810]	[10.590]	[3.550]	[2.370]	[2.280]	[9.900]
$ln(A_{BR\text{-}ICT})$		0.265	0.051	0.138	0.027	0.314	0.094	0.212	0.120
		[14.860]	[12.660]	[14.290]	[2.150]	[14.420]	[13.840]	[13.190]	[1.920]
CONSTANT	5.191	6.048	6.712	5.981	5.155	6.206	7.544	7.092	5.032
	[17.440]	[24.960]	[17.100]	[15.960]	[17.380]	[25.030]	[17.780]	[15.460]	[15.320]
R^2 (within group)	0.295	0.56	0.623	0.671	0.30	0.552	0.779	0.755	0.198
Obs.	465	465	310	293	465	465	196	181	465
Countries	97	97	74	70	97	97	51	51	97
	In the G2SLS panel estimate $ln(A_{BR\text{-}ICT})_t$ is instrumented with $ln(A_{BR\text{-}ICT})_{t-2}$, $ln(A_{BR\text{-}ICT})_{t-3}$, and $ln(A_{BR\text{-}ICT})_{t-4}$								

Table 3.6a Sensitivity Analysis on Panel Regressions (panel fixed effects)

		PANEL FIXED EFFECTS						
Regressors		Coefficient	T-stat.	R^2	Obs	ADDITIONAL VARIABLES		
ln(S$_k$)-ln(n+g+d)	*High*	0.203	4.770	0.441	317	GOV	EXP	GDC
	Base	0.166	6.090	0.304	465			
	Low	0.141	5.300	0.354	460	EXP	INFL	POLFREE
ln(S$_h$)-ln(n+g+d)	*High*	0.515	9.180	0.465	256	GOV	INTSPREAD	CIVFREE
	Base	0.434	10.590	0.304	465			
	Low	0.397	9.610	0.367	446	EXP	GDC	POLFREE
ln(A$_{BR-ICT}$)	*High*	0.085	4.270	0.465	256	GOV	INTSPREAD	CIVFREE
	Base	0.027	2.150	0.304	465			
	Low	0.035	2.870	0.354	460	EXP	INFL	CIVFREE

Table 3.6b Sensitivity Analysis on Panel Regressions (G2SLS fixed effects)

		G2SLS (FIXED EFFECTS)						
Regressors		Coefficient	T-stat.	R^2	Obs	ADDITIONAL VARIABLES		
ln(S$_k$)-ln(n+g+d)	*High*	0.213	4.740	0.292	339	EXP	INTSPREAD	POLFREE
	Base	0.205	5.280	0.198	465			
	Low	0.138	2.110	0.12	328	GOV	INFL	POLFREE
ln(S$_h$)-ln(n+g+d)	*High*	0.473	9.130	0.313	339	EXP	INTSPREAD	CIVFREE
	Base	0.436	9.900	0.198	465			
	Low	0.128	0.990	0.12	317	GOV	EXP	GDC
ln(A$_{BR-ICT}$)	*High*	0.389	3.280	0.12	256	GOV	INTSPREAD	POLFREE
	Base	0.120	1.920	0.198	465			
	Low	0.122	2.110	0.263	460	EXP	INFL	POLFREE

Note: the sensitivity analysis is run by adding to the benchmark model all three by three combinations of the following variables: GOV: average government consumption to GDP, EXP: export to GDP, INFL: inflation, standard deviation of inflation, GDC: average growth rate of domestic credit; SD_GDC: standard deviation of domestic credit, ECONFREE: economic freedom, CIVFREE: civil freedom, INTSPREAD: average difference between lending and borrowing rate in the domestic banking system. In the table we select for each regressor of the base model only the benchmark estimate and the two replications in which the coefficient has the highest and the lowest significance.

additional regressors (Table 3.6a). Our results are a direct answer to Islam's (1995) interpretation of country-specific fixed effects in its MRW-type panel estimate which he finds significantly and positively correlated with growth rates and human capital and interprets as country-specific technology effects. Since our BR-ICT variables are positive and significant and their inclusion reduces the impact of human capital, they are formally (in definition) and substantially (in data) a relevant part of the fixed effects measured by Islam (1995).

Table 3.7a Subsample Split Results on Panel Regressions

	ICT1			
	PANEL FIXED EFFECTS		G2SLS (FIXED EFFECTS)	
Variable	OECD	NON-OECD	OECD	NON-OECD
$ln(S_k)-ln(n+g+d)$	0.055	0.126	0.055	0.118
	[0.920]	[5.660]	[0.910]	[5.210]
$ln(S_h)-ln(n+g+d)$	0.328	0.067	0.326	0.006
	[5.380]	[1.490]	[5.290]	[0.130]
$ln(A_{BR-ICT})$	0.400	0.273	0.405	0.324
	[5.840]	[14.850]	[5.710]	[14.100]
CONSTANT	4.851	6.526	4.837	6.789
	[8.410]	[23.840]	[8.360]	[23.720]
Obs	125	340	125	340
Countries	25	72	25	72
R^2 (within groups)	0.559	0.601	0.559	0.590
	ICT COMPOSITE INDEX			
	PANEL FIXED EFFECTS		G2SLS (FIXED EFFECTS)	
Variable	OECD	NON-OECD	OECD	NON-OECD
$ln(S_k)-ln(n+g+d)$	0.026	0.180	-0.182	0.206
	[0.380]	[5.890]	[-1.200]	[4.660]
$ln(S_h)-ln(n+g+d)$	0.427	0.400	0.085	0.414
	[6.400]	[7.550]	[0.420]	[7.260]
$ln(A_{BR-ICT})$	0.134	0.023	0.741	0.076
	[2.580]	[1.680]	[2.310]	[1.180]
CONSTANT	6.532	5.058	9.708	4.928
	[9.640]	[14.570]	[5.020]	[12.670]
Obs	125	340	125	340
Countries	25	72	25	72
R^2 (within groups)	0.443	0.277	0.157	0.234
	In the G2SLS panel estimate $ln(A_{BR-CT})_t$ is instrumented with $ln(A_{BR-ICT})_{t-2}$, $ln(A_{BR-ICT})_{t-3}$, *and* $ln(A_{BR-ICT})_{t-4}$			

Table 3.7b Financial Market Freedom, BR-ICT and Growth on Fixed Effect and G2SLS Panel Regressions

Variable	PANEL FIXED EFFECTS				G2SLS (FIXED EFFECTS)			
	High Financial Freedom	*Low Financial Freedom*	*High Financial Freedom*	*Low Financial Freedom*	*High Financial Freedom*	*Low Financial Freedom*	*High Financial Freedom*	*Low Financial Freedom*
	ICT1		ICT COMPOSITE INDEX		ICT1		ICT COMPOSITE INDEX	
$ln(S_k)-ln(n+g+d)$	0.122	0.093	0.199	0.147	0.110	0.090	0.214	0.148
	[3.170]	[3.490]	[4.020]	[4.050]	[2.810]	[3.350]	[3.970]	[2.800]
$ln(S_h)-ln(n+g+d)$	0.229	0.040	0.510	0.326	0.174	0.021	0.476	0.327
	[5.010]	[0.650]	[10.220]	[4.310]	[3.630]	[0.330]	[8.400]	[4.220]
$ln(A_{BR\text{-}ICT})$	0.333	0.253	0.072	0.027	0.394	0.269	0.190	0.029
	[11.990]	[11.330]	[3.350]	[1.410]	[12.600]	[9.640]	[2.900]	[0.280]
CONSTANT	5.566	6.827	4.814	5.549	5.720	6.911	4.963	5.547
	[15.990]	[18.320]	[10.880]	[11.500]	[16.150]	[18.060]	[10.280]	[11.300]
Obs	233	193	233	193	233	193	233	193
Countries	46	41	46	41	46	41	46	41
R^2 (within groups)	0.667	0.567	0.440	0.204	0.658	0.565	0.351	0.204
	In the G2SLS panel estimate $ln(A_{BR\text{-}ICT})_t$ is instrumented with $ln(A_{BR\text{-}ICT})_{t-2}$, $ln(A_{BR\text{-}ICT})_{t-3}$, *and* $ln(A_{BR\text{-}ICT})_{t-4}$							

Note: *high financial freedom*: countries ranked in the highest half according to the ECFREE (VII) indicator described in Table 3.4. *Low financial freedom*: countries ranked in the lowest half according to the ECFREE (VII) indicator described in Table 3.4.

This type of estimate, though, generates an endogeneity problem since the contribution of BR-ICT is no more split into the two components of initial levels and rates of growth and is therefore not completely lagged with respect to the dependent variable.

To overcome the endogeneity problem we use the G2SLS methodology which combines fixed effect panel estimates with instrumental variables. We use as instruments two period to four period lagged values of BR-ICT indicators and find that BR-ICT variables are still significant (Tables 3.5-3.7b).

Results from Table 3.4 seemed to show that the governance of financial and trade markets was a fundamental factor for growth. The development of financial markets though may even have an impact on the relationship between BR-ICT and growth.[24] Technological innovation and investment in technologies which may reduce ICT bottlenecks (optic fibres, power enhanced mobile phones) are in fact easier to implement in well-developed capital markets where they can be equity financed since equity financiers are residual claimants of the expected increase in value generated by the innovation and find it instantaneously incorporated into their share prices. Furthermore, in well-developed financial markets, the unobserved quality of BR-ICT innovation is therefore expected to be higher and our BR-ICT proxies (not corrected for quality) to have an increased significance on levels and growth of income per capita.

Exogenous subsample splits help us to investigate whether the BR-ICT–growth relationship is stronger, as we postulated, in countries with more developed financial markets. Consistently with our assumption, we find that the significance of BR-ICT variables is much more pronounced in the OECD and in the higher economic freedom subsample than in their complementary samples (Table 3.7a). Since our index of economic freedom measures at most the development of the banking system (which may proxy but does not coincide with the development of equity markets), we propose an additional indicator based on the stock market capitalisation to GDP. Results from this indicator are consistent with those on the development of the banking system with the BR-ICT factor being more significantly related to income per worker in the high stock market development subgroup in panel fixed effect estimates (Table 3.7c).

To check whether our results are affected by endogeneity we perform G2SLS panel estimates on these samples. Unfortunately the limited number of degrees of freedom available when we use lagged instruments allows us to estimate the model with sufficient confidence only for the financial freedom split and for the ICT1 and composed index indicators. In these specific cases G2SLS estimates show that, once endogeneity is taken into account, differences between countries with high and low economic freedom persists (Table 3.7b).

---

[24] Saint Paul (1992) identifies a trade-off between technological diversification (which implies despecialisation and no choice of the more specialised technology) and financial diversification. The development of financial markets allows the entrepreneur to achieve diversification on financial market and therefore to reduce technological diversification by choosing the riskier and more profitable technology.

Table 3.7c Equity Market Development, BR-ICT and Income Per Working-age Person

DEPENDENT VARIABLE: LOG GDP PER WORKING-AGE PERSON 1997				
	PANEL FIXED EFFECTS			
Variable	*High stock market development*	*Low stock market development*	*High stock market development*	*Low stock market development*
	ICT1		ICT COMPOSITE INDEX	
$ln(S_k)-ln(n+g+d)$	0.071	0.060	0.209	0.087
	[1.440]	[2.120]	[3.810]	[1.930]
$ln(S_h)-ln(n+g+d)$	0.249	-0.011	0.334	0.633
	[4.950]	[-0.170]	[5.990]	[8.410]
$ln(A_{BR\text{-}ICT})$	0.336	0.325	0.219	0.031
	[10.860]	[14.030]	[7.540]	[1.510]
CONSTANT	5.738	7.299	6.012	4.209
	[13.470]	[18.640]	[12.000]	[8.200]
Obs	172	166	172	166
Countries	34	35	34	35
R^2 (within groups)	0.654	0.758	0.544	0.396

Note: *high stock market development*: countries ranked in the highest half according to the stock market capitalisation to GDP indicator described in Table 3.4. *Low stock market development*: countries ranked in the lowest half according to the stock market capitalisation to GDP indicator described in Table 3.4.

3.3 Econometric Estimates of Convergence in Rates of Growth of Income Per Worker

The reduced interval for which we dispose of ICT data limits our analysis to short-medium term convergence and prevents us from estimating convergence with panel data. Nonetheless, since the best specification of (10'') explains almost 95 per cent of the observed cross-sectional heterogeneity, our attempt at estimating convergence with a cross-sectional estimate is not severely affected by the *cross-country heterogeneity critique* (Evans, 1997). The results we obtain are roughly in line with the existing literature and with our theoretical predictions formulated in section 2. Table 3.8 shows that our ICT-growth model performs better than the

MRW model in the 1990s. The level of income per working-age person in the starting period (Y/L_{1985}) becomes significant only once we proxy the labour-augmenting technological progress with our BR-ICT variables. This suggests that evidence of convergence in the short run can be found only when we consider its conditionality to investment not only in physical capital,[25] but also in BR-ICT.[26] It is also slightly larger when we introduce BR-ICT variables. In interpreting our result of faster convergence, we must consider that we are working on a reduced and almost non-overlapped sample period with respect to MRW (1983-1997 against 1960-1985). In this period convergence looks faster when it is conditioned to variables relevant in our model.

Sensitivity analysis on this result finds that it is confirmed even when we use bootstrap standard errors (and we consider the composite BR-ICT index or the PC diffusion variable) and that it is robust to the inclusion of three by three combinations of all additional variables used in Levine and Renelt (1995) sensitivity analysis plus all different attributes of economic freedom (Tables 3.9 and 3.10).

---

25 The lack of significance of the coefficient of human capital is a well-known result in the literature. Islam (1995) explains it by arguing that the positive cross-sectional effect of human capital is likely to be outweighted by the negative temporal effect (higher levels of investment in human capital did not produce positive changes in growth). This is not the case for BR-ICT investment which is shown to have also positive time effects in our estimate.

26 If we arbitrarily set $(n+\delta+g)$ equal to 0.05 for all countries, our implied λ is larger than that in MRW and lower than in Solow (1956) and in Islam (1995).

Table 3.8 Growth Regressions with and without BR-ICT Indicators

Dependent variable: log difference GDP per working-age person (1985-1997)							
	(1991-1997)					(1983-1997)	
	MRW-type estimate	Equation (1) with ICT1	Equation (1) with ICT3	Equation (1) with ICT4	Equation (1) with the composite index	MRW	Equation (1) with the composite index
$ln(S_k)-ln(n+g+d)$	0.010	0.144	0.009	0.011	0.143	0.407	0.312
	[4.818]**	[3.080] **	[3.437] **	[4.903] **	[3.440] **	[5.140]**	[4.370]**
$ln(S_h)-ln(n+g+d)$	0.002	0.031	0.001	0.001	0.036	0.081	-0.0004
	[2.814] **	[0.930]	[1.146]	[1.089]	[1.280]	[1.510]	[-0.010]
$g_{BR\text{-}ICT}$		0.020	0.030	0.105	0.021		0.124
		[0.790]	[1.955]*	[2.225]**	[1.100]		[5.500]**
$Ln(A_{BR\text{-}ICT(1985)})$		0.131	0.060	0.121	0.063		0.102
		[3.040] **	[3.297] **	[4.199] **	[4.590] **		[4.500]
$Ln(Y/L)_{1985}$	-0.038	-0.041	-0.169	-0.240	-0.075	-0.095	-0.227
	[-1.414]	[-1.050]	[-3.399] **	[-4.124] **	[-2.140] **	[-2.140]*	[-4.630]**
Constant	0.170	-0.585	1.409	1.664	-0.171	-1.495	0.783
	[0.857]	[-1.410]	[3.028] **	[3.457] **	[-0.420]	[-4.010]**	[1.330]
R^2	0.311	0.4208	0.520	0.557	0.4549	0.369	0.5346
Test: β=0	0.006	0.363	0.258	0.282	0.272	0.129	
Implied λ						0.024	0.034
Countries	94	88	47	47	94	95	94

** 95 per cent significance with bootstrap standard errors, * 90 per cent significance with bootstrap standard errors. We use the percentile and bias corrected approach with 2000 replications.

Table 3.9 Sensitivity Analysis on Growth Regressions (with composite BR-ICT indicator)

DEPENDENT VARIABLE: LOG DIFFERENCE GDP PER WORKING-AGE PERSON (1985-1997)								
Regressors		Coefficient	T-stat	R-sq	Obs	Additional variables		
$ln(S_k)-ln(n+g+d)$	*High*	0.425	5.860	0.660	74	GOV	INTSPREAD	CIVFREE
	Base	0.312	4.370	0.535	94			
	Low	0.254	3.500	0.671	83	EXP	SD_GDC	ECONFREE
$ln(S_h)-ln(n+g+d)$	*High*	0.064	1.290	0.685	74	GOV	EXP	INTSPREAD
	Base	0.000	-0.010	0.535	94			
	Low	-0.006	-0.110	0.662	84	EXP	SD_INFL	ECONFREE
$Ln(A_{BR\text{-}ICT(1985)})$	*High*	0.094	4.060	0.553	91	EXP	GDC	CIVFREE
	Base	0.102	4.500	0.535	94			
	Low	0.070	3.260	0.685	74	GOV	EXP	INTSPREAD
$g_{BR\text{-}ICT}$	*High*	0.115	5.060	0.553	91	EXP	GDC	CIVFREE
	Base	0.124	5.500	0.535	94			
	Low	0.093	4.220	0.660	74	GOV	INTSPREAD	POLFREE
$(Y/L)_{1985}$	*High*	-0.206	-4.230	0.685	74	GOV	EXP	INTSPREAD
	Base	-0.227	-4.630	0.535	94			
	Low	-0.314	-6.260	0.670	83	EXP	GDC	ECONFREE

Note: the sensitivity analysis is run by adding to the benchmark model for growth estimated in Table 3.8 all three by three combinations of the following variables: GOV: average government consumption to GDP; EXP: export to GDP; INFL: inflation, standard deviation of inflation; GDC: average growth rate of domestic credit; SD_GDC: standard deviation of domestic credit; ECONFREE: economic freedom; CIVFREE: civil freedom; INTSPREAD: average difference between lending and borrowing rate in the domestic banking system. In the table we select for each regressor of the base model only the benchmark estimate and the two replications in which the coefficient has the highest and the lowest significance.

Table 3.10 Growth Regressions with and without BR-ICT and Economic Freedom Indicators

	DEPENDENT VARIABLE: LOG DIFFERENCE GDP PER WORKING-AGE PERSON (1985-1997)								
Variable	MRW-type estimate	ECFREE COMPOSITE	ECFREE (I)	ECFREE (II)	ECFREE (III)	ECFREE (IV)	ECFREE (V)	ECFREE (VI)	ECFREE (VII)
$ln(S_k)-ln(n+g+d)$	0.312	0.277	0.331	0.339	0.312	0.317	0.205	0.324	0.332
	[4.370]**	[3.950] **	[4.230] **	[4.640] **	[3.950] **	[4.400] **	[2.420]*	[4.130] **	[4.730] **
$ln(S_h)-ln(n+g+d)$	0.000	-0.009	-0.029	-0.026	-0.030	-0.011	-0.068	-0.041	-0.010
	[-0.010]	[-0.170]	[-0.490]	[-0.480]	[-0.520]	[-0.210]	[-1.200]	[-0.700]	[-0.190]
$g_{BR\text{-}ICT}$	0.124	0.107	0.132	0.119	0.129	0.111	0.182	0.127	0.115
	[5.500] **	[4.960] **	[5.610] **	[5.310] **	[5.520] **	[4.980] **	[5.760] **	[5.270] **	[5.360] **
$Ln(A_{BR\text{-}ICT(1985)})$	0.102	0.091	0.109	0.095	0.108	0.093	0.159	0.109	0.093
	[4.500] **	[4.220] **	[4.580] **	[4.150] **	[4.580] **	[4.160] **	[5.200] **	[4.570] **	[4.270] **
$Ln(Y/L_{1985})$	-0.227	-0.304	-0.203	-0.232	-0.217	-0.265	-0.341	-0.234	-0.279
	[-4.630] **	[-6.110] **	[-3.790] **	[-4.750] **	[-4.230] **	[-5.330] **	[-5.380] **	[-4.110] **	[-5.700] **
ECFREE		0.104	0.012	0.041	0.014	0.040	0.046	0.019	0.048
		[4.820] **	[0.640]	[3.320] **	[1.390]	[3.760] **	[2.140]*	[0.930]	[4.370] **
CONSTANT	0.783	1.053	0.568	0.660	0.801	0.883	2.558	0.922	0.895
	[1.330]	[1.940]	[0.830]	[1.150]	[1.320]	[1.570]	[3.230] **	[1.460]	[1.630]*
Countries	94	84	85	85	85	85	82	85	85
R-squared	0.535	0.660	0.567	0.619	0.576	0.632	0.607	0.570	0.651

As BR-ICT indicator we use the composite ICT index wich is an unweighted average of normalised values of the following four ICT variables (when available): i) main telephone lines per 1,000 people; ii) the number of computers with active Internet Protocol (IP) addresses connected to the Internet, per 10,000 people; iii) Mobile phones (per 1,000 people); iv) Personal computers (per 1,000 people). For the definition of the index of economic freedom see Table 3.4.

T-stats are reported in square brackets.
** 95 per cent significance with bootstrap standard errors, * 90 per cent significance with bootstrap standard errors. We use the percentile and bias corrected approach with 2000 replications.

Conclusions

The technological revolution originated by the progressive convergence of software and telecommunications and fostered by the advancements in digital technology is dramatically changing the world. This revolution has sharply reduced transportation costs, deeply modified geographical patterns of productive factors across the world and significantly increased the productivity of human capital.

We believe that Information and Communication Technology mainly consists of a core of reproducible and implementable knowledge incorporated in quasi-public 'knowledge products' such as software and database libraries which can be accessed by everyone 'with' some conditions. These conditions are represented by capacity and access to the network and by the availability of efficient terminal nodes which allow the processing, exchange and reproduction of these knowledge products. The wealth of nations therefore crucially depends on the quality of telephone lines, on the number of personal computers, mobile phones and Internet hosts as these factors reduce bottlenecks which may limit the diffusion of technological knowledge.

The empirical literature of growth has so far neglected this phenomenon because of limits in the available information or under the theoretical assumption that technology is a public good which can be easily and costlessly incorporated into domestic aggregate production functions. Our empirical evidence demonstrates that this is not the case and finds – even though for a limited time span with respect to the traditional empirical analyses on growth – some interesting results which support the theoretical prediction of a significant role of BR-ICT in explaining levels and rates of growth of income per worker. Our results clearly show that the BR-ICT factor is an additional crucial factor of conditionality for convergence in levels and rates of growth. These findings are robust to changes in specification and in the estimation approach.

Table 3.11 sums up the rationales, critical issues and main results of our empirical approaches showing how we rationally moved from the simplest to more sophisticated approaches in order to provide answers to the most important critical issues raised in the empirical literature. Results obtained from the methodological path followed are satisfactory when we look at both level and convergence estimates whose robustness has been tested under several alternative methods.

We may therefore conclude that BR-ICT is another crucial variable in conditional convergence. It therefore bridges the gap between pessimistic views arguing that differences in personal income across countries are a structural element of the economic system which is going to persist and even widen, and optimistic views believing that those who lag behind will be able to catch up.

By collecting additional information on ICT diffusion in the coming years, we will be able to know whether BR-ICT contribution to growth is also likely to persist in the future so that our conclusions may be extended to a longer time period.

Table 3.11 Synthesis of Rationales, Critical Issues and Main Results of Empirical Approaches Followed in the Chapter

Estimation approach	Main results with alternative specifications of the BR-ICT variable	Critical issues	Potential solutions
The determinants of levels of income per worker (cross-section approach)			
Cross-sectional estimate of the determinants of levels of income per worker. The specification of the labour-augmenting technological progress overcomes the *cross-sectional constant critique* (Islam, 1995; Temple, 1999).	Levels and rates of growth of BR-ICT are always significant in any specification. The goodness of fit is higher with BR-ICT variables than in the traditional MRW estimate. In the larger time span with the composite index regressors elasticities are higher than expected.	i) Dependent and explanatory variables are non-normal. ii) Additional individual country factors (governance, preferences) are unspecified.	i) Estimate with bootstrap standard errors. ii) Panel fixed effects or inclusion of additional proxies of country specific effects.
Cross-sectional estimate of the determinants of levels of income per worker with bootstrap standard errors.	Results are the same as above.	Additional individual country factors (governance, preferences) are unspecified	Panel fixed effects or inclusion of additional proxies of country specific effects.
Levine-Renelt (1992) sensitivity analysis in the cross-sectional estimate of the determinants of levels of income per worker with and without bootstrap standard errors.	Levels and rates of growth of BR-ICT variables are robust to the inclusion of additional regressors.		
The determinants of levels of income per worker (panel approach)			
Estimation of the determinants of levels of income per worker with panel fixed effect to allow for country-specific effects not captured by BR-ICT variables.	BR-ICT variables are significant in any specification.	i) Endogeneity problem.	i) G2SLS estimates. ii) Estimates for subsample splits.

Exogenous subsample split of the estimate of the determinants of levels of income per worker with panel fixed effects.	The significance of BR-ICT variables is strong but confined only to OECD, EU and high economic freedom subsample, while much weaker or not existing in their complementary samples (non-OECD, non-UE, low economic freedom).	i) Endogeneity problem.	G2SLS estimates.
G2SLS estimates to avoid endogeneity.	BR-ICT variables are still significant.		
CONVERGENCE			
Cross-sectional estimate of the determinants of rates of growth in income per worker. The high fit of the cross-sectional estimate in levels partially overcomes the cross-country heterogeneity critique.	Initial period levels and rates of growth of BR-ICT are positive and significant.	Dependent and explanatory variables are non-normal. Unexplained cross-country hetereogeneity critique may generate correlation between the lagged dependent variable and the disturbance.	i) Estimate with bootstrap standard errors. ii) Inclusion of additional proxies of country-specific effects.
Cross-sectional estimate of the determinants of rates of growth in income per worker with bootstrap standard errors.	Initial period levels and rates of growth of BR-ICT are positive and significant.	Cross-country heterogeneity critique still partially unsolved and additional individual country factors are unspecified. Potential solutions: a) panel fixed effect estimate, or b) sensitivity analysis with the inclusion of additional proxies for country specific effects.	Inclusion of additional proxies of country-specific effects.
Levine-Renelt (1992) sensitivity analysis on growth estimates.	Initial period levels and rates of growth of BR-ICT are positive and significant.		

Table A1 Data Appendix

Variability ICT		Telephone mainlines (per 1,000 people)				Internet hosts (per 10,000 people)				Mobile phones (per 1,000 people)				Personal computers (per 1,000 people)			
id	Country Name	First year		Last year		First year		Last year		First year		Last year		First year		Last year	
1	Algeria	1965	6.0	1997	47.5	1994	0.004	1997	0.011	1990	0.019	1997	0.508	1990	0.996	1997	4.200
2	Angola	1960	1.3	1997	5.3	1994	0.000	1997	0.015	1993	0.107	1997	0.608	1997	0.700	1997	0.700
3	Argentina	1960	44.3	1997	191.0	1994	0.368	1997	5.321	1989	0.072	1997	56.303	1988	4.430	1997	39.216
4	Australia	1960	148.0	1997	505.0	1994	90.037	1997	381.828	1987	0.271	1997	264.324	1988	103.030	1997	362.162
5	Austria	1960	60.8	1997	492.0	1994	34.002	1997	108.283	1985	1.291	1997	143.742	1988	39.474	1997	210.657
6	Bangladesh	1977	0.9	1996	2.6	1994	0.000	1996	0.000	1992	0.002	1995	0.021		#N/D		#N/D
7	Barbados	1960	30.0	1997	404.0	1994	0.000	1997	0.755	1991	1.884	1997	29.888	1995	57.471	1995	57.471
8	Belgium	1960	85.1	1997	468.0	1994	17.250	1997	84.511	1986	0.385	1997	95.490	1988	50.556	1997	235.294
9	Benin	1960	0.9	1997	6.3	1994	0.000	1997	0.022	1995	0.192	1997	0.752	1995	0.547	1997	0.900
10	Bolivia	1980	25.2	1997	68.8	1994	0.000	1997	0.693	1991	0.074	1997	14.929		#N/D		#N/D
11	Botswana	1970	7.3	1997	56.0	1994	0.000	1997	1.553	1995	0.000	1996	0.000	1994	6.993	1996	13.400
12	Brazil	1975	20.3	1997	107.0	1994	0.383	1997	4.196	1990	0.005	1997	27.500	1988	1.786	1997	26.250
13	Burkina Faso	1970	0.2	1997	3.2	1994	0.000	1997	0.046	1995	0.000	1997	0.135	1990	0.113	1997	0.700
14	Burundi	1965	0.4	1997	2.5	1994	0.000	1997	0.012	1993	0.061	1997	0.100		#N/D		#N/D
15	Cameroon	1960	0.5	1997	5.3	1994	0.000	1997	0.054	1994	0.124	1997	0.302	1990	1.304	1995	1.504
16	Canada	1960	278.4	1997	609.0	1994	63.728	1997	227.928	1985	0.463	1997	138.900	1980	4.065	1997	270.627
17	Cape Verde	1960	0.9	1997	81.8	1994	0.000	1997	0.399	1995	0.000	1997	0.049		#N/D		#N/D
18	Central African Repub ic	1978	1.1	1997	2.8	1994	0.000	1997	0.018	1995	0.013	1997	0.200		#N/D		#N/D
19	Chad	1965	0.4	1997	1.1	1994	0.000	1995	0.000	1995	0.000	1997	0.000		#N/D		#N/D
20	Chile	1960	17.3	1997	180.0	1994	2.181	1997	13.109	1989	0.376	1997	28.082	1988	4.688	1997	54.110
21	China	1975	1.8	1997	55.7	1994	0.005	1997	0.209	1987	0.001	1997	10.476	1988	0.268	1997	5.952
22	Colombia	1960	17.2	1997	148.0	1994	0.327	1997	1.724	1994	2.516	1997	34.807	1992	9.581	1997	33.425
23	Comoros	1970	1.1	1997	8.4	1994	0.000	1995	2.656	1995	0.000	1997	0.000	1970	0.000	1995	0.266
24	Costa Rica	1970	23.1	1997	169.0	1994	2.440	1997	12.295	1992	1.003	1997	18.559		#N/D		#N/D
25	Denmark	1960	182.0	1997	633.0	1994	35.396	1997	259.278	1982	1.406	1997	272.727	1988	58.480	1997	360.200

26	Dominican Republic	1980	19.0	1997	87.5	1994	0.000	1997	0.031	1990	0.442	1997	16.049		#N/D		#N/D
27	Ecuador	1965	9.3	1997	75.2	1994	0.290	1997	0.903	1994	1.598	1997	13.445	1991	1.905	1995	13.043
28	Egypt, Arab Rep.	1960	7.9	1997	55.6	1994	0.027	1997	0.314	1987	0.052	1997	0.116	1994	3.368	1997	7.300
29	El Salvador	1965	4.0	1996	56.1	1994	0.000	1997	0.337	1993	0.302	1997	6.779		#N/D		#N/D
30	Ethiopia	1960	0.3	1997	2.6	1994	0.000	1997	0.000	1995	0.000	1997	0.000		#N/D		#N/D
31	Fiji	1960	13.1	1997	91.9	1994	0.065	1997	0.000	1994	1.438	1997	6.658		#N/D		#N/D
32	Finland	1960	96.6	1997	556.0	1994	133.847	1997	653.631	1982	0.549	1997	417.476	1990	100.000	1997	310.680
33	France	1960	48.0	1997	575.0	1994	14.447	1997	49.840	1986	0.163	1997	99.487	1988	55.258	1997	174.359
34	Ghana	1965	2.2	1997	5.7	1994	0.000	1997	0.153	1992	0.025	1997	1.200	1983	0.000	1997	1.600
35	Greece	1960	21.8	1997	516.0	1994	3.381	1997	18.733	1993	4.615	1997	89.333	1988	12.000	1997	44.762
36	Guatemala	1960	4.4	1997	40.8	1994	0.000	1997	0.839	1990	0.033	1997	6.114	1993	1.047	1995	3.006
37	Guinea	1960	0.6	1997	2.5	1994	0.003	1997	0.003	1993	0.006	1997	0.377	1994	0.054	1997	0.344
38	Guinea-Bissau	1960	0.5	1997	6.8	1994	0.000	1997	0.088	1995	0.000	1997	0.000		#N/D		#N/D
39	Haiti	1981	3.6	1997	8.0	1994	0.000	1997	0.000	1995	0.000	1997	0.000		#N/D		#N/D
40	Honduras	1975	5.6	1997	36.8	1994	0.000	1997	0.986	1995	0.000	1997	2.271		#N/D		#N/D
41	Hong Kong, China	1960	25.7	1997	565.0	1994	20.591	1997	74.839	1984	0.186	1997	343.077	1988	25.688	1997	230.769
42	Hungary	1960	24.3	1997	304.0	1994	6.627	1997	33.302	1990	0.255	1997	69.314	1988	8.286	1997	49.020
43	Iceland	1960	187.5	1997	617.0	1994	169.551	1997	521.481	1986	10.864	1997	241.544	1990	39.063	1995	205.224
44	India	1960	0.7	1997	18.6	1994	0.004	1997	0.050	1995	0.083	1997	0.924	1988	0.185	1997	2.094
45	Indonesia	1960	0.8	1997	24.7	1994	0.009	1997	0.542	1984	0.011	1997	4.557	1988	0.581	1997	7.960
46	Ireland	1960	39.0	1997	411.0	1994	15.281	1997	90.224	1985	0.085	1997	146.027	1990	106.286	1997	241.300
47	Israel	1960	30.6	1997	450.0	1994	22.645	1997	104.764	1990	3.207	1997	282.572	1988	44.346	1997	186.125
48	Italy	1960	60.9	1997	447.0	1994	4.951	1997	36.849	1985	0.112	1997	204.100	1986	9.353	1997	113.043
49	Ivory Coast	1960	0.9	1997	9.3	1994	0.000	1997	0.175	1995	0.000	1997	2.353	1996	1.351	1997	3.268
50	Jamaica	1960	12.2	1996	140.0	1994	0.308	1997	1.366	1991	1.059	1996	21.667	1994	3.457	1996	4.563
51	Japan	1960	38.9	1997	479.0	1994	7.731	1997	75.794	1981	0.113	1997	303.968	1985	17.355	1997	202.381
52	Jordan	1960	13.7	1997	69.7	1994	0.000	1997	0.383	1990	0.338	1995	2.114	1994	5.769	1997	8.700
53	Kenya	1965	2.8	1997	8.1	1994	0.000	1997	0.160	1992	0.044	1997	0.162	1990	0.348	1997	2.300
54	Korea, Rep.	1965	7.7	1997	444.0	1994	4.020	1997	28.782	1986	0.172	1997	150.217	1988	11.190	1997	150.652
55	Luxembourg	1960	116.1	1997	669.0	1994	12.525	1997	91.435	1985	0.109	1997	160.766	1996	375.303	1996	375.303
56	Madagascar	1965	1.5	1997	2.7	1994	0.000	1997	0.029	1994	0.021	1997	0.300	1997	1.300	1997	1.300

57	Malawi	1965	0.9	1997	4.0	1994	0.000	1997	0.000	1995	0.039	1996	0.366		#N/D		#N/D
58	Malaysia	1960	5.8	1997	195.0	1994	0.815	1997	18.707	1986	0.675	1997	113.364	1988	4.142	1997	46.083
59	Mali	1960	0.3	1997	2.0	1994	0.000	1997	0.028	1995	0.000	1997	0.247	1995	0.278	1997	0.600
60	Malta	1960	29.7	1997	498.0	1994	0.000	1997	20.933	1991	6.333	1997	47.074	1990	14.045	1995	80.645
61	Mauritania	1970	0.4	1997	5.4	1994	0.000	1997	0.000	1995	0.000	1997	0.000	1996	5.319	1996	5.319
62	Mauritius	1960	9.1	1997	195.0	1994	0.000	1997	1.838	1990	2.075	1997	32.456	1987	0.456	1997	78.947
63	Mexico	1960	9.7	1997	96.0	1994	0.720	1997	3.735	1988	0.018	1997	18.154	1988	4.469	1997	37.344
64	Morocco	1960	6.7	1997	49.9	1994	0.000	1997	0.325	1987	0.003	1997	2.709	1993	1.149	1997	2.545
65	Mozambique	1960	1.2	1997	3.6	1994	0.000	1997	0.026	1995	0.000	1997	0.137	1996	0.843	1997	1.600
66	Myanmar	1960	0.5	1997	4.6	1994	0.000	1997	0.001	1993	0.015	1997	0.183		#N/D		#N/D
67	Namibia	1981	31.1	1997	58.0	1994	0.000	1997	2.157	1995	2.258	1997	7.764	1996	12.658	1997	18.600
68	Nepal	1975	0.5	1997	7.7	1994	0.000	1997	0.074	1995	0.000	1997	0.000		#N/D		#N/D
69	Netherlands	1960	90.8	1997	564.0	1994	55.807	1997	218.851	1985	0.331	1997	109.554	1988	50.676	1997	280.255
70	New Zealand	1960	225.9	1997	486.0	1994	87.193	1997	413.927	1987	0.738	1997	149.077	1991	96.802	1997	263.852
71	Nicaragua	1970	8.2	1997	29.3	1994	0.114	1997	1.589	1993	0.079	1997	1.818		#N/D		#N/D
72	Niger	1960	0.2	1997	1.6	1994	0.000	1997	0.035	1995	0.000	1997	0.010	1997	0.200	1997	0.200
73	Nigeria	1960	0.4	1996	3.5	1994	0.000	1997	0.001	1993	0.086	1995	0.117	1993	3.810	1997	5.100
74	Norway	1960	126.8	1997	621.0	1994	111.438	1997	474.635	1981	0.407	1997	380.700	1991	145.540	1997	360.800
75	Pakistan	1960	1.3	1997	18.5	1994	0.000	1997	0.075	1990	0.018	1997	0.797	1990	1.339	1996	4.478
76	Panama	1978	59.6	1997	134.0	1994	0.066	1997	1.434	1995	0.000	1997	6.250		#N/D		#N/D
77	Papua New Guinea	1965	1.9	1996	10.6	1994	0.000	1997	0.176	1995	0.000	1996	0.693		#N/D		#N/D
78	Paraguay	1960	4.6	1997	42.8	1994	0.000	1997	0.470	1992	0.332	1997	16.600		#N/D		#N/D
79	Peru	1965	7.2	1997	67.5	1994	0.073	1997	2.671	1990	0.076	1997	17.869	1995	5.957	1997	12.300
80	Philippines	1965	2.5	1997	29.0	1994	0.050	1997	0.586	1991	0.557	1997	17.687	1988	2.058	1997	13.600
81	Poland	1960	18.1	1997	194.0	1994	2.796	1997	11.225	1992	0.057	1997	22.145	1988	3.968	1997	36.176
82	Portugal	1960	11.5	1997	402.0	1994	5.100	1997	18.247	1989	0.284	1997	151.911	1988	14.344	1997	74.447
83	Puerto Rico	1975	81.1	1997	351.0	1994	0.222	1997	0.298	1987	1.153	1996	45.187		#N/D		#N/D
84	Qatar	1960	13.3	1997	249.0	1994	0.000	1997	4.787	1990	7.856	1997	76.450	1994	46.555	1996	62.724
85	Reunion	1970	18.2	1997	351.0	1994	0.000	1997	0.000	1991	4.484	1997	39.673		#N/D		#N/D
86	Romania	1965	16.0	1997	167.0	1994	0.230	1997	2.659	1993	0.035	1997	8.900	1990	0.431	1997	8.900
87	Rwanda	1960	0.4	1996	2.7	1994	0.000	1997	0.008	1995	0.000	1997	0.000		#N/D		#N/D

88	Senegal	1960	2.9	1997	13.2	1994	0.000	1997	0.313	1994	0.012	1997	0.792	1981	0.002	1997	11.400
89	Seychelles	1965	4.9	1996	196.0	1994	0.000	1997	4.508	1995	4.329	1996	15.132		#N/D		#N/D
90	Sierra Leone	1965	1.1	1997	3.9	1994	0.000	1997	0.000	1995	0.000	1997	0.000		#N/D		#N/D
91	Singapore	1960	22.7	1997	543.0	1994	15.631	1997	195.502	1988	3.789	1997	273.400	1988	42.105	1997	399.500
92	Solomon Islands	1982	6.1	1997	19.3	1994	0.000	1997	0.050	1994	0.393	1997	1.629		#N/D		#N/D
93	Somalia	1960	0.3	1996	1.5	1994	0.000	1995	0.000	1995	0.000	1997	0.000		#N/D		#N/D
94	South Africa	1960	37.3	1997	107.0	1994	6.693	1997	28.932	1989	0.107	1997	36.951	1988	4.144	1997	41.570
95	Spain	1960	42.1	1997	403.0	1994	7.053	1997	30.980	1986	0.044	1997	110.433	1988	17.857	1997	122.137
96	Sri Lanka	1960	2.3	1997	17.0	1994	0.000	1997	0.329	1990	0.059	1997	6.183	1990	0.176	1997	4.086
97	Sudan	1960	1.5	1997	4.0	1994	0.000	1997	0.001	1995	0.000	1997	0.136	1994	0.195	1997	1.147
98	Suriname	1975	28.8	1997	146.0	1994	0.000	1997	0.000	1993	2.609	1997	9.359		#N/D		#N/D
99	Swaziland	1970	5.9	1996	24.0	1994	0.000	1997	2.504	1995	0.000	1997	0.000		#N/D		#N/D
100	Sweden	1960	279.3	1997	679.0	1994	84.741	1997	321.464	1981	2.452	1997	358.192	1988	59.242	1997	350.282
101	Switzerland	1960	203.4	1997	661.0	1994	67.597	1997	208.843	1987	0.827	1997	146.685	1988	52.317	1997	394.922
102	Syrian Arab Republic	1960	8.5	1997	87.7	1994	0.000	1997	0.000	1995	0.000	1997	0.000	1994	0.362	1997	1.700
103	Tanzania	1960	0.7	1997	3.3	1994	0.000	1997	0.020	1994	0.013	1997	0.641	1997	1.600	1997	1.600
104	Thailand	1960	1.4	1997	80.0	1994	0.294	1997	2.111	1986	0.016	1997	33.003	1988	1.842	1997	19.802
105	Togo	1960	0.7	1997	5.8	1994	0.000	1997	0.014	1995	0.000	1997	0.694	1995	3.623	1997	5.787
106	Trinidad and Tobago	1965	24.7	1997	190.0	1994	0.000	1997	3.236	1991	0.361	1997	13.594	1991	4.237	1995	20.000
107	Tunisia	1960	6.2	1997	70.1	1994	0.061	1997	0.016	1987	0.030	1997	0.821	1990	2.602	1997	8.574
108	Turkey	1960	6.4	1997	250.0	1994	0.308	1997	3.602	1986	0.007	1997	25.596	1988	2.235	1997	20.668
109	Uganda	1965	1.2	1997	2.4	1994	0.000	1997	0.013	1995	0.091	1997	0.240	1995	0.518	1997	1.400
110	United Kingdom	1960	96.1	1997	540.0	1994	38.713	1997	148.834	1985	0.883	1997	151.300	1985	37.102	1997	242.373
111	United States	1960	272.7	1997	644.0	1994	121.807	1997	442.013	1984	0.386	1997	206.343	1981	9.217	1997	406.716
112	Uruguay	1965	52.7	1997	232.0	1994	0.543	1997	3.135	1992	0.546	1997	45.732	1995	21.944	1995	21.944
113	Venezuela	1965	19.5	1997	116.0	1994	0.247	1997	2.054	1988	0.098	1997	46.121	1988	5.435	1997	36.638
114	Yemen, Rep.	1980	2.0	1997	13.3	1994	0.000	1996	0.001	1992	0.124	1996	0.554	1997	1.200	1997	1.200
115	Zambia	1965	4.7	1996	9.4	1994	0.087	1997	0.270	1995	0.165	1996	0.329		#N/D		#N/D
116	Zimbabwe	1975	13.2	1997	17.2	1994	0.017	1997	0.237	1995	0.000	1997	0.900	1990	0.202	1997	9.000

References

Alesina, A. and Perotti, R. (1994), 'The political economy of growth: a critical survey of the recent literature', *World Bank Economic Review*, 8:3, pp. 351-71.

Barro, R. and Sala-i-Martin, X. (1992), 'Convergence', *Journal of Political Economy*, 100, pp. 223-251.

Barua, A., Kriebel, C. and Mukhopadhyay, T. (1991), 'Information Technology and Business Value: An Analytic and Empirical Investigation', University of Texas at Austin Working Paper, (May).

Becchetti, L., Londono Bedoya, D.A. and Paganetto, L. (2000), 'ICT investment, productivity and efficiency: evidence at firm level using a stochastic frontier approach', CEIS Working paper n.126.

Bender, D.H. (1986), 'Financial Impact of Information Processing', *Journal of Management Information Systems*, 3(2), pp. 22-32.

Berndt, E.R., Morrison, C.J. and Rosenblum, L.S. (1992), 'High-tech Capital Formation and Labor Composition in U.S. Manufacturing Industries: an Exploratory Analysis', National Bureau of Economic Research Working Paper No. 4010 (March).

Brunetti, A. (1997), 'Political variables in cross-country growth analysis', *Journal of Economic Surveys*, 11:2, pp. 162-190.

Brynjolfsson, E. and Hitt, L. (1996), 'Paradox Lost? Firm-Level Evidence on the Returns to Information Systems Spending', *Management Science* (April).

Caselli, F., Esquivel, G. and Lefort, F. (1996), 'Reopening the convergence debate; a new look at cross-country growth empirics', *Journal of Economic Growth*, 1:3, pp. 363-90.

Dawson, J.W. (1998), 'Institutions, Investment, and Growth: New Cross-Country and Panel Data Evidence', *Economic Inquiry*, 36(4), October, pp. 603-19.

Durlauf, S.N. and Quah, D.T. (1998), 'The new empirics of economic growth', Center for Economic Performance Discussion Paper N. 384.

Easterly, W. and Rebelo, S. (1993), 'Fiscal Policy and Economic Growth', *Journal of Monetary Economics*, 32:3, pp. 417-58.

Easton, S.T. and Walker, M.A. (1997), 'Income, Growth, and Economic Freedom', *American Economic Review*; 87(2), May 1997, pp. 328-32.

Evans, P. (1997), 'How fast do economies converge?', *The Review of Economics and Stati*stics, pp. 219-225.

Gwartney, J., Lawson, R. and Samida, D. (2000), *Economic Freedom of the World: 2000*, Vancouver, B.C.: The Fraser Institute.

Islam, N. (1995), 'Growth empirics: a panel data approach', *Quarterly Journal of Economics*, pp. 1127-1169.

Jorgenson, D. and Stiroh, K.J. (1999), 'Information technology and growth', *American Economic Review*, 89:2, pp. 109-115.

King, R.G. and Levine, R. (1992), 'Finance and growth: Schumpeter might be right', *The Quarterly Journal of Economics*, August.

Knack, S. and Keefer, P. (1997) 'Does Social Capital Have an Economic Payoff? A Cross-Country Investigation', *Quarterly Journal of Economics* 112, pp. 1251-88.

Lehr, B. and Lichtenberg, F. (1999), 'Information Technology and Its Impact on Productivity: Firm-Level Evidence from Government and Private Data Sources, 1977-1993', *Canadian Journal of Economics*; 32(2), pp. 335-62.

Levine, R. and Renelt, D. (1992), 'A sensitivity analysis of cross-country growth regressions', *American Economic Review*, 82(4), pp. 942-63.

Loveman, G.W. (1988), 'An Assessment of the Productivity Impact of Information Technologies', MIT Management in the 1990s, Working Paper # 88-05, July.

Mankiw, N.G., Romer, D. and Weil, D. (1992), 'A contribution to the empirics of economic growth', *Quarterly Journal of Economics*, May, pp. 407-437.

Mauro, P. (1995), 'Corruption and growth', *Quarterly Journal of Economics*, 110:3, pp. 681-712.

Milgrom P. and Roberts R. (1988), *The Economics of Modern Manufacturing: Products, Technology and Organization*, Stanford Center for Economic Policy Research Discussion Paper 136.

Oliner, S.D. and Sichel, D.E. (1994), 'Computers and Output Growth Revisited: How Big is the Puzzle?', Brookings Papers on Economic Activity, 1994(2), pp. 273-334.

Pagano, M. (1992), 'Financial markets and growth: an overview', *European Economic Review* 37, pp. 613-622.

Perotti, R. (1996), 'Growth, income distribution and democracy: What the data say', *Journal of Economic Growth*, 1, pp. 149-87.

Persson, T. and Tabellini, G. (1994), 'Is inequality harmful for growth?', *American Economic Rev*iew, 84:3, pp. 600-21.

Quah, D. (1999), 'Technology and Growth, The Weightless Economy in Economic Development', *LSE Discussion Paper* no. 417.

Roach, S.S. (1989), 'America's White-Collar Productivity Dilemma', *Manufacturing Engineering*, August, pp. 104.

Roach, S.S. (1991), 'Services under Siege: the Restructuring Imperative', *Harvard Business Review* 39(2), pp. 82-92, (September-October).

Sichel, A. (1997), *The Computer Revolution: An Economic Perspective*, Washington, DC: Brookings Institution Press.

Solow, R.M. (1956), 'A contribution to the theory of economic growth', *Quarterly Journal of Economics*, LXX, pp. 65-94.

Stiroh, K.J. (1998), 'Computers productivity and input substitution', *Economic Inquiry*, 36:2, April, pp. 175-91.

Strassmann, P.A. (1990), *The Business Value of Computers: An Executive's Guide*, New Canaan, CT: Information Economics Press.

Temple, J. (1999), 'The new growth evidence', *Journal of Economic Literature*, XXXVII, pp. 112-156.

Chapter 4

Growth and Finance: What Do We Know and How Do We Know It?

Paul Wachtel

Development economics has changed profoundly in the course of one generation. Twenty-five years ago the emphasis among development economists was on planning and allocation mechanisms, which separated the development community from the core of mainstream market-oriented economics. Academicians who followed development issues were often peripheral to the cutting edge in the economics literature. However, that has all changed in recent years and development issues are now at the forefront. As part of this transformation, the term development (which connotes a directed process) has been largely replaced by the term emerging markets. The very term emphasizes the private sector and the market-oriented paradigm of contemporary economics. In no other area is the change in thinking more striking than in analysis of the role of the financial sector – banks and capital markets – in the development process.

The modern literature on economic growth starts with Robert Solow's work in the mid 1950s for which he was awarded the Nobel Memorial Prize in Economics. The early theoretical and empirical literature focused on the role of capital and labor resources and the use of technology as the sources of growth. For the most part, any possible role of the financial sector in the growth process was ignored. To the contrary, development economists up until the 1970s would often advocate explicit manipulation of the financial sector in order to achieve development goals. Credit subsidies to favored activities were the rule rather than the exception. Inflation was attractive since a tax on financial assets gave governments with an otherwise weak tax base the resources that could be given to development industries.

A few influential economists began to draw attention to the contribution of the financial structure to growth (in particular, see Goldsmith, 1969; McKinnon, 1973) and the benefits of liberalization. The term financial repression took hold and economists slowly acknowledged that credit allocation, interest rate ceilings and high reserve requirements were undesirable. Generally, high inflation, negative real rates and inflation taxes create distortions that lead to extensive resource misallocations and discourage saving and the use of intermediaries. In 1973 (p. 12) McKinnon could write with confidence that: 'Now, however, there is widespread agreement that flows of saving and investment should be voluntary and significantly decentralized in an open capital market at close to equilibrium interest rates.' However, the path toward liberalization is characterized by McKinnon as a minefield where one misstep might be the last.

The financial sector – both domestic markets and international capital flows – was often the most heavily controlled and regulated component of the economy. However, a major shift towards a market-oriented approach began about twenty-five years ago. Since then, capital controls that prevailed around the world in both developed and less developed economies have largely disappeared. Today countries that maintain capital controls are almost self-conscious pariahs in the international community. The domestic corollary of capital account liberalization is financial sector liberalization that has occurred at a somewhat slower pace. Nevertheless, support for directed credit, interest rate ceilings and government ownership of financial institutions have also disappeared. The prevailing paradigm is that competitive private sector capital markets should be able to gather savings at market rates of interest and allocate capital to the most efficient private sector projects.

The contemporary paradigm hardly needs restatement. Contemporary economists take it for granted that a well-developed, market-oriented financial sector contributes to economic growth. However, it is curious how little evidence there is that relates the financial sector to economic growth and stability. The paradigm of financial liberalization was widely accepted before there was evidence to relate it to economic growth. The objective of this paper is to review some of that evidence.

We will begin with two related observations about growth and the financial sector. First, the financial sector, particularly in developed economies, is a large industry. What are we buying from this industry? Second, although growth rates are related to levels of investment, there are wide differences in growth for any given level of investment. What are the reasons for this?

We will then turn to the empirical literature on the relationship between financial sector development and economic growth. Only recently – since the 1990s – has a large body of empirical knowledge accumulated that relates financial sector development – the depth and activity of financial intermediaries – to growth. The standard approach used in the literature will be described and the results are summarized. Finally, we also discuss the relationship between the financial sector and economic stability. Banking crises and currency crises seem to occur with great frequency – although it is not at all clear that they are more common than in the past. Our interest is whether crises are more or less likely to occur in countries with developed financial sectors.

Two Observations about Growth and the Financial Sector

About eight per cent of U.S. GDP is produced by the financial services industry – depository and non-depository institutions, brokers, insurance carriers and agents. The largest part of the industry – depository institutions or banks – accounts for two-fifths of the industry total. Financial services are an extraordinarily large part of the U.S. economy, larger than agriculture and mining together and half as big as manufacturing.[1]

What are we buying from this large industry? Are we getting our money's worth? What does this industry contribute to the economy and the well-being of its citizens?

From the individual's point of view the industry is providing two related types of services:

- Payments services – transactions assets that facilitate safe and rapid payments in a single unit of account
- Savings services – instruments and institutions that enable economic agents to move consumption around over time.

For sure, these services are of great value but still the size of the industry in the U.S. defies understanding. Are these financial services of sufficient value to warrant the size of the industry? Or does society get other payoffs from the industry?

The additional payoffs to society as a whole come in the form of the allocative role of financial intermediation. Financial intermediaries channel savings into capital investment projects. A well-working intermediary sector has two valuable implications:

- improves the efficiency of allocation of capital resources
- encourages savings and leads to more capital formation.

We get our money's worth from the financial industry because it expands our opportunities and leads to more productive allocations of resources.

The efficiency-enhancing value of the financial sector cannot be over emphasized. Think of countries with high rates of investment and savings and poor growth experience. The Soviet Union always had high savings rates; there was always an abundance of machinery and equipment. It simply was not allocated to effective uses.

That is not to say that the amount of capital formation is not an important indicator of economic growth. Generally speaking, countries with higher investment to GDP ratios experience higher growth rates. Table 4.1 shows average annual real per capita GDP growth rates for countries grouped by their average investment ratios. There is a clear but not overwhelming tendency for countries with higher investment rates to have higher real per capita growth in the subsequent decade. The simple correlation of investment ratios and subsequent growth rates was 0.43 in the 1980s and 0.24 in the 1990s (see the table note for exact data definitions). For the whole period, the correlation of contemporaneous growth rates and investment ratios is 0.41.

---

[1] Detailed data on product by industry are from Lum and Moyer (2000).

Table 4.1 Growth Rates and Investment to GDP Ratios

Investment Ratio	<20%	20-25%	25-30%	30-35%	>35%
(1) Growth rate 1980-88	1.0%	0.6%	2.3%	4.8%	3.4%
(2) Growth rate 1989-98	-0.9	0.5	0.3	-0.1	2.9
(3) Growth rate 1980-98	-0.4	0.7	1.9	1.3	4.3

Note: for row (1) the investment to GDP ratios are for 1979-83 and for row (2) 1988-92. For row (3) average growth rates and investment rates for the 1980-98 period are used. GDP growth is based on GDP converted to international dollars using PPP rates and further corrected for U.S. inflation. There are 87 countries with data for the entire period and a population of at least two million. Calculated from the World Development Indicators, 2000.

There is substantial variation in growth rates among countries with similar investment ratios. Table 4.2 summarizes the relationship between investment to GDP ratio in 1990 and the average annual growth rate in the 1990s for 50 countries with population in excess of 15 million (six former Communist countries are excluded). These data also indicate that growth rates tend to increase with investment ratios. However, the standard deviations of growth rates across countries in each investment ratio group are always large.

Table 4.2 Average Annual Growth Rates and Investment to GDP Ratios

Investment GDP ratio	<15%	15-20%	20-25%	25-30%	>30%
Number of countries	10	12	15	8	5
Average annual growth rate, 1990-99 MEAN	3.6	3.5	3.1	4.7	4.6
STANDARD DEVIATION	3.7	1.6	1.2	3.1	1.9

Source: World Development Report 2000/2001 World Bank, 2001.

A look at a few large countries, all with similar investment ratios, further illustrates the point that growth rates differ considerably (Table 4.3).

Our first observation is that countries devote a lot of resources to the financial sector for the provision of intermediary services. Our second observation is that growth rates differ a lot even when countries have similar levels of investment. These two observations are linked by a burgeoning literature that suggests financial sector development is related to economic growth.

Table 4.3 Investment to GDP and Average and Growth Rates for Selected Countries

	Investment as a percentage of GDP, 1990	Average annual GDP growth, 1990-99
Australia	21	3.8
Brazil	20	2.9
Canada	21	2.3
France	22	1.7
Germany	23	1.5
Netherlands	22	2.7
U.K.	19	2.2
U.S.	17	3.4

Source: World Development Report, 2000/2001.

Sources of the Growth-Finance Relationship

The financial sector of the economy provides two basic and essential services. First, it provides a money asset and payments service, and second, it provides vehicles for the intermediation of savings to investors. We will start this section with a little more detail on the nature of intermediary services. Often the same institutions – banks – provide these functions. Sound provision of money services and sound monetary policy call for a very conservative approach while financing of investment projects is inherently a risky activity. Thus, the role of banks, when they provide all financial services, can be problematic. Countries with more developed financial sectors will have a range of institutions and markets that provide intermediation services. The second part of this section will describe the variety of financial sector institutions.

Functions of Intermediaries

Surveys by Pagano (1993) and Levine (1997) list several theoretical channels of causation from financial sector development to growth:

- Financial sector improves the screening of fund-seekers and the monitoring of recipients which improves the allocation of resources.
- Encourage the mobilization of savings – by providing attractive instruments and savings vehicles, they may well increase the savings rate.
- Lower costs of project evaluation and origination and facilitate the monitoring of projects through corporate governance.
- Provide opportunities for risk management and liquidity – intermediation promotes the development of markets and instruments with attractive characteristics that enable risk sharing.

The advantage of a wide variety of intermediaries providing different services is clear once we consider the myriad functions that financial intermediaries perform.

Broadly speaking, the role of the financial sector in all economies is to channel resources from savers to investment projects. A single institution –a bank – can provide these various functions or it can be provided by a variety of institutions. Modern economies have a wide range of market-oriented institutions for facilitating intermediation. In planned economies, this process is conducted by administrative arrangements and there were few market-oriented elements of the financial sector. In many less developed and transition economies, the only ubiquitous financial institutions are banks.

Variety of Financial Institutions

Financing arrangements fall along a continuum that starts with the entrepreneur, who collects the savings of friends and family, and extends to the large firm that raises capital in a variety of ways, ranging from the issuance of publicly traded equity to internationally syndicated loans and private placements. There are many modes of financing and different intermediary institutions and instruments. The broad array can be grouped in three categories:

- *Entrepreneurial finance* Entrepreneurial financing starts with the efforts of start-ups to utilize self-financing, e.g., the personal saving of the entrepreneurs' friends and family. It is quite important in all economies, emerging markets as well as developed economies. However, the paucity of data on the financial activity of new enterprises often makes it difficult to examine how much investment goes on and how well it is channeled.

  In many places, there are governmental efforts to provide some formal institutional structures to provide financing for start-ups. These can include government development banks and government-sponsored micro lending programs. Another example is technology centers that channel physical resources to favored scientific enterprises and help them obtain financing, often with some form of guarantee.

  Finally, trade credit provides an important source of informal interfirm financing that is particularly valuable to small firms. It is often provided by large firms to small firms and provides them with working capital and enables them to cope with financial difficulties. Although trade credit often has a bad reputation (when it takes the form of interfirm arrears and soft budget constraints), it is of vital importance.

- *Bank lending* As firms grow, they will turn to formal financial sector institutions for financing needs, starting with banks. In some countries, bank lending to the business sector is a simple extension of government soft budget lending, but in more advanced economies, bank lending at the behest of the government ceases, and bank lending to business is on commercial terms.

  There is a considerable debate concerning the relative merits of bank-dominated financial sectors as compared to those that give equal weight to capital markets. In any event, banks are crucial institutions that provide transactions services and credit ratings and relationships with customers that are important sources of information to other credit market sources.

- *Capital market financing* The next step in business financing is access to capital markets. Capital market activity can start at the early stages of a firm's development with venture capital. Initially, institutions provide *angel financing*, i.e., start up capital when an entrepreneur lacks the track record needed for bank financing or even trade credit. As a firm develops, venture capitalists provide *long-term loans* or *private equity* or *private placements* that supplements any short-term financing available to the firm. A fully developed enterprise is likely to turn to public capital market flotation such as *publicly traded equity or bonds*. Private sector bond markets have developed in only a few countries while equity markets are quite common.

This continuum of financing applies both to the sources of financing usually available to a firm as it grows from a start-up to a large publicly held corporation and to the development and maturation of the financial sector of a developing economy. There are wide differences among countries in the development of financial sector institutions. Many of these differences are due to historical accidents that led to the adoption of one or another set of institutions or the consequence of government policies.

U.S. Flow of Funds data gives some idea of the size of the different components. In 1999, the total non-financial business sector raised $678 billion (excluding foreign direct investment in the U.S.). Of this capital market financing (corporate bonds, commercial paper, equity etc.) was 19 per cent, loans from banks and other financial intermediaries and all mortgage lending came to 47 per cent, and finally, other sources – trade credit and all other sources of financing came to 34 per cent of the total.[2] U.S. business relies on all three main financing categories.

A distinguishing characteristic of U.S.A. capital markets is the broad variety instruments and institutions and the fact that no particular mode of financing dominates. It is tempting to conclude that the depth of the financial system in the U.S. is a strong determinant of its success although there is little formal testing of such a hypothesis. Many countries, including highly developed ones, have more limited financial sectors than the U.S. Banks dominate corporate finance in the so-called German or European model compared to the greater importance of capital markets in the Anglo-Saxon model.[3]

---

[2] The capital markets proportion is small for two reasons. First, many mortgages included under bank financing are really directly capital market instruments and second, in 1999 there was almost $150 billion in stock buy backs by corporations.

[3] The differences have been diminishing in recent years as a result of globalization, technological and regulatory changes. One of the consequences of European unification is the increased importance of capital markets on the continent. In the U.S., regulatory changes

A few studies emphasize the importance of a broad variety of financial sector activities. Bonin and Wachtel (2001) and United Nations (1999) emphasize the role of capital markets as well as banks in the financial sector development of emerging and transition economies. Furthermore, recent financial crises have led policy makers to focus on the development of the financial sector beyond banks and equity markets. Herring and Chatusripitak (2000) conclude that 'the absence of a bond market may render an economy less efficient and significantly more vulnerable to financial crisis'.

The Evidence on Financial Sector Development and Growth

As noted earlier, economists seemed to have fully accepted the liberal orthodoxy in support of financial liberalization before there was much firm evidence demonstrating the relationships between financial sector development and economic growth. The empirical literature is only now beginning to examine how and whether different financial sector structures matter and whether the absence of specific market structures affects the operation of the financial sector and impacts on growth.

Empirical investigations of the relationship between financial sector development and economic growth began to appear in the 1990s with King and Levine's (1993) cross-country studies for the post-war period and Wachtel and Rousseau's (1995) evidence from long time series for several countries. These studies showed that the depth of financial sector development and greater provision of financial intermediary services are associated with economic growth. In the decade since those studies appeared, there has been a veritable explosion of empirical interest in the finance-growth relationship.

The empirical efforts to show a relationship between financial sector development and economic growth began with very broad measures of the existence of a financial sector such as the degree of monetization in the economy. Further work looked at the most important or best known institutions: bank lending and equity financing. Most recent empirical investigations have moved in two new directions. First, there are some efforts, limited by the paucity of data, to examine the role of non-bank financial intermediaries and the specific characteristics of the financial industry. Second, there has been considerable interest in the quality of financial institutions and the environment in which they operate. For example, the legal and regulatory frameworks in a country affect the ability of given institutions to contribute.

In his extensive survey article Levine (1997) cites Goldsmith (1969) as the first cross-country study of growth and financial development. Goldsmith introduces the idea of using a broad measure of the size of financial intermediaries (his specific choice is the value of intermediary assets to GDP) as an indicator of the provision of intermediary services. Looking at decade averages for 35 countries

---

virtually allow continental style universal banking where banks are involved in the entire spectrum of financing.

for about 100 years, he finds broad indications of a relationship between finance and growth. Goldsmith's work was econometrically unsophisticated and did not seem to spur much research interest at that time. More extensive econometric work was needed to (a) hold constant other determinants of growth and (b) identify the direction of causality. Efforts in this direction did not appear until the 1990s.

King and Levine and Barro and Sala-i-Martin published several papers in the early 1990s with cross-country data sets for the post-war period that have become the benchmark for other studies. Their empirical specifications are widely used and they introduced new measures of intermediary activity, developed from IMF and World Bank data sources and available for a large number of countries for the post-war period. The King and Levine financial measures include:

- A measure of the amount of intermediation. Although this measure reflects the overall size of the intermediary sector, it is not informative about the quality of services provided by the sector. Furthermore, there are distortions due to inter-financial institution holdings.
- DEPTH = ratio to GDP of liquid liabilities of the financial system (currency plus demand and interest bearing accounts of banks and non-bank intermediaries).
- A measure of the role of commercial bank vs. the central bank as a source of credit. BANK = Ratio of bank credit (domestic deposit money banks) to bank credit + central bank.
- Measures of the proportion of credit extended to the private sector. PRIVATE = Claims on the non-financial private sector to total domestic credit. PRIVY = Gross claims on private sector to GDP.

Table 4.4 reproduced from Levine (1997, p. 705) shows values for the indicators in 1985 for 116 countries divided into quartiles by real GDP per capita. The relationships are clear: richer countries have more developed intermediary sectors. Financial intermediary liabilities are over two-thirds of GDP in very rich countries and about half as much in below median income countries. Commercial banks allocate about 90 per cent of bank credit in very rich countries while commercial banks and central banks each allocate about one-half of the credit in below median countries.

Formal econometric investigations have developed a now standard form for regression estimates with these data (the consensus approach is due to King and Levine):

$$X_{it} = \alpha F_{it} + \beta Z_{it} + u_{it}$$

Where X_{it} is the growth of per capita real GDP or the real capital stock or a measure of total factor productivity growth in the rich country for some time period, t. Z_{it} is a standard set of conditioning variables that usually includes log of initial real GDP per capita (a convergence effect) and the log of initial secondary school enrollment rate (human capital investment). Additional conditioning variables may include the ratio of government consumption to GDP (measure of private sector activity), the inflation rate, a black market exchange rate premium and a measure of openness of the economy among others. Finally, F_{it} is one of the measures of financial sector development.

Table 4.4 Financial Indicators and Per Capita GDP

	Very Rich	Rich	Poor	Very Poor	CORRELATION With real per capita GDP
DEPTH	0.67	0.51	0.39	0.26	0.51
BANK	0.91	0.73	0.57	0.52	0.58
PRIVATE	0.71	0.58	0.47	0.37	0.51
PRIVY	0.53	0.31	0.20	0.13	0.70
REAL GDP per capita (87 $)	13053	2376	754	241	

There are at least two serious econometric problems with regressions of this type. First, there may be simultaneity or reverse causality between the finance variable, F, and economic growth, X. Simply speaking, rich countries might have well-developed financial sectors because the income elasticity of the demand for financial services is large. That is, wealthy people demand banking services. Second, the regression specification assumes that any unobserved country-specific effects are part of the error term. Thus, correlation between the error term and included variables in F or X is likely which leads to biased estimation of the regression coefficients. Modern econometrics offers a number of approaches to solving these problems.

To deal with simultaneity, researchers have used predetermined (initial) values for the independent variables or instrumental variable estimation. Since the underlying relationship is a long run one, the time period for observations is often set as a five or ten-year period. To avoid simultaneity, the independent variables are then measured as the initial (first year) values of the observation period. For example, if X is the average growth rate for 1960-65, then F and Z are the 1960 values for the respective variables. More recent studies by Levine, Loayza and Beck and Rousseau and Wachtel have introduced the use of instrumental variables to ameliorate the effects of simultaneity between F and X. Typically, the instruments are initial values of the regressors and perhaps some contemporaneous indicators not included as regressors such as the inflation rate and relative size of the government sector and the degree of openness.

Rousseau and Wachtel (2000) argue that neither of these approaches does an adequate job at solving the simultaneity problem. The predetermined components of the F measures remain correlated with the contemporaneous measures. In addition, the X measures tend to be serially correlated. Thus, the techniques described do not remove all doubt of causality from X to F.

Techniques for examining dynamic interactions among variables have long been available for time series where extensive data series are available. Vector auto regression (VAR) is a widely used technique procedure for looking at causality from lagged F to current X and vice versa. Wachtel and Rousseau and Rousseau and Wachtel among others have applied VAR to the handful of countries with adequate data for very long periods of time. The results are consistent with the cross-country data analyses for the post-war period.

Panel VARs with a large number of cross-country observations and relatively few time series observations can be estimated with recently developed econometric techniques (see Holtz-Eakin, Newey and Rosen, 1988). Estimating panel VARs is made more accessible when the panel techniques introduced by Arrelano and Bond (1991) are used. Rousseau and Wachtel (2000) implement their technique to estimate panel VARs and develop Granger causality tests. We use the cross-country data for 47 countries with annual data from 1980 to 1995 to examine causality directly.

The second econometric problem noted above was the estimation bias introduced in any panel estimation from unobserved country-specific influences. One way of dealing with this is to include country fixed effects (dummy variables) in all estimated equations. However, the co-linearity between the fixed effects and the phenomenon under investigation leads to very imprecise and unstable coefficient estimates. A measure of the financial structure such as the ratio of credit to GDP varies considerably among countries but changes slowly over time in any given country. Thus, the country fixed effects explain much of the panel variation in the financial structure variable. Although many econometricians would argue in favor of such country fixed effects, most analysts reject this approach on practical grounds. Another approach is to difference the data so that the country-specific effects disappear. Finally, the Arrelano-Bond estimator ameliorates the country-specific effects and leads to better estimates.

Review of the Evidence on Financial Depth and Growth

Despite the formidable econometric problems, a wide body of literature has firmly established a consensus in support of a relationship between financial sector development and economic growth. In this section, I examine some of my work with Peter Rousseau to illustrate both the approaches taken and the results established. I will also present some results that illustrate the importance of estimation issues. Finally, the relationship to other papers and the direction that research is taking will be discussed.

Summary of Results

Rousseau and Wachtel (2000) examine the ratio of the broad money supply to GDP with panel data that includes two eight-year average observations for 47 countries. Similarly, Rousseau and Wachtel (2001) use seven five-year averages (1960-95) for 84 countries. These studies present results with panel data sets using instrumental variables. The first paper also presents panel VAR models with 47 countries and 16 annual observations, estimated with our application of the Arrelano and Bond procedures.

The ratio of broad money to GDP averages about 40 per cent; it is larger in countries where the depository institutions are more actively intermediating between savers and investors and it is smaller where the banks do little more than provide transactions services. Our results indicate that increasing that ratio by ten percentage points (increasing the activity and depth of the depository institutions) will, particularly in countries without high inflation, increase the rate of growth by between 0.6 and 1.0 percentage points a year.

To address the issue of causality more directly, we estimate VAR systems with the same data using the Arrelano and Bond approach. We find evidence of significant causality from financial measures to real GDP and no evidence of feedback from GDP to the financial variables. These estimates indicate that an increase in M3 that raises its average share in output by ten percentage points would raise output per capita over five years by 4.1 per cent or 0.8 per cent per year.

A change in the ratio of M3/GDP of ten percentage points is quite large. For any given country, the ratio is serially correlated and trends occur slowly. However, there is a lot of variation among countries at different stages of financial development and at any given time the distribution of the ratio across countries is quite diffuse. In 1987, the ratio is less than 40 per cent in 38 per cent of the countries, between 40 and 60 per cent in 34 per cent of the countries and over 60 per cent in 38 per cent.[4] Thus, an increase of ten percentage points is not unreasonable for a country experiencing financial sector deepening. Both the VAR and panel results indicate that such a change would have profound effects on growth.

Importance of Estimation

In some respects the standard panel model is very robust, but in other respects estimation issues lead to problematic results.[5] In Table 4.5 we use the panel data from Rousseau and Wachtel (2001) to show the effects of different estimation procedures on the standard cross-section specification of the growth. The first equation is estimated by Ordinary Least Squares (OLS) and the independent variables are all initial values (value for the first year of each five-year period). Estimates are indistinguishable from the second equation that uses average values and instrumental variables observation. The choice of technique to correct for simultaneity is immaterial. Both of these equations include fixed effects for time periods but not for countries. Country fixed effects are included as well in the last column.

---

4 This is based on our sample of 46 countries with active equity markets.

5 Temple (1999) discusses why ad hoc growth equations are difficult to interpret and estimate.

The introduction of country fixed effects has a profound effect on the results, particularly on the finance variable. Including country fixed effects leads to an insignificant role for financial sector development on growth. The finance results in cross-section or panel growth regressions are generally not robust to the inclusion of country fixed effects.

Defenders of the finance effects would argue that growth rate equations (an already differenced specification) do not require country dummies. But the simple fact that they enter the equation significantly suggests that the country effects are still present. Moreover, the effects of finance on growth cannot be readily distinguished from country-specific characteristics. This observation points to the importance of the recent papers with panel VAR estimates that remove the country fixed effects by differencing. Rousseau and Wachtel (2000) and Beck, Levine and Loayza (2000) and Levine, Loayza and Beck (2000) find that measures of financial sector development have a significant causal effect on growth in panel VAR estimates.

Table 4.5 Panel Estimates for 5-Year Average Real Per Capita GDP Growth

	OLS	**IV**	**OLS**
Constant	-0.726 (1.0)	-0.766 (1.1)	29,29 (6.0)
Log of initial Real GDP	-0.204 (1.5)	-0.196(1.5)	-3.46 (5.4)
Log initial secondary school enrollment	0.839 (3.7)	0.821 (3.7)	-1.70 (3.7)
Government expenditure to GDP		-0,062 (2.5)	
Initial government expenditure to GDP	-0.060 (2.7)		-0.080 (2.3)
Liquid liabilities to GDP		0.028 (4.9)	
Initial liquid liabilities to GDP	0.027 (4.8)		0.001 (0.1)
Fixed effects	Time periods	Time periods	Time periods and countries
Corrected R^2	0.232	0.246	0.438

Source: Panel with 431 observations from Rousseau and Wachtel (2001) for 84 countries, 1960-95. Absolute values of t-statistics are shown in parentheses.

Related Research and the Direction of Recent Work

The results in Beck, Levine and Loayza (2000), which extend Levine's earlier work and also introduce panel estimation, are very similar to Rousseau and Wachtel (2000). This chapter introduces an improved measure of financial sector development – the ratio to GDP of credits from financial intermediaries to the private sector from a World Bank data set. This measure excludes credits from the central bank and government and also credits among financial intermediaries. They estimate a variant of the now standard specification with data for 77 countries for 1960-95 in two ways. First, they estimate a cross-section regression with instrumental variables (using 35-year average data). Second, they estimate a panel of five-year averages with the Arrelano and Bond technique.

When initial income and average years of schooling are the only conditioning variables, both estimation procedures give very similar results. An increase of the private credit to GDP ratio of ten percentage points from its mean of 27.5 per cent results in an increase in the annual growth rate of 0.69 per cent with the cross section and 0.74 per cent with the panel. When a broader set of conditioning variables is used the estimates vary between 0.5 and 1 per cent.

The consensus result seems well established. There are, of course, questions that can be posed. For example, Luintel and Khan (1999) find some evidence of bi-directional causality between financial sector development and growth in a VAR analysis of developing countries. The econometric issues are complex and efforts to address them have left the empirical consensus in tact.

Estimation issues aside, there are at least two reasons why the consensus model is only the first stage of an important research agenda. First, even the refined measure of financial depth introduced by Levine, Loayza and Beck provides a highly aggregated picture. There is wide variation in these financial sector ratios that are hard to understand. For example, the 1987 ratio of M3 to GDP is 73 per cent in Spain and 51 per cent in Sweden. Does this reflect more advanced financial sector development in Spain or greater reliance on bank-based financing? Second, a thrust of our earlier discussion was the variety of financial sector institutions and activities that contribute to efficient intermediation. The aggregate measures mask a rich and diverse set of activities and tells us little about how intermediation affects growth.[6]

Equity Markets and Growth

The first efforts to extend the empirical literature start with a look at the activities of specific financial institutions. In particular, there are quite a few research papers devoted to equity markets. This is probably due to the attention given to equity markets in the transition economies because the stock market – Wall Street – is the paramount symbol of capitalism. In fact, many countries have organized equity markets and in some instances they are quite active. In this section, we will discuss why equity markets – even when they are small – can make important contributions to growth and examine the evidence on the effects of equity markets.

In the last section we examined literature that uses measures of financial intermediation since most financing comes from banks or related institutions.

[6] Kenny and Williams (2001) provide a scathing critique of the empirical growth literature (without any reference to the role of finance). In their view there is little consensus or robustness and most models are overly simple.

Banks dominate financing in many places and even in the most advanced industrialized countries; equity markets are only a small part of the overall financial markets. Most new investment is funded either internally by firms, through banks and other intermediaries or directly through capital markets. New issuance of stock is never a large fraction of total sources of funds. Nevertheless, the existence of a stock market is more important, even when equity issuance is a relatively minor source of funds.

Why is this so? First, an equity market provides investors and entrepreneurs with a potential exit mechanism. An equity market gives the venture capital investor the ability to realize the gains from a successful project when the company makes an initial public offering. The option to exit through a liquid market mechanism makes venture capital investments more attractive and might well increase entrepreneurial activity generally.

Second, capital inflows – both foreign direct investment and portfolio investments – are potentially important sources of investment funds for emerging market and transition economies (see the discussion in International Monetary Fund, 1997b). International portfolio investments have grown rapidly in recent years as portfolio managers around the world have begun to understand the importance of international diversification.[7] Portfolio flows tend to be larger to countries with organized and liquid markets. Thus, the existence of equity markets facilitates capital inflow and the ability to finance current account deficits.[8]

Third, the provision of liquidity through organized exchanges encourages both international and domestic investors to transfer their surpluses from short-term assets to the long-term capital market, where the funds can provide access to permanent capital for firms to finance large, indivisible projects that enjoy substantive scale economies.

Finally, the existence of a stock market provides important information that improves the efficiency of financial intermediation generally. For traded companies, the stock market improves the flow of information from management to owners and quickly produces a market evaluation of company developments. As firms increasingly link the compensation of their managers to stock price performance, a deep equity market may also provide managers with incentives to exert more effort in monitoring risky, high-return projects. Finally, the valuation of company assets by the stock market provides benchmarks for the value of business assets, which can be helpful to other businesses and investors, thereby improving the depth and efficiency of company assets generally.

There are arguments to the contrary as well. The higher returns from improved efficiency, the additional liquidity, and the ability to realize capital gains

---

7 Foreign direct investment in emerging markets rose from $11.3 billion in 1985 to a record $90.3 billion in 1995, while portfolio equity flows increased from $0.14 billion in 1985 to $22.1 billion in 1995, which was down from a high of $34.9 billion in 1994 (International Finance Corporation, 1996, p. 6).

8 Portfolio flows can also be destabilizing since a change in market sentiment can lead to massive outflows, which often lead to exchange rate crises (as in Mexico in 1995 and the Czech Republic in 1997).

from the stock market might discourage savings because of income effects. Similarly, a stock market can affect perceptions of risk. If risk falls, there might be less precautionary saving and if risk rises, then savings might be discouraged. However, the ability of equity markets to provide investors with better opportunities to diversify is usually viewed positively as it may lower the risk premia charged by financiers for funding new projects and thus lower the hurdle rate on new investments.

There have been several efforts to examine empirically the specific role of equity markets in real sector activity starting with Atje and Jovanovic (1993) who construct a cross-country panel for the 1980s and show that trading volume has a strong influence on growth after controlling for lagged investment while bank credit does not. Demirguc-Kunt and Levine (1996) provide a descriptive investigation. Levine and Zervos (1996, 1998) introduce equity market measures to the standard growth-finance cross-section specifications discussed earlier. Finally, a more comprehensive effort to examine the dynamic relationships is found in my paper with Peter Rousseau (Rousseau and Wachtel, 2000).

In our paper, we use two measures of stock market development as financial sector indicators in the panel regressions: the ratio of market capitalization to GDP and the ratio of total value traded to GDP. Both have a positive coefficient but only the latter is significant at the one per cent level. We also use a VAR model to examine causality and dynamic interactions among growth, a measure of financial intermediation and a stock market indicator. Table 4.6 summarizes the results of panel equations with alternative measures of financial sector development.

Table 4.6 Financial Indicators and Growth Rates

Ratio to GDP of	Country Mean		Effect on growth rate of a 10 percentage point increase	
	1987	1995	Panel Regression	VAR Model (5-year horizon)
Liquid Liabilities (M3)	58.73		0.15	0.8
Market Capitalization	29.12	65.11	0.08	0.4
Total Value Traded	10.75	24.22	0.52	1.0

Source: Calculated from Rousseau and Wachtel (2000).

The results indicate that the development of a liquid and highly capitalized equity market increases growth. The equity market effects are of similar magnitude as the effect of more developed financial intermediaries. Since new equity issuance is always small, equity markets are important because they improve the flow of information which, in turn, improves the efficiency of allocation. How equity markets provide information and affect efficiency improvements is an issue that merits further investigation (see some suggestion in Morck, Yeung and Yu, 2000).

Further Evidence on Financial Sector Characteristics and Growth

Research efforts so far have not examined the impact of other financial markets or instruments on economic growth in a similar cross-country framework. A major reason for this is that data on other types of financial intermediaries (e.g. private placements, venture capital, bond issuance, commercial paper, etc.) are not part of any standardized data collection efforts and are often simply not available. Furthermore, the number of countries with these other instruments and markets is not large. Although banks and related intermediaries are found everywhere and equity markets are found in most places, bond markets, commercial paper, organized venture capital industry, etc. are really quite rare. Thus, research efforts have turned in a slightly different direction. Recent research has focused on the relationship between economic growth and the characteristics of financial institutions.

The performance of the major financial sector institutions such as banks can be measured by quantitative indicators of the extent of their activities and by qualitative or descriptive measures of the nature of intermediary activity. These measures might characterize the sound institutions, the legal framework for the operation of sound institutions, the economic environment that allows competition and the regulatory environment.

This approach in the literature examines the environment issues that allow for and encourage the operation of financial intermediaries. For example, clear and universally applied accounting standards and auditing practices provide more reliable information for decision making by intermediaries. Similarly, a legal framework that defines the relationship between creditors and debtors will encourage intermediation.

The effect of accounting, bankruptcy and governance standards and procedures on growth and on financial sector development has been recently examined in a cross-country framework by Levine, Loayza and Beck (2000). Among other things they explore the influence of difference in creditor rights in bankruptcy procedures. There are wide differences in the rights of creditors to obtain and liquidate assets, in the rights of management to retain control in corporate reorganizations, in the enforcement of rules and the application of procedures and the transparency of accounting information. They find that countries with better creditor rights, rigorous enforcement and better accounting information tend to have more highly developed financial intermediaries.

Another avenue for further empirical research is the structure of the banking system. We have already established that 'more banking' – a larger ratio of bank liabilities to GDP – is an important correlate of economic growth. Further investigation examines the type of banking activity, the environment in which it is conducted and by whom it is conducted. A country may have a high ratio of bank liabilities to GDP because banks subject to government influence (whether they are state-owned or not) make loans to state-owned (or favored) enterprises and accumulate large portfolios of bad loans and ultimately require government-sponsored recapitalization. Such activity presumably does not have the same effect on economic growth as an expanding market-oriented banking sector. The research literature has begun to look at the characteristics of the banking sector to see if they are associated with higher growth rates and greater economic stability. Clearly, better banking systems create a more stable environment by leading to a reduced likelihood of systemic banking crises and international currency crises.

Within the last year or so, a number of working papers that address some of these issues have begun to circulate. Results indicate that the following banking industry characteristics may be related to growth and stability:

- More competitive and less concentrated banking industry
- More private as opposed to government ownership or control
- More foreign participation in banking.

There is of course an enormous literature on bank competition but I only know of one paper that relates concentration to economic growth. Cetorelli and Gambera (2001) find a depressing effect on economic growth of a concentrated banking industry. However, their industry analysis suggests that concentrated banking sectors may successfully target industries in need of external financing and promote the growth of new firms.

La Porta, Lopez-de-Silanes and Shleifer (2001) examine the implications of government ownership of commercial banks. First it is astounding that extensive government ownership of banks is quite common and not restricted to formerly planned economies. They find that the median government ownership of the ten largest banks in each of 92 countries in 1995 is 33.4 per cent (and still 30 per cent if the transition economies are excluded). Although the numbers have fallen since 1970 (from 57 per cent and from 53 per cent without the transition economies), they are still quite large. Government control (as the holder of a large or largest block of stock) is even stronger – almost half of all bank assets. Table 4.7 shows overall state ownership for selected emerging markets. Privatization efforts that have resulted in state divestiture are common but not prevalent.

Government ownership of banks is more common in poorer countries and less common in democracies. Government ownership of banks can come about in several ways. In some instances, it reflects the attempts of politicians to use the financial system to the advantage of those in power. The ruling party might just want to use bank lending to shift resources to its supporters. In other instances, public bank ownership is the result of efforts by the government to respond to market failure. An undeveloped financial system might not provide intermediary services but government-owned banks might create the critical mass of activity to start the industry. In many instances, both motivations are probably relevant.

Table 4.7 State-Owned Banks' Share of Total Assets

	One year prior to reform (%)	Recent year (%)
Argentina	52	39
Bangladesh	74	68
Brazil	50	48
Chile	100	14
India	90	87
Korea	81	32
Mexico	100	18
Pakistan	89	63
Taiwan	78	58
Turkey	50	48

Source: Beim and Calomiris (2001).

La Porta et. al. examine the relationship between government ownership and financial sector performance and growth as well as overall economic growth. They find that government ownership does not lead to rapid growth of financial intermediation. They examine the effect on economic growth with the standard panel framework introduced earlier. They consistently find that higher initial government bank ownership has a negative impact on real per capita growth rates. A ten percentage point increase in the proportions of assets of the largest banks owned by the government is associated with a decline in the annual growth rate of about 0.2 per cent. These preliminary regressions do not address all of the econometric problems but the overall thrust of these results will probably withstand a more careful empirical investigation.

Many governments have restricted foreign ownership of banks or foreign entry into the financial industry. I have argued elsewhere (Wachtel, 2001) that foreign entry has many positive benefits, including:

- leads to the rapid introduction of product and service innovations and the development of financial markets
- results in economies of scale and scope
- attracts FDI.

Nevertheless, there is a long history of resistance of foreign entry into banking. This is based on political fears of foreign control and, more importantly, resistance to competition by entrenched and vulnerable local banks and their allies.

Foreign bank entry and cross-border banking have begun to increase rapidly in the 1990s. Foreign banking activity in the transition economies and the changes induced by currency union in Europe have started to affect the rest of the world. Bankers have become much bolder and cross-border bank mergers and acquisitions have mushroomed in the last few years. Table 4.8 shows foreign control of banking in selected emerging markets in Europe, Asia and Latin America.[9] Foreign control of bank assets has increased rapidly in just the last five years. The situation in Venezuela where foreign control went from virtually zero in 1994 to over 40 per cent in 1999 is not unusual. There are a few exceptions to the recent internationalization of banking such as Turkey and South Asia where there are still barriers to foreign entry. In many other countries, such as Brazil and Poland, there was substantial resistance to foreign bank entry that disappeared in the last few years. However, it is too early to judge the impact of these industry changes on economic performance.

There is one additional line of empirical research that relates economic growth to characteristics of the financial sector. There are a group of papers that relate the legal environment for the financial sector to economic growth. Part of the motivation for these inquiries is econometric. The origins of the legal system (i.e. English common law, French penal system, German, etc.) are a completely exogenous variable determined by accidents of history (and colonialism). However, the legal structures have different approaches to creditor-debtor relationships than could be relevant to the performance of the financial system. The line of inquiry started with La Porta et. al. (1998); Levine (1999 and 2000) relates it to economic growth. The exogenous characteristics can be used as instruments to improve econometric estimates of the basic growth-finance relationships. In addition, the results indicate that countries with better contract law, more informative accounting and accurate financial reporting will have more developed financial systems and more growth.

A related issue addressed by Levine (2000) is whether bank-dominated (the German model) or market-dominated (the Anglo-Saxon model) financial systems generate better growth performances. The evidence indicates that more financial services matter rather than the structure of the industry that provides them. Convergence of financial systems around the world will probably make this specific question moot over time.

Most of the work so far on the characteristics of the financial sector has looked at banks and the environment in which they operate. There have been some efforts to examine characteristics of equity markets. Lundblad, Harvey and Bekaert (2000) examine the effect on growth of a specific type of financial sector liberalization. They identify the dates when domestic equity markets were opened up to foreign investors and find evidence that this liberalization move has a positive effect on growth.

9 For a description of recent developments see United Nations (1999) and IMF (2000).

Table 4.8 Foreign Control of Banking in Selected Emerging Markets (per cent of total bank assets in banks where foreigners own more than half of total equity)

	1994	1999
Argentina	18	49
Brazil	8	17
Chile	16	54
Colombia	6	18
Czech Republic	6	49
Hungary	20	57
Korea	1	4
Malaysia	7	12
Mexico	1	19
Peru	7	33
Poland	2	53
Thailand	1	6
Turkey	3	2
Venezuela	0.3	42

Source: IMF, 2000.

Economic Crises and Financial Sector Development

Most of the literature reviewed so far discusses the extent of financial sector development and its implications for growth. However, there is another dimension of economic well-being that could be related to financial sector development – stability. In this section we examine the relationship between financial sector development and the ability of a country to avoid systemic crises. Systemic crises are either banking system failures or currency crises. Are countries with more developed financial structures better able to avoid such crises?

With regard to banking crises, it is not at all obvious that specific financial sector characteristics or developments can help a country avoid crises. Systemic banking crises are often due to regulatory failure in the face of countrywide shocks. They occur in both large and small economies including many with sophisticated (albeit flawed) financial systems. The bank crises in Japan, the U.S. Savings and Loan crisis and in Scandinavia are examples of well-developed financial systems that endured systemic crises.

Currency crises occur with some frequency around the world, as policy makers are unable to maintain a fixed exchange rate in the face of macroeconomic disequilibrium and speculative pressures.

In both crises instances, the question that needs to be answered is whether well-developed capital markets and banks help a country withstand the pressure of crisis. Did the U.S. financial system enable the country to absorb the shock of massive failures of Savings and Loan associations in the 1980s without any major effects on long-term growth? Did the financial systems of some Asian countries help them absorb the impact of exchange rate crises?

It is difficult to untangle the relationship between crises and financial sector development. Take the case of a barter economy – it is immune from banking and currency crises and also has no financial sector. Once the country develops a fractional reserve banking system and a currency traded on open markets, it may be subject to crises. Thus, it can appear that financial sector development causes crises. Clearly that would be a mistaken conclusion but the example illustrates the problem of disentangling the phenomenon.

The increased concern in recent years with financial sector (banking or currency) crises has led to much interest in creating warning systems. There has been wide research interest in identifying crisis indicators. A good way to judge the empirical relationship between the occurrence of crises and financial sector development would be to see if characteristics of the financial sector are found to be crisis indicators or whether they are related to identified indicators. There have been several efforts to examine and evaluate crisis indicators and there has been particular interest since the Asian crisis in developing early warning systems.

Kaminsky and Reinhart (1999) develop a series of indicators of banking and currency crises. Their list indicates the difficulty in disentangling financial sector development and crisis vulnerability. Among their indicators of crisis are a number of measures that we would associate in the long run with beneficial financial sector development. A high ratio of credit to GDP or lending to deposits can signal a lending boom and declining loan quality, which are precursors of crisis. However, these indicators create crises when they develop in conjunction with other phenomenon.

Some preliminary investigation of the relationship between the incidence of bank crises and the characteristics of the financial system is found in Barth, Caprio and Levine (2000). There are some broad indications that crises are more likely to occur in countries where the corporate ownership and governance activities of banks are restricted. Policy discussions of bank crises discuss the structure of financial systems and regulation, as well as best practices that will avoid crises (see Caprio et al. 1998). Accounting and financial reporting standards that are consistently and clearly applied are a dominant prescription.

The interesting thing about the indicators of banking and currency crises is that they are often related to the banking and financial sector. Financial development can be associated with financial fragility and vulnerability to crisis, especially when the regulatory and legal environments are wanting. The implication is that financial liberalization and the development of sound financial institutions and regulatory structure should be carefully sequenced (Demirguc-Kunt and Detragiache, 1999).

One element of financial sector development that might reduce the likelihood of financial crises is foreign bank ownership. Indeed, it would have significantly reduced the seriousness of the recent financial crises in Asia. Making foreign investors – the bank owners in emerging markets – responsible for the consequences of their lending practices creates a disincentive for damaging speculative short-term financial flows. Foreign banking interest is a genuine market test of the value and soundness of domestic banks. So it is a useful signal when local financial markets are too thin or too small to draw such attention. Making foreign investors – the bank owners in emerging markets – responsible for the consequences of their lending practices creates a disincentive for deleterious, speculative short-term financial flows. Hence, lending by foreign-owned banks can avoid the problems associated with cross-border lending by international banks to local banks (see Radelet and Sachs, 1998).

Conclusions

There is no doubt in my mind that ample empirical evidence makes a convincing case that financial sector development promotes economic growth. However, deeper and more active financial institutions and markets may also be more vulnerable to crisis. When steps towards liberalization are not sequenced or when the development of regulatory capabilities lags behind changes in the industry, financial sector development can lead to crises that inhibit growth. But this observation surely does not mitigate in favor of restricting the development of a variety of capital market institutions. It merely reiterates the importance of sequencing liberalization steps.

Although research on these issues has mushroomed in just the last few years, much still needs to be done. The specific characteristics of growth-enhancing capital market institutions have not yet been identified. Moreover, how to fill in for market failures so as to promote institutional development remains a challenge.

References

Barro, R.J. (1991), 'Economic Growth in a Cross Section of Countries', *Quarterly Journal of Economics*, 56.

Barth, J., Caprio, G. and Levine, R. (2000), *Banking Systems Around the Globe: Do Regulation and Ownership Affect Performance and Stability?*, Milken Institute Policy Brief #15, July.

Beck, T., Levine, R. and Loayza, N. (2000), 'Finance and the Sources of Growth', *Journal of Financial Economics*, 58, pp. 261-300.

Beim, D.O. and Calomiris, C.W. (2001), *Emerging Financial Markets*, McGraw-Hill Irwin.

Bonin, J. and Wachtel, P. (1999), 'Towards Market-Oriented Banking in the Economies in Transition', in M. Blejer and M. Skreb (eds), *Financial Sector Transformation*, Cambridge University Press.

Bonin, J. and Wachtel, P. (2001), 'Financial Sector Development in Transition Economies: A Retrospective on the First Ten Years', in M. Blejer and M. Skreb (eds), *Ten Years of Transition: The Lessons and the Prospects*, Cambridge University Press, forthcoming.

Caprio, G. Jr., Hunter, W., Kaufman, G.C. and Leipziger, D. (eds) (1998), *Preventing Bank Crises: Lessons from Recent Global Bank Failures*, World Bank.

Cetorelli, N. and Gambera, M. (2001), 'Banking Structure, Financial Dependence and Growth: International Evidence from Industry Data', *Journal of Finance*.

Demirguc-Kunt, A. and Detragiache, E. (1999), 'Financial Liberalization and Financial Fragility', in B. Pleskovic and J.E. Stiglitz (eds), *Annual World Bank Conference on Development Economics 1998*, World Bank.

Goldsmith, R. (1969), *Financial Structure and Development*, Yale University Press.

Holtz-Eakin, D., Newey, W. and Rosen, H.S. (1988), 'Estimating Vector Autoregressions with Panel Data', *Econometrica*, 56, 1371-95.

International Monetary Fund (2000), *International Capital Markets*, September.

Kaminsky, G.L. and Reinhart, C.M. (1999), 'The Twin Crises: The Causes of Banking and Balance of Payments Problems', *American Economic Review*, 89, pp. 473-500.

Kenny, C. and Williams, D. (2001), 'What Do we Know About Economic Growth? Or, Why Don't We Know Very Much?', *World Development*, 29, pp. 1-22.

Khan, A. (2000), 'The Finance and Growth Nexus', *Business Review*, Federal Reserve Bank of Philadelphia, January/February.

King, R.G. and Levine, R. (1993), 'Finance and Growth: Schumpeter Might Be Right', *Quarterly Journal of Economics*, 108.

La Porta, R., Lopez-de-Silanes, F., Shleifer, A. and Vishny, R. (1998), 'Law and Finance', *Journal of Political Economy*, 106, pp. 1133-55.

La Porta, R., Lopez-de-Silanes, F. and Shleifer, A. (2001), 'Government Ownership of Banks', January.

Levine, R. (1997), 'Financial Development and Economic Growth: Views and Agenda', *Journal of Economic Literature*, 35(2), June.

Levine, R. (1999), 'Law, Finance and Economic Growth', *Journal of Financial Intermediation*, 8, pp. 8-35.

Levine, R. (2000), 'Bank-Based or Market-Based Financial Systems: Which is Better?', January.

Levine, R., Loayza, N. and Beck, T. (2000), 'Financial Intermediation and Growth: Causality and Causes', *Journal of Monetary Economics*, 46.

Luintel, K. and Khan, M. (1999), 'A quantitative reassessment of the finance-growth nexus: Evidence from a Multivariate VAR', *Journal of Development Economics*, 60, pp. 381-405.

Lum, S.K.S. and Moyer, B.C. (2000), 'Gross Domestic Product by Industry for 1997-1999', *Survey of Current Business*, December, pp. 24-35.

Lundblad, C., Harvey, C. and Bekaert, G. (2000), 'Emerging Equity Markets and Economic Development', September.

McKinnon, R.I. (1973), *Money and Capital in Economic Development*, Washington, D.C., The Brookings Institution.

Morck, R., Yeung, B. and Yu, W. (2000), 'The Information Content of Stock Markets: Why do emerging markets have synchronous stock price movements?', *Journal of Financial Economics*, 58, 215-60.

Pagano, M. (1993), 'Financial Markets and Growth: An Overview', *European Economic Review*, 37, pp. 613-22.

Radelet, S. and Sachs, J.D. (1998), 'The East Asian Financial Crisis: Diagnosis, Remedies, Prospects', *Brookings Papers on Economic Activity 1*.

Rousseau, P.L. and Wachtel, P. (1998), 'Financial Intermediation and Economic Performance: Historical Evidence from Five Industrialized Countries', *Journal of Money, Credit and Banking*, 30, pp. 657-78.

Rousseau, P.L. and Wachtel, P. (2000), 'Equity Markets and Growth: Cross Country Evidence on Timing and Outcomes, 1980-95', *Journal of Banking and Finance*, 24, pp. 1933-57.

Rousseau, P.L. and Wachtel, P. (2001), 'Inflation, Financial Development and Growth', in T. Negishi, R. Ramachandran and K. Mino (eds), *Economic Theory, Dynamics and Markets: Essays in Honor of Ryuzo Sato*, Kluwer, forthcoming.

Temple, J. (1999), 'The New Growth Evidence', *Journal of Economic Literature*, 37, pp. 112-56.

United Nations, Department of Economic and Social Affairs (1999), *World Economic and Social Survey, 1999*, New York.

Wachtel, P. (2001), 'Globalization of Banking: Why does it matter?', in *Presente y Futuro del Sistema Financiero en Paises Emergentes*, Caracas, Venezuela.

Wachtel, P. and Rousseau, P.L. (1995), 'Financial Intermediation and Economic Growth: A Historical Comparison of the U.S., U.K. and Canada', in M. Bordo and R. Sylla (eds), *Anglo-American Finance*, Irwin.

Chapter 5

Globalization, the New Economy and Growth in the Leading Industrial Countries

Dominick Salvatore

1. Introduction

Growth in the United States accelerated and far exceeded growth in the other leading industrial (G-7) countries during the past decade. The only exception was in 2001 when the United States was in recession. The more rapid growth of the United States during the past decade has been attributed to the greater degree of globalization, more flexible economic system and more rapid spread of the New Economy.[1]

This chapter first examines the process of globalization in the world economy and how this, together with more liberalization and restructuring of the economy, made the United States the most competitive economy in the world. Subsequently, the chapter discusses the meaning, measurement and spread of the New Economy among the G-7 countries and how the much better U.S. performance in this area sharply increased labor productivity and growth in the economy relative to that in the other leading industrial nations during the past decade, but especially since 1995.

2. Globalization in the World Economy

There is a strong trend toward globalization in production and labor markets in the world today and this increased the efficiency and competitiveness of firms and nations that took full advantage of this trend. Global corporations are companies that are run by an international team of managers, have research and production facilities in many countries, use parts and components from the cheapest source

---

1 The 2001 recession in the United States does not contradict the existence of the New Economy but represented simply a necessary correction from the exaggerated growth and profit expectations engendered by the New Economy. Proof is given by the fact that labor productivity continued to grow rapidly even during the recession and growth resumed sooner and much faster in the United States than in Europe and Japan.

around the world, and sell their products, finance their operation, and are owned by stockholders throughout the world.

More and more corporations operate today on the belief that their very survival requires for them to be one of a handful of global corporations in their sector. This is true in automobiles, steel, aircrafts, computers, telecommunications, consumer electronics, chemicals, drugs, and many other products. Nestlé, the largest Swiss company and the world's second largest food company, has production facilities in 59 countries and America's Gillette in 22. Ford has component factories in 26 different industrial sites around the world, assembly plants in six countries, and employs more people abroad (181,000) than in the United States (169,000).

One important form that globalization in production often takes in today's corporation is in foreign 'sourcing' of inputs. There is practically no major product today that does not have some foreign inputs. Foreign sourcing is often not a matter of choice for corporations to earn higher profits, but simply a requirement for them to remain competitive. Firms that do not look abroad for cheaper inputs face loss of competitiveness in world markets and even in the domestic market. This is the reason that $625 of the $860 total cost of producing an IBM PC was incurred for parts and components manufactured by IBM outside the United States or purchased from foreign producers during the mid-1980s. Such low-cost offshore purchase of inputs is likely to continue to expand rapidly in the future and is being fostered by joint ventures, licensing arrangements, and other non-equity collaborative arrangements. Indeed, this represents one of the most dynamic aspects of the global business environment of today.

Foreign sourcing can be regarded as manufacturing's new *international* economies of scale in today's global economy. Just as companies were forced to rationalize operations within each country in the 1980s, they now face the challenge of integrating their operations for the entire system of manufacturing around the world to take advantage of the new international economies of scale. What is important is for the firm to focus on those components that are indispensable to the company's competitive position over subsequent product generations and 'outsource' other components for which outside suppliers have a distinctive production advantage.

Globalization in production has proceeded so far that it is now difficult to determine the nationality of many products. For example, should a Honda Accord produced in Ohio be considered American? What about a Chrysler minivan produced in Canada, especially now that Chrysler has been acquired by Daimler-Benz (Mercedes)? Is a Kentucky Toyota or Mazda that uses nearly 50 per cent of imported Japanese parts American? It is clearly becoming more and more difficult to define what is American and opinions differ widely. One could legitimately even ask if this question is relevant in a world growing more and more interdependent and globalized. Today, the ideal corporation is strongly decentralized to allow local units to develop products that fit into local cultures, and yet at its very core is very centralized to coordinate activities around the globe.

Even more dramatic has been the globalization of labor markets around the world. Work which was previously done in the United States and other industrial countries is now often done much more cheaply in developing countries. And this is the case not only for low-skilled assembly-line jobs but also for jobs requiring high computer and engineering skills. Most Americans have only now come to fully realize that there is a truly competitive labor force in the world today willing and able to do their job at a much lower cost. If anything, this trend is likely to accelerate in the future.

Even service industries are not immune to global job competition. For example, more than 3,500 workers on the island of Jamaica, connected to the United States by satellite dishes, make airline reservations, process tickets, answer calls to toll-free numbers, and do data entry for U.S. airlines at a much lower cost than could be done in the United States. Nor are highly skilled and professional people spared from global competition. A few years ago, Texas Instruments set up an impressive software programming operation in Bangalore, a city of four million people in southern India. Other American multinationals soon followed. Motorola, IBM, AT&T and many other high-tech firms are now doing even a great deal of basic research abroad. In 2004, IBM indicated that it was going to shift about 7,500 hi-tech jobs abroad to lower costs.

American workers are beginning to raise strong objections to the transfer of skilled jobs abroad. Of course, many European and Japanese firms are setting up production and research facilities in the United States and employing many American professionals. But all advanced countries are outsourcing more and more of their work to emerging markets in order to bring or keep costs down and remain internationally competitive. In the future, more and more work will simply be done in places best equipped to do the job most economically. Try to restrict the flow of work abroad to protect jobs in the United States, and firms risk losing international competitiveness or end up moving all of its operations abroad.

3. Globalization and the International Competitiveness of Nations

Globalization of production and labor markets is a crucial determinant of the international competitiveness of firms, industries and nations. During the 1970s and 1980s the United States lost relative competitiveness in one industry after another with respect to Japan and, in some industries, even with respect to Europe and the Newly Industrializing Economies (NIEs) of Asia. Since the late 1980s and early 1990s, however, the United States has recaptured most of the lost competitiveness ground and in 1994 ranked once again as the most competitive economy in the world, displacing Japan, which had occupied that position since 1985. Since 1994, the United States not only retained its number one position but it even increased its lead over Japan and many other industrialized countries.

There are several measures of the overall international competitiveness of nations. One of the best is that calculated by the Institute for Management Development (2003) in Lausanne, Switzerland. IMD found that, assigning a value of 100 to the competitiveness index of the United States in 2003, the index of Canada was 84.17; that is, Canada was about 16 per cent less competitive than the United States on an overall basis in 2003. The competitive index for the remaining five of the G-7 (largest industrialized) countries was 69.8 for Germany, 66.5 for the United Kingdom, 66.4 for France, 56.3 for Japan, and 51.8 for Italy. To be noted is that although Canada ranked second among the G-7 countries, it was actually in third place after the United States and Australia among large countries (those with more than 20 million people) and 11th when the competitive index for all 51 countries (including the small ones) was calculated. Ahead of Canada, among all 51 countries, were the United States, Finland, Singapore, Denmark, Hong Kong, Switzerland, Australia, Luxembourg, Sweden and the Netherlands.

Competitiveness was defined as the ability of a country or company to generate more wealth for its people than its competitors in world markets and was calculated as the weighted average of four competitive factors. These are (1) economic performance, which includes domestic economy, international trade, international investment, employment and prices; (2) government efficiency, which includes public finance, fiscal policy, institutional framework, business legislation, and societal framework; (3) business efficiency, which includes productivity, labor market, finance management practices, and attitudes and values; and (4) infrastructure, which includes basic infrastructure, technological infrastructure, scientific infrastructure, health infrastructure and education.

The United States ranked first among the G-7 countries on all competitive factors in 2003. Canada ranked second on government efficiency, business efficiency and infrastructure, but fifth on economic performance. Germany ranked second on economic performance, fourth on government efficiency and third on business efficiency and infrastructure. The United Kingdom ranked fourth on economic performance, third on government efficiency and sixth on infrastructure. France ranked third on economic performance and fifth on the other three indices. Japan ranked sixth on economic performance and government efficiency, seventh on business efficiency and fourth on infrastructure. Italy ranked last on all indices, except business efficiency in which it outranked Japan. Japan suffered a dramatic reduction in international competitiveness over the past decade. It ranked sixth among the G-7 countries and 18th among all 51 countries for which the index was calculated in 2003 because it performed badly on all four competitiveness factors. This was a sharp fall from consistently being the most competitive economy in the world from 1980 to 1993. This resulted from the serious economic and financial problems that Japan has been facing since the early 1990s.

Measuring international competitiveness, however, is a very ambitious and difficult undertaking. Although useful, the competitiveness study discussed above faces a number of serious shortcomings. One is the grouping and measuring of international competitiveness of developed and developing countries together. It is well known, however, that developed and developing countries have very different industrial structures and face different competitiveness problems. Thus, using the same method of measuring the international competitiveness for all types of countries may not be appropriate and the results may not be very informative and may also be difficult to interpret.

Another serious shortcoming with the above competitiveness measure is that the correlation between real per capita income and the standard of living of the various nations may not be very high. For example, the United Kingdom has a higher competitiveness index than Japan's even though its real per capital income is more than a quarter lower than Japan's. Similarly, the United Kingdom has a competitiveness index much higher than Italy even though its real per capita income is practically the same as Italy's. The questions that naturally arise are (1) If the United Kingdom is more competitive than Japan, how can its per capita income and standard of living be so much lower? (2) Similarly, if Italy is so much less competitive than the United Kingdom, how can it have a similar real per capita income? Specifically, where is Italy's high per capita income and standard of living coming from?

These questions are troublesome because in economics we believe that productivity determines per capita income and the standard of living and it is disconcerting to see such a blatant variance between expectations and reality. Furthermore, a nation may score low on its overall competitiveness index and still have some sectors in which it is very productive and efficient.

IMD answers the criticism of low correlation between the competitiveness index and per capita income by saying that the international competitiveness index measures the ability and prospect for the future growth of the country, while per capita income and standard of living measure past successes and growth. In addition, entrepreneurs and managers around the world are known to rely on these indices or measures in deciding whether to invest in one nation or another. Thus, the index of overall international competitiveness and similar measures are useful and important.

Displeased by how the world competitiveness index was measured, the World Economic Forum (WEF), which had previously collaborated with IMD in measuring the international competitiveness of nations, started to prepare its own index. WEF (2003), which is also based in Switzerland, defines international competitiveness as 'the ability of a country to achieve sustained high rates of growth in GDP per capita'. One of the major differences between the two competitiveness indices is that the WEF, unlike IMD, excludes such variables as GDP growth, export growth, and the inflow of foreign direct investments in arriving at its overall index because it regards these as the result or consequence, rather than the cause, of a country's level of international competitiveness. The ordinal competitiveness ranking of the G-7 countries in 2003, however, is very similar to the IMD's results (with the United States far ahead among the G-7 countries, Canada in second place, but with the United Kingdom ahead of Japan in third and fourth places respectively, followed by France, Italy and Germany.

4. International Competitiveness and Economic Restructuring

Not everyone considers the concept of international competitiveness significant, however. In a 1994 article, Paul Krugman stated that the concept is irrelevant and dangerous because nations do not compete with each other in the way that corporations do. Increases in productivity are all that count for increasing the standard of living of a nation. Krugman points out that U.S. trade represents only about 10-15 per cent of U.S. GDP (so that international trade cannot significantly effect its standard of living), international trade is a positive-sum game (so that all nations gain), and concern with international competitiveness can lead governments to the wrong policies (such as adopting trade restrictions and engaging in industrial policies).

All of these statements are true, but Krugman's conclusion does not follow. The reason is that if a nation's corporations innovate and increase productivity at a faster rate than foreign corporations, the nation will export products which are increasingly technologically advanced and this permits faster growth in the future. For example, the U.S. superiority in software makes possible faster productivity growth based on computer-aided design (CAD) and computer-aided manufacturing (CAM), and this increases its standard of living.

Krugman's statement that some high-tech sectors artificially protected by trade policies and/or encouraged by industrial policies have grown less rapidly than some low-tech sectors, such as cigarettes and beer production, misses the point. This only proves that wrong policies can be costly. Productivity growth and international competitiveness must be encouraged not by protectionist or industrial policies but by improving the factors that affect its degree of international competitiveness (such as liberalizing its economy and improving its industrial structure). In short, a country's future prosperity depends on its growth in productivity and this can certainly be influenced by government policies. Thus, nations compete in the sense that they choose policies that promote productivity. As pointed out by Dunning (1995) and Porter (1990), international competitiveness does matter.

That industrial policies and protectionism only provide temporary benefits to the targeted or protected industries but slows down the growth of productivity and standards of living in the long run is clearly evidenced by the competitiveness situation in Europe *vis-à-vis* the United States and Japan today. Aside from banking, biotechnology, the space industry, and, maybe, the chemical industry, there is practically no industry in which Europe can stand up to U.S. and Japanese competition. This is the case for the steel industry, the automobile industry, the commercial aircraft industry, and many other industries. Without the billions of dollars that some of these industries receive in subsidies or for repeated restructuring and trade protection, and without alliances with U.S. or Japanese firms, most European firms in this industry would be unable to compete. Seven of the top ten computer firms (including the top five) in Europe are American, one is Japanese and only two are European. In software, America has an undisputed lead. In telecommunications, online services, biotech, and aircraft the United States also has a big lead over Europe. In automobiles, Japan has an undisputed lead and even U.S. automakers are much more efficient than Europeans. To be sure, European automobiles are of high quality, but command a much higher price than Japanese and a higher price than even American automobiles of comparable quality.

Although Europe has been able to keep wages and standards of living relatively high and rising during the past two decades, the rate of unemployment is now more than double the U.S. and the Japanese rates. And while the United States, with a smaller population than Europe, has created many more jobs during the past thirty years, employment has stagnated in Europe. The Unites States has also been much more successful than European countries in meeting the growing competition from NIEs and other emerging economies in Asia (see Rausch, 1995).

The restructuring and downsizing that rapid technological change and increasing international competition made necessary resulted in average wages and salaries not rising very much in real terms in the United States during the past decade, but millions of new jobs were created. In Europe, on the other hand, real wages and salaries grew but very few new jobs were created, and this left Europe less able to compete on the world market than the United States. Being unable to fire workers when not needed, firms have tended to increase output by increasing capital per worker rather than hiring more labor and this has made the return to capital lower and the wage of labor higher in Europe than in the United States.

Since the 1970s, the United States has moved faster than Japan, Germany, France and other nations in deregulating (i.e. in removing government regulations and controls of economic activities on airlines, telecommunications, trucking, banking, and many other sectors of the economy). For example, cutithroat competition makes American airlines about one third more productive than the larger regulated or government-run foreign airlines. General merchandise retailing is twice as efficient in the Unites States than in Japan, and so is American telecommunications in relation to German telecommunications. Most American firms today face much stiffer competition from domestic and foreign firms than their European and Japanese counterparts. Stiff competition makes most American firms lean and mean – and generally more efficient than foreign firms.

5. Labor Productivity, Market Efficiency and Growth Potential

In a 1997 study of the labor productivity of German and French industry relative to U.S. industry, the McKinsey Global Institute (1997) found that German and French productivity increased over the past decade but at a slower rate than U.S. productivity, and so it is now further behind U.S. industry today than it was a decade ago. Overall, McKinsey found that German industry is 30 per cent less efficient than U.S. industry. In general, the higher U.S. labor productivity is not due to bigger firms, more automation, or better managers (although these factors might be determinant in some specific industries), but it is the result of greater competition and much more flexible labor practices. Specifically, the higher U.S. productivity depends on the ability of U.S. managers to introduce new and improved products much faster than abroad and the ability of U.S. engineers to invent new and more efficient ways of making and designing products.

Furthermore, despite the fact that the United States has in recent years been saving and investing less than Japan, Germany, and France (and, for that matter, less than most other nations), it seems to have gotten more mileage out of its investments. In fact, the McKinsey Global Institute (1996) found that Germany and Japan use their physical capital only about two-thirds as efficiently as the United States. The institute looked at the entire economy and in-depth at five industries: telecommunications, utilities, auto manufacturing, food processing, and retailing. It found that Germany uses excessive capital for the job at hand. For example, the phone cables for Deutsche Telekom are built to withstand being run over by a tank, even though the cables are underground and may become obsolete in a few years. Such 'gold-plating' of equipment is expensive and wasteful. Japan keeps massive electrical generating capacity idle most of the time in order to meet peak demand on hot summer days, while the Unites States avoids this great capital waste by creative time-of-day and summer electricity pricing schemes that discourage usage at peak times. Such higher capital productivity translates into higher financial returns for U.S. savers – 9.1 per cent compared with 7.4 per cent in Germany and 7.1 per cent in Japan. This higher U.S. capital productivity more than makes up for its lower saving rate than Germany and Japan.

Another reason for the higher productivity of U.S. over Japanese and European labor is the much higher degree of computerization in the United States than Japan or Europe. Labor flexibility is still another reason for the larger productivity of U.S. labor. While labor practices abroad are often constrained by unions, social policies and regulation, U.S. firms are much freer to hire, fire, reorganize, and use labor and other resources where they are most productive. This makes life difficult for U.S. workers, who can lose their jobs when caught in a competitive squeeze, but it also enhances firm efficiency and labor productivity. Coupled with adequate job creation, this higher labor productivity is responsible for the higher GDP per capita and standard of living in the United States than abroad.

Table 5.1 presents data on the growth of labor productivity in the United States in relation to the other G-7 nations from 1993 to 2002 (with 1992=100). It shows that the growth of output per hour in U.S. manufacturing was higher (and in some cases much higher) than for the other G-7 countries (except France) from 1993 to 2002.

Table 5.1 Growth of Output per Hour in Manufacturing in the G-7 Countries, 1993-2002 (1999=100)

	1993	1995	1997	1999	2000	2001	2002
U.S.	102.1	113.8	121.3	133.7	142.1	142.7	151.9
Japan	101.7	111.0	121.0	126.9	135.9	133.8	140.7
Germany	109.6	114.7	122.0	121.3	126.7	128.4	131.4
France	100.7	113.8	121.8	133.0	143.4	149.3	153.3
U.K.	104.2	106.4	107.0	113.4	120.1	123.2	123.7
Italy	101.4	108.0	109.9	109.7	112.7	114.8	113.0
Canada	105.8	112.4	113.5	116.0	118.4	116.1	117.9
Ratio of U.S. to trade partners	99.0	102.3	103.8	111.5	112.6	116.5	123.5

Source: Bureau of Labor Statistics, U.S. Department of Labor, September 2003, p. 19.

This represents a reversal of the experience in the previous decade. The last row in the table shows the ratio of the index of output per hour in U.S. manufacturing in each year to the trade-weighted index of nine U.S. trade partners (the other G-7 countries, as well as Belgium, Norway and Sweden). According to this measure, the international competitiveness of the United States increased continuously and reached 123.5 in 2002.

Table 5.2 provides data on the functioning of labor markets, the efficiency of financial markets, the degree of price competitiveness and the growth potential of the G-7 countries in 2001 (the last year for which data were available). It shows that the United States performed better than the other G-7 countries in all of these areas. That is, the United States has more efficient labor markets, more sophisticated financial markets, the highest degree of price competitiveness and, as a result, it has the highest growth potential among the G-7 countries.

Table 5.2 Growth Potential in the G-7 Countries in 2001 (10=Best Result; 0=Worst)

Nation	Labor Market Flexibility	Financial Market Sophistication*	Price Competitiveness	Growth Potential
United States	6.8	6.8	6.8	5.9
Canada	6.3	5.8	6.0	5.4
U.K.	6.3	6.7	5.8	5.3
France	4.4	5.1	4.8	5.1
Japan	5.2	4.2	4.2	5.1
Germany	4.6	5.6	4.7	4.6
Italy	4.6	4.5	4.1	4.0

* = 2003
Source: Lehman Brothers (2001), pp. 21-23 and World Economic Forum (2003), p. 557.

6. The Spread of the New Economy

The New Economy refers to the rapid improvements and spread in the use of information and communication technology (ICT) based on computers, software, and communications systems. Table 5.3 shows that the New Economy has spread the most in the United States among the group of G-7 countries. Specifically, the U.S. economy is the most computerized, has the largest number of Internet connections per 1000 people, and is the heaviest user of new technology and electronic commerce among the G-7 countries.

The New Economy has spread much faster in the United States than abroad not only because the United States is at the frontier in the development and production of ICT but also because it is the nation where ICT has spread the most and permeated more sectors of the economy. The greater use of the new technologies has been stimulated by the more rapid globalization of the U.S. economy and by the fact that the U.S. economy has the most liberalized and restructured economy among the G-7 countries. In short, there has been a more rapid increase in the supply and the demand of new technologies in the United States and that increased its labor and multifactor productivity much more than in the other leading industrial countries during the past decade, especially since the mid-1990s.

Table 5.3 The Spread of the New Economy among the G-7 Countries in 2002

Nation	Computers per 1,000 People	Internet Users per 1,000 People	New Information Technology (10=Highest; 0=Lowest)	Electronic Commerce* (10=Highest; 0=Lowest)
United States	739	556	8.8	8.1
Japan	477	509	7.6	4.7
Germany	480	369	8.3	6.2
France	419	280	7.4	5.0
U.K.	526	456	7.4	6.2
Italy	310	362	6.2	3.6
Canada	647	570	8.6	6.9

* = refers to 2000
Source: Institute for Management Development (2003).

The widespread use of the new technology also led to more changes in business organization in the United States than elsewhere in the form of new production methods and human resource management practices, new types of relationships with suppliers and customers, and new forms of finance and compensation. It also led to new business strategies, such as spreading the scope of the enterprise through mergers and acquisitions and streamlining their operations to best utilize their core competencies. To be sure, these results occurred in the other leading industrial countries, but to a much smaller extent than in the United States because of the slower progress of globalization, more rigid labor markets, and generally less liberalized and restructured economies.

7. The New Economy, Multifactor Productivity, and Growth

We can measure the spread of the New Economy by the growth of multifactor productivity. This involves starting by calculating labor productivity (LP), which measures how much output (Y) is produced, on average, by each unit of labor (L) employed in production. That is,

$$LP=Y/L \tag{1}$$

In terms of growth rather than the level of labor productivity, we have

$$Lp=y-l \tag{2}$$

The growth of labor productivity (lp) can, in turn, be decomposed into the contribution of (1) capital deepening, (2) the growth of the capital-labor ratio (K/L), and (3) multi-factor-productivity (MFP). MFP measures the increase in productivity attributable to technological advances or improvements in the organization of production, as opposed to increases in the quantity used of factor inputs. This requires specifying the following production function:

$$Y=F\ (K,L,MFP) \tag{3}$$

Thus, MFP is obtained by subtracting the combined growth of total factor inputs (L and K) from the growth of total output (Y). Total input growth is calculated as the weighted average of labor and capital growth, with the marginal contribution of each of these factors to output being used as the weights. Assuming that the marginal contribution of each factor of production is proportional to the share of total production that it receives in compensation, we have

$$q = (wl)l+(wk)k \tag{4}$$

where q represents the combined growth of labor and capital, wl is the weight of labor (usually the share of labor compensation in total income), l is the growth rate of labor input, wk is the weight of capital (usually the share of capital compensation in total income) and k is the growth rate of capital services, assumed to be proportional to the capital stock.

Given the measure of overall input growth, multifactor productivity growth (mfp) can be defined as

$$\begin{aligned} mfp &= y-q \\ &= y-[(wl)l+(wk)k] \end{aligned} \tag{5}$$

In this framework, any increase in the growth of output (y) in excess of contribution of the growth in the quantity used of factor inputs is attributed to an increase in multifactor productivity growth (mfp).

Rearranging equation (5), we can express output growth as the sum of total factor input growth (q) and multifactor productivity growth (mfp)

$$y = q + mfp$$
$$= [(wl)l + (wk)k] + mfp \quad (6)$$

Subtracting the growth of the labor input (l) from both sides and keeping in mind that wl=1-wk, we further rearrange equation (6) to decompose the growth of labor productivity into its two components: (1) (k-l)wk, or the rate of capital deepening adjusted by the contribution of capital to the production process, and (2) mfp and get:

$$y - l = (k - l)wk + mfp$$

If capital is relatively unimportant (i.e. if the wk term is small) then labor and mfp would be virtually identical. Similarly, if the K-L ratio remains constant then l and mfp would also remain practically identical. If, on the other hand, capital is an important factor and the K-L ratio is not constant then l and mfp need not move together.

Table 5.4 provides data on the growth of real GDP, the growth of labor productivity, and the growth of multifactor productivity (mfp) – the latter used as an estimate of the relative contribution of the New Economy to the growth of the G-7 countries from 1981 to 1999. The table shows that, after growing at a similar rate from 1981 to 1989 and at a slightly higher rate from 1990 to 1995, the growth of real GDP grew much faster in the United States than in the other G-7 countries from 1996 to 1999 (it was 4.43 in the United States, 3.53 in Canada, 2.78 in the United Kingdom, 2.53 in France, 1.38 in Italy, and 1.321 in Japan).

Table 5.4 also shows that after growing less rapidly between 1981 and 1995, labor productivity grew much faster in the United States than in the other G-7 countries in the 1996-1999 period. As we have seen in the previous section, the growth of labor productivity reflects the growth in capital deepening (i.e. the increase in the K-L ratio) and the growth in multifactor productivity (the difference between the growth of real output and the growth in the quantity of labor and capital used in production).

Finally, Table 5.4 shows that after growing less rapidly between 1981 and 1995 (except for Canada), multifactor productivity grew much faster (about 2.3 times faster, on average) in the United States than in the other G-7 countries between 1996 and 2000 (it was 2.0 in the United States, 1.7 in France, 1.1 in the United Kingdom, 1.1 in Germany, 0.6 in Japan, 0.5 in Canada, and 0.4 in Italy). As pointed out earlier, the growth of multifactor productivity (mfp) can be used as a rough measure of the contribution of the New Economy to the growth of the nation. Thus, the New Economy contributed more than twice as much to the growth of the United States than to the growth of the other G-7 countries between 1996 and 2000.

Table 5.4 Average Yearly Growth of Real GDP, Labor Productivity, and Multifactor Productivity (MFP) in the G-7 Countries, 1981-2000

COUNTRY	1981-1995	1996-2000
United States		
GDP	3.0	4.0
Labor Productivity	1.3	2.5
of which MFP	1.1	2.0
Japan		
GDP	3.3	1.5
Labor Productivity	3.0	1.6
of which MFP	1.8	0.6
Germany		
GDP	2.2	1.8
Labor Productivity	2.4	1.8
of which MFP	1.2	1.0
France		
GDP	2.0	2.8
Labor Productivity	2.9	2.6
of which MFP	1.5	1.7
United Kingdom		
GDP	3.1	2.9
Labor Productivity	2.1	1.5
of which MFP	1.8	1.1
Italy		
GDP	2.1	1.9
Labor Productivity	2.4	1.3
of which MFP	1.3	0.4
Canada		
GDP	2.6	4.0
Labor Productivity	1.5	1.1
of which MFP	0.3	0.5

Source: Gust and Marquez (2002) and the author's calculations.

8. The Future of the New Economy

The time period for the exceptional U.S. growth performance and the spread of the New Economy is rather brief and we cannot be sure that 1996 represents the beginning of a new trend of superior U.S. growth performance, especially in view of the sharp reduction in the U.S. growth rate (that no one anticipated) in the fall of 2000 and the recession in 2001. The fact that labor productivity continued to increase at a rapid pace in the United States even during 2001 (a recession year) and 2002 (a year of much slower growth of real GDP) is evidence, however, that the New Economy is not a mirage, but is real and is here to stay.

The recession in the United States in 2001 arose from the necessity to correct the excesses that developed in the U.S. economy (especially in the information and communications technology (ICT) and the financial sectors) during the high-growth period in the second half of the 1990s. Some people believed that new ICT technology, by permitting better inventory management, would prevent excesses and help avoid bubbles and recessions. This was not the case, and a bubble and a recession did occur in the United States in 2001. But the growth of labor productivity and mfp did continue. It even accelerated and this is clear evidence that the New Economy is likely to continue to expand.

What no one can deny is that, after two decades of disappointing performance, the second half of the 1990s does represent one of the most rapid and consistent periods of growth in the United States. During this period, the United Stated was able to reconcile what until then seemed irreconcilable: a rapid growth rate, a low and declining core inflation rate, and a low and declining rate of unemployment – and it is this that gave rise to the belief that the United States created a New Economy.

Jorgenson (2000), Stiroh (2001) and others predicted that the growth of labor productivity will average from 2.0 per cent to 2.6 per cent per year and that the growth of mfp will remain high during this decade. Thus, a general consensus is emerging that the New Economy is here to say. There are, to be sure, skeptics such as Gordon (2002) who expect the growth of labor productivity at a much lower rate than indicated above, but they are in a minority. The general belief is that, despite slower growth of real GDP in 2001 and 2002 when compared to the growth of GDP during the second half of the 1990s, the U.S. economy has experienced a structural change based on the production and utilization of ICT that will lead to continued large increases in labor and mfp productivities in the future.

European countries have also invested heavily in new ICT during the past decade and, as a result, they are also very likely to experience the spread of the New Economy and more rapid growth during this decade (after the present period of uncertainty and slow growth comes to an end).

As the U.S. experience indicates, it takes time before ICT can become a significant part of the economy and result in a rapid increase in labor and mpf productivity. We all remember Robert Solow's U.S. productivity paradox of the 1980s, where he uttered the now famous phrase: 'Computers are everywhere but in the productivity statistics'. The answer, of course, was that computers were not everywhere in the United States at the time he was writing to make a significant difference in its productivity and growth statistics. Those benefits only came later (i.e. with a lag) after a period of learning to use the new technology effectively. As a late starter, Europe is in a similar situation today. But if Europe continues to invest in ICT as heavily as during the past decade, it will very likely also experience rapid growth during this decade.

Invest heavily in ICT is not, however, the only requirement to create the New Economy. The nation must also (1) restructure firms to cut costs, improve flexibility and make better use of technology, (2) increase the pace of deregulation, especially in telecoms and labor markets, (3) encourage an entrepreneurial culture and make it easier to start new businesses, (4) liberalize financial markets to funnel capital to the best uses, (5) develop venture capital to finance innovative companies, and (6) adjust monetary policy to the realities of the New Economy by waiting for inflation to appear before raising interest rates.

If European nations fail to restructure and liberalize their economies adequately, they will be unable to make the most effective use of the new ICT and match U.S. growth. At the Lisbon Summit in March 2000, the European Union (EU) set the goal of becoming 'the most competitive economy in the world by 2010'. Four years have now passed since the EU heads of state met in Lisbon and not much has happened toward realizing their goal.

References

Barro, R.J. and Sala-i-Martin, X. (1995), *Economic Growth*, New York: McGraw-Hill.

Council of Economic Advisors (2004), *Economic Report of the President*, Washington, D.C.

Dunning, J.H. (1995), 'Think Again Professor Krugman: Competitiveness Does Matter', *The International Executive*, Vol. 37, No. 4, pp. 315-324.

Gordon, R.J. (2002), 'Technology and Economic Performance in the American Economy', NBER Working Paper 8771, February.

IMD (2003), *The World Competitiveness Yearbook*, IMD, Lausanne.

Jorgenson, D. (2000), 'Raising the Speed Limit: U.S. Economic Growth in the Information Age', *Brooking Papers on Economic Activity* 1, pp. 125-211.

Krugman, P. (1994), 'Competitiveness: A Dangerous Obsession', *Foreign Affairs*, March-April, pp. 28-44.

McKinsey Global Institute (1993), *Manufacturing Productivity*, Washington D.C.: McKinsey Global Institute.

McKinsey Global Institute (1996), *Capital Productivity*, Washington D.C.: McKinsey Global Institute.

McKinsey Global Institute (1997), *Removing Barriers to Growth and Employment in France and Germany*, Washington D.C.: McKinsey Global Institute.

OECD (2003), *Information and Technology Outlook*, Paris: OECD.

Porter, M. (1990), *The Comparative Advantage of Nations*, New York: Free Press.

Rausch, L.M. (1995), *Asia's New High-Tech Competitors*, Washington, D.C.: National Science Foundation.

Salvatore, D. (1990), *The Japanese Trade Challenge and the U.S. Response*, Washington D.C.: Economic Policy Institute.

Salvatore, D. (1993), *Protectionism and World Welfare*, New York: Cambridge University Press.

Salvatore, D. (1998), 'Europe's Competitiveness Problems', *The World Economy*, March 1998, pp. 189-205.

Stiroh, K. (2001), 'Information Technology and the U.S. Productivity Revival: What Do the Industry Data Show?', New York, Federal Reserve Bank of New York, January.

Stiroh, K. (2001), 'What Drives Productivity Growth?', New York, Federal Reserve Bank of New York, January.

U.S. Department of Labor (2003), *International Comparisons of Labor Productivity and Unit Labor Costs in Manufacturing*, Washington D.C., September.

WEF (2003), *The Global Competitiveness Report*, Geneva.

PART TWO

Chapter 6

Finance, Technology and Risk

Luigi Paganetto and Pasquale Lucio Scandizzo

1. Introduction

In the second part of the 1990s, the experience of large differences in the rates of GNP and TFP (Total Factor Productivity)growth between the USA and Europe has generated a debate on the existence and on the role of the so-called 'new economy'. Gordon (2000), for example, argues that the increases in productivity have been occurring only in the computer industry. Jorgenson (2001) claims that the expansionary phase of the US economy was linked to the dynamics of the semiconductor industry. The available empirical evidence shows, however, that the massive introduction of new technologies, in particular the so-called ICTs, has determined two different effects: an increase of productivity in the computer sector and an important increase in TFP linked to new organizational models of the firm, the use of more skilled human capital and new workplace practices (Brynjolfsson and Hitt, 2000).

In this context, the role of finance in supporting and facilitating the introduction of the new technologies is not an established fact and is a matter of considerable discussion. First of all, the 'causality nexus', from finance to growth, is controversial. In a recent review on 'The new growth evidence', J. Temple (1999) pointed out that 'some prominent economists have tended to dismiss the role of financial factors, arguing (from little evidence) that financial development is simply a passive consequence of growth. There are now a number of papers looking at the effect on growth of initial financial development including both banking system and stock market variables'.

Secondly, economists are divided on the issue of the channels by which finance works, since these depend on the model of growth adopted. In the AK endogenous growth approach (Romer, 1986), the main focus is on capital accumulation. The financial system, mobilizing and influencing the saving rate and its allocation, affects capital accumulation. Most empirical studies have found significant links between some indicators of finance development (liquid liabilities, money deposit, stock market capitalization) and the level of investment. In the so-called Schumpeterian approach to endogenous growth, on the other hand (Aghion and Howitt, 1992), the 'driver' is technological change. The financial system, in this case, affects growth altering the rate of technological innovation. As R. Levine (1997) has pointed out, financial markets and institutions ease the 'trading, hedging and pooling of risk', that is inherent to high return innovating projects and related long-term commitment of capital. Efficient financial markets are also useful to monitor managers and exert corporate control, compensating for the often prohibitively high costs for outsider investors to evaluate and monitor project returns.

The empirical studies based on the East Asian experience seem to support the view that financial markets affect growth, despite their relative inefficiency, by channeling savings and contributing to capital accumulation. The main idea emerging from these studies is the need to link any evaluation of the relative efficiency of the financial systems to the different stages of development.

If we accept the Schumpeterian idea that capitalism achieves its dynamism from the new projects, selected in an efficient way by financial markets, growth can be seen as a process in which innovation is proportional to the risk taken. In this respect, Phelps (1999) noted that the diseconomies of scale connected to risk can be attenuated by a good governance and adequate selection of projects and entrepreneur.

In this chapter, we examine first the appropriateness of different institutional regimes for financing innovation and then present a simple model of endogenous growth that tries to capture, in a stylized way, the nexus between finance, innovation and growth. The model is based on the idea that the dynamism of a developed economy depends on the degree of risk taken in innovative business, on the possibility of risk sharing (which is a function of the efficiency of financial markets), on the effect of innovation on the increase of TFP of the economy and the opposite, negative effect of capital accumulation on the marginal productivity of capital.

The plan of the chapter is as follows: in section 2, we look at the problem of innovation and finance, and explore the microeconomic aspects which make the financing of innovation a particularly difficult endeavor both for traditional intermediaries and for the entrepreneurs. In section 3, we examine more explicitly the issue of the effectiveness of banking versus equity as a source of financing for innovation, with special reference to the recent, and still unfolding, Internet story. In section 4, we present the mathematical model and in section 5 we study its possible steady states. Section 6 elaborates some conclusive remarks. Numerical simulations and diagrams for two test cases are presented in the Appendix.

2. Innovation and Finance

Finance represents a problem for technology at two different levels: first, research projects have to be funded and their results properly developed to ensure effectiveness and applicability; second, these results have to be transferred from universities and research centers to firms in order to foster innovation and growth. For both these stages adequate financing instruments hold a *prima facie* claim as an important element for economic success.

The importance of finance for technology, in reality, is not easily established and, in spite of its intuitive plausibility, rests on so many different arguments that it is ultimately difficult to ascertain with clarity. *A priori* arguments for finance as a key determinant of technology success range from its effect on the actual applicability of innovation, to the comparative disadvantage of high tech firms in obtaining capital. For example, no less an economist than John Hicks (1969, pp. 143-145) claims that the industrial revolution in England did not occur when the main inventions were made, but only, much later, when the financial system was sufficiently developed to offer the appropriate financial instruments to develop and apply the innovations.

From a more microeconomic angle, economists such as Arrow (1962) and Stiglitz (1993) have argued that firms engaging in innovation are likely to be more highly constrained by liquidity, and the financial market imperfections arising from informational asymmetries and moral hazard. Others, such as Bhattacharya and Ritter (1983), have pointed out that innovators may themselves be unreliable as information sources for would-be financiers, because the defense of property rights implies that a crucial part of the information on the projects undertaken remains closely guarded against potential competitors. In the United States, for example, patent law cannot be applied unless the invention is considered sufficiently unrelated to 'prior art', and even if applied, in many cases 'would be held invalid if ever litigated. Trade secret laws (protection against the theft of ideas) is also difficult to implement because of the strategies used by firms to avoid legal challenges and the difficulty to establish legal proofs' (Anton and Yao, 1994, p. 191).

Empirical evidence on the effects of finance on technology has been initially based on the sensitivity of R&D expenditure to the cash flow of the enterprise. The results of these tests have been originally mixed, in spite of the strength of prior arguments, and only recently appear more convincing. Cross-sectional studies conducted in the 1960s by, among others, Scherer (1965), Hamburg (1966), and Muller (1967) failed to turn up significant effects of the cash flow on R&D. The studies conducted in the 1990s and based on panel data, instead, are more successful. For example, Hall (1992) measures a strong effect of the cash flow on R&D over a large panel of US manufacturing firms. Himmelberg and Petersen (1994), by investigating a short panel of high tech firms, find also a similar, strong and positive effect, and so do Hao and Jaffe (1993) on a small and long panel of US firms and Guiso (1997) on a panel of Italian firms. Event studies by Greenwald, Salinger and Stiglitz (1990) point to the same result for the US automotive and airline industry.

The credit instrument, especially for small and medium enterprises (SME), represents by far the main source of finance of technology and innovation. Most of the recent empirical evidence shows that, in spite of the development of financial markets, R&D projects are still financed in order of importance: (1) by the entrepreneur with possible recourse to his family and friends; (2) by a short-term credit relation with a bank; (3) by third party equity investors and venture capitalists (Berger and Udell, 1998).

Because R&D as well as innovation projects are generally affected by high, non-diversifiable risks, the financial structure of the firm provides an allocation of risks between the participants to the enterprise. Any change in that structure thus implies subsequent changes in the risk borne by each class of claimants, as well as in the expected value of their claims. By its very nature, however, investment in technology requires very specific expertise for expert evaluation; it does not provide collateral because of intangibility and may modify substantially the expected value of the owners' (e.g. shareholders') claims in the course of project life.

Not only SMEs may thus face severe constraints in capital-scarce countries with low capital labor ratios and undeveloped financial markets (Cobham, 1999), but they may be affected by a specific anti-innovation bias.

Risk transfers between claimants – due to debt financing – may affect shareholders' investment incentives in two different ways. On the one hand, shareholders can undertake a negative Net Present Value (NPV) project if debt financing allows them to capture part of the project gains by transferring part of their risk to debt-holders (over-investment incentive). Conversely, shareholders can reject a positive NPV project if most of the gains accrue to debt-holders (under-investment incentive) without a corresponding increase in the risk level. The resulting sub-optimal investment decisions cause deadweight losses which are commonly referred to as agency costs of debt.

The standard framework of the agency costs of debt assumes that investment decisions go before the firm financing strategy and that operating decisions are taken by shareholders (or managers) in order to maximize the value of equity. When there is no debt in the financial structure, an equity maximizing policy is equivalent to a value maximizing policy. When debt is present, on the contrary, investment incentives can be distorted by the conflict of interest that originates when the project NPV is shared between claimants according to their relative 'seniority'. This distortion of incentives induces sub-optimal investment decisions that result in a difference between the levered and unlevered value of the firm (agency costs of debt).

The impact of the agency costs of debt have been envisaged in situations like 'asset substitution' (Jensen and Meckling, 1976), 'over-investment' and 'under-investment' (Myers, 1977; Berkovitch and Kim, 1990). Jensen and Meckling (1976) show how the shareholders of a levered firm have incentives to increase the riskyness of a firm's assets, thus increasing the risk for debt-holders, even if the greater risk is associated with lower present values of future cash flows. Shareholders are, in fact, interested only in the 'upper' side of the probability distribution of firm results, that is the part where cash flows are greater than the face value of debt. Debt-holders, in contrast, receive only the full payment of debt as specified in the contractual provision but nothing of the cash flows greater than the face value of debt. Therefore, they are interested in the 'lower' part of the probability distribution of firm results: the addition of risk-increasing projects to the firm reduces the expected value of their claim. In this case, the agency cost of debt consists in the increased cost of financing that debt-holders require when they assess the shareholders incentive to accept a risk-increasing investment project.

Myers (1977) shows how shareholders of a levered firm can have incentives not to accept a positive NPV project: the 'under-investment' incentive arises because existing debt-holders get a share of the project NPV while shareholders suffer the investment cost. In the presence of risky debt in the financial structure, debt-holders appropriate the positive results of the project financed with internal funds up to the face value of their claim, leaving to the shareholders only the residual. The agency cost of debt is directly related to the change in firm value that the project would have produced if adopted, but that was lost because of the decision to reject the project.

While in the Myers contribution the agency costs of debt are due to the under-investment incentives that originate from risky debt, Berkovitch and Kim (1990) show that risk-shifting incentives can also produce significant deviations from the NPV rule. Using a model based on a different probability level for each state (high and low) and on a project entirely financed with an exogenous specified amount of debt, the authors show how under- and over-investment incentives can arise from the 'seniorship' of debt. In particular, the issuance of senior debt to finance a new investment project can have two effects on the shareholders' investment incentives. On the one hand, a greater seniority of new debt with respect to existing debt makes the former less risky because it increases its probability to be paid back in case of default. This reduces the cost on new debt and makes it easier to use senior debt to finance the investment, thus reducing the under-investment incentives. On the other hand, however, the low cost of new debt, if senior to the existing one, can generate incentives for excessive investment expenses and can result in the acceptance of negative NPV projects (over-investment). Also in this case, the agency costs of debt depend on the relative weight of the two incentives and can be defined as the difference between the firm values that originate from the acceptance/rejection of the project.

Scandizzo (1997) shows how this effect is exacerbated in the case of R&D projects. Once an SME has achieved a given threshold of leverage, in fact, it is in the interest of shareholders, i.e. both the owners, partners and venture capitalists, to engage in risky innovation since the debt-holders will bear part of the risk without participating in the possible payoffs. While this effect may partly counteract the under-incentive problem that affects R&D projects for private entrepreneurs, its consequence is that financial institutions will have to step up supervision activities for innovative firms. They will thus be more reluctant to fund projects that concern firms likely to invest in new technology, *even when these projects do not directly involve R&D activities or innovation*.

Traditional managerial economics (e.g. Reekie and Crook, 1995) predicts that financing of the firm will follow a 'pecking order' depending on the degree of control of each financing source. Because ownership resists the relinquishing of control and residual rights, internal finance, i.e. the re-investment of profits, will be the favored option. This will be followed by debt, which is simply a commitment to repay without any foregoing of control rights, and only as an extreme ratio, by enlarging the platform of residual and control rights to other equity partners. According to Brouwer and Hendrix (1998), however, this order is reversed in the case for high-tech start-ups, because of *actual* constraints, rather than a reversal in pecking *preferences* (Cobham, 1999): 'Since internal finance (cash flows) cannot meet (the firm's) capital demands and debt is hard to come by, equity capital figures as the prime financial resource' (Brouwer and Hendrix, 1998, p. 334).

Financing technology may thus engineer a dilemma for the owner-manager of an SME. Her natural preference for debt financing, magnified by the possibility of risk shifting offered by high risk technology projects, in fact, may be frustrated by the unwillingness of banks to grant her credit. According to this approach, high-tech firms may be perceived by banks, and also by potential bondholders, as subjects continually threatening to disrupt the basic conditions of credit contracts. This would be accomplished through the shift of the risk burden that innovation could induce by incorporating increasingly risky projects into the financial structure of the firm.

On the other hand, the reluctance of the potential creditors to supply finance to high-tech start-ups would not be matched by an equal reluctance by management to relinquish control over the firm to equity owners, for two main reasons. In the first place, in fact, the SME-high-tech manager may see debt as a too great commitment, in the face of the uncertainty created by the investment in innovation. Because debt repayment appears dominated by external constraints, owner-managers of small start-ups may feel less inclined to be fussy about control rights in exchange for the clear risk sharing agreement provided by the equity contract. In the second place, the financial constraints for SMEs will appear much more stringent in the case of enterprises that are more dependent on innovation for success.

Financial constraints prevent external finance from being made available to firms, rather than merely reducing it (Carpenter et al., 1995). They can be summarized under three hypotheses: (1) the collateral hypothesis states that the collateral value of a firm will reduce the discounted value of its expected cash flow, thereby reducing the creditworthiness of firms depending on intangible factors more than proportionally; (2) the bank lending hypothesis states that restrictive monetary policy will cause a reduction of activity for bank dependent firms; (3) the internal finance hypothesis, finally, implies that capital market imperfections and agency costs arising from asymmetric information will cause profit levels, rather than growth, to be the main determinant of investments. Given that large corporations (LCs) themselves face finance constraints under these three hypotheses, SMEs, and, even more, SMEs operating in the high-tech sectors, can be expected to face more stringent constraints. In support of this contention, we may add the result by Brown (1997) that innovative firms are financially constrained because 'the assumption of perfect capital markets is least likely to be satisfied for the class of firms which devote resources towards the development of innovative products or processes'.

3. Banking, Equity Financing and Risk

The considerations developed in the previous section suggest that the banks are an inadequate source of financing for innovative business and that the equity market is a critical element to support and encourage innovation. According to econometric studies conducted at the World Bank (Levine and Zervos, 1995), the size of the equity market and the volume of trading are robust indicators of market efficiency, low transaction costs and market liquidity. These studies further found that countries with more developed equity markets and more intense activities of non-banking intermediaries were, *ceteris paribus*, better performers in terms of capital accumulation, long-term growth, and efficiency. While this evidence appears to be convincing and, indeed, compelling, it is difficult to pinpoint the elements of clear advantage of the Anglo-Saxon system, based on public companies and equity financing, on the European system, based on traditional banking and a system of companies with concentrated property rights. In general one can say that countries with large and active equity markets appear more dynamic and competitive. Furthermore, although equity markets have been growing in all countries, where banks are the predominant source of financing, the financial resources of domestic origin are still trapped in large bureaucratic institutions (public banks and insurance companies), while foreign capital is often subject to discouraging restrictions.

While large and well-organized equity markets are generally credited to be a positive factor of development and innovation, some evidence of the higher risks implied by their modes of functioning, governance and transaction costs emerges from the recent story of Internet financing. As a spectacular example of inversion of the traditional financing 'pecking order' in financing innovative business, in fact, Internet companies have almost foregone conventional credit. At least during the 'boom' years, they were mostly financed by venture capitalists, with initial public offerings (IPOs) coming very fast after the first deal between the financial partners was struck. The venture capitalists responsible for most of the financing were a handful of financial houses and investment banks that still dominate the market, and the risk, of the new business. These firms, who were often strategic partners for the new ventures, ranged from VC kingpin Kleiner Perkins Caufield & Byers to Japanese renegade Softbank and built networks of companies that are often referred to as Keiretsu.

Kleiner Perkins is perhaps the most important venture capitalist on the Internet market, with a record of financing that includes, among others, Netscape, Amazon, AtHome, Excite and many others. Others that can be cited are: Benchmark Capital, with investments in companies like eBay, Ariba and Critical Path, Sequoia Capital that invested in Yahoo, Vulcan Ventures, Idealab and Softbank and few more worth mentioning.

These venture capitalists (VCs), however, do not work alone. While they specialize in identifying the firms with highest potential and helping them develop their strategies, they have to resort to different specialists when the time comes to bring the new born to the market. Goldman Sachs and Morgan Stanley Dean Witter are the top investment banks to back and advise the best Web companies that want to go public. Just behind them is Credit Suisse First Boston and, as the best 'technology' financial boutique, Hambrecht & Quist.

The role of venture capitalists in financing the Internet firms has been critical for more than one reason. First, VCs have played a broad function in 'picking the winners'. This has been achieved by actively searching for ideas and companies with the highest potential, by investing in networks and strategic partnerships, and by developing imaginative ways to combine venture capital with different and new forms of financing.

The main indicator of success in these different strategies is the exit of the IPOs. Some of the most spectacular deals occurred in the summer of 1999. For example, Benchmark Capital, one of the leading VCs based in Menlo Park, California, scored two peaks in 1999: Red Hat, whose IPO in August offered shares at $14 and closed its first day of trading at $52.06 a share, and Ariba, which in June offered 5 million shares at $23 each and saw them close at $90 the same day. In July, the public sale of Net2Phone shares, handled by H&Q, from an offering price of $15 a share scored $26.50 on the first day of trading, with shares soaring afterwards as high as $92.63 handled. In June and July, Juniper Networks and Drugstore.com, both backed by Kleiner, respectively soared from a $34 opening price to $98.88 at the close of the day; and from $18 per share to $50.25 at the close of the first day of trading.

More successes and special deals followed through the rest of 1999 and the first part of 2000. At the end of this year, and in the first three months of 2001, however, the bubble burst, with Internet stock prices falling at rates and speed which were almost as spectacular as the earlier rise. Much of this fall was due to the growing evidence of companies under-performing in terms of growth and revenues with respect to investors' expectations. Financing appears to have played a role, however, since the earlier euphoria had been based on the belief that companies might almost do away with credit financing. As the price of the stocks fell, Internet companies found that they had a very hard time in obtaining credit from ordinary credit sources. Extraordinary sources, such as corporate bonds and other market-linked deals were precluded by the loss of reputation created by the revenue warnings and the fall in the prices of their previously overvalued stock. A significant part of earlier financing, on the other hand, had been obtained through convertible bonds and other types of options, which, once left unexercised by investors, turned into further loads for their income accounts and balance sheets.

The recent Internet story, therefore, provides material for thought, in the sense that it forces us to focus on the key issue of risk taking: equity financing being a clear case where risk is encouraged by sharing and by the desire of collecting large gains over relatively short time spans. The rise of the Internet economy has demonstrated, in fact, somewhat spectacularly and not without the danger of a negative feedback, that high-tech firms may be almost entirely financed by equity, provided that the prospects for acquiring rents are sufficiently high (Scandizzo, 2001). But is this true for other innovative businesses as well? While available empirical research on this topic is almost nil, business angels appear to be the main source of third party financing (TPF), at least in Anglo Saxon economies. Nevertheless, even in the most developed countries, this source of finance, at least at first sight, appears to be of minor importance. In the USA, for example, according to SBIC data, only 3.59 per cent of total finance to small businesses is provided by TPF and only 1.85 per cent by venture capitalists. These figures, however, may give a false impression, since both business angels and venture capitalists '... invest very selectively and target small companies with significant upside potential'. (Berger and Udell, 1998, p. 15). While a small proportion of the total, therefore, TPFs, venture capitalists and business angels may account for a much larger share of the outside finance obtained by successful firms.

As for innovation, one may reasonably argue that, because of the comparatively lower incidence of traditional credit, enterprises engaging in riskier projects involving research and new technology would also be more represented among the firms financed by venture capitalists and business angels. This would be the result of mutual signaling of preference for growth, as well as a result of greater competence in evaluating high-tech and start-up projects. Furthermore, the improved financial management obtained through the involvement of equity partners could have positive results on the performance of the firm. This conjecture has received some support in a study of venture capital in the US (Kortum and Lerner, 1998), which shows that, even though it financed only 3 per cent of total R&D, it was associated with 15 per cent of industrial innovation.

Venture capitalists and business angels differ in their objectives in a substantial way. While venture capitalists are interested in capital gain, business angels aim at finding enterprises that can be reliable income sources. Further differences concern the *modus operandi* in the partnership. Because of their concern with maximizing returns to capital, venture capitalists generally operate through intermediaries (closed funds or other financial entities), they typically take small equity positions in the firm selected and always combine these positions with carefully designed exit strategies. Among these, the initial private offering (IPO) is the elective one. In contrast, business angels do not operate through intermediaries, are not committed to exit designs and tend to become involved in the management of the companies financed in a major way. Involvement in the company management appears indeed to hold a positive value for angels, to the point of justifying their financing of companies comparatively riskier and less liquid than those that TPFs and venture capitalists would fund.

Business angels are also characterized by the fact that they tend to operate in anonymity, often work in groups, tend to share databases and news about the best companies and generally rely on networks of consultants and special services. These services, which are increasingly on-line, have a matching function and, by combining an application process to a growing database, look for mutuality of preferences between investors and entrepreneurs. According to Marcia Schirmer, who is President of the Colorado Capital Alliance Inc., a Colorado-based angel network, 82 per cent of BAs expect a role in the venture, with investment ranging from \$50K up to over \$1 million – (Bill Gates is the largest angel of all, and has a slightly higher range) – 18 of 20 investments do not produce a positive return, while investment costs for angels are very high (due diligence – patent attorneys for example). The sectors of involvement are mostly technological, with innovation in the forefront: high-tech services companies, telecom, computers, Internet, manufacturing, with financing distributed over project life: 31 per cent seed, 46 per cent early stage, 23 per cent mid-stage or established – 56 per cent have sales.

According to the latest SBIC data, there are more than two million angels in the US (of which only 250,000 are investing), who invest \$20 billion annually. While angels look for companies that have strong management, they are also interested in very high returns (40 per cent within a few years is a common target). As a consequence, they often seek direct involvement in the company in a way that may allow them to exercise some control on growing strategies, but also effective monitoring of management practices and performance.

In sum, the fuller 'capitalistic system' characteristic of the Anglo-Saxon economies, and based on large and active equity markets, also appears to be specially adaptive in the area of financing innovation and encouraging risky undertaking. On the contrary, the more traditional system followed in Europe and in its area of influence, based as it is on banking and debt financing, seems more hampered by adverse selection and asymmetric information and, at least *prima facie*, it appears less capable of efficiently handling risk and progressive technologies.

4. A Model of Finance, Innovation and Growth

Consider an economy where the representative consumer seeks to maximize over time her utility as a function of two control variables: the expected value of per capita consumption level $c(t)$ and the risk level $\sigma(t)$, where t denotes time. The risk indicator can be defined in general as an expected loss and, as such, it is comprised between zero and an upper bound representing the maximum amount of bearable risk in a given society and time: $0 \leq \sigma \leq \overline{\sigma}$. The state variables are represented by the expected level of capital per capita $k(t)$ and by expected total factor productivity (TFP) $A(t)$, whose relation with the control variables is described by the two differential equations:

$$\frac{\partial k}{\partial t} = \dot{k} = Af(k) + g(\sigma) - \theta k - c \tag{1}$$

$$\frac{\partial A}{\partial t} = \dot{A} = bA\sigma \tag{2}$$

where $Af(k)$ is a well-behaved, neoclassical production function, $(\frac{\partial f}{\partial k} < 0)$, $g(\sigma)$ represents the private effect of risk taking on the performance of the representative firm, while $\frac{\partial A}{\partial t}$, as defined through the differential equation in (2), is the external effect of risk taking on TFP and can be interpreted as neutral technological progress. In (1) and (2) the time argument has been suppressed for simplicity, dots denote time derivatives and θ is the sum of the exogenous rates of depreciation and population growth. Note that expressions (1) and (2) are consistent with the usual formulation of endogenous growth made popular by Lucas (1988) and Romer (1986). They may be given, however, a Schumpeterian interpretation, along the lines of Aghion and Howitt (1992). If we characterize innovation as a gamble whose value is proportional to the risk taken (as well as to a parameter representing the amount of resources per unit of risk, given by b in expression (2)), we may think of production as ultimately depending only on innovation. As capital accumulates, in fact, its marginal productivity, aside from the technical progress part, tends to zero. This is equivalent to the hypothesis that, given sufficient time, any addition to the existing capital stock is instantly scrapped (has zero value) unless it carries sufficient innovation (via risk taking). The private effect of risk, in this context, is also modeled as a segment of the production process, that is independent of the capital stock of the representative enterprise. This is so because a successful risky undertaking may correspond to the fact that a certain number of firms profit from the opportunity of gaining through a 'risky' innovation. Thus, the private effect of risk does not imply that the existing stock of capital becomes more productive, but that an innovation can be considered equivalent to scrapping ordinary capital and substituting it with risky capital.

An alternative way to interpret the separation hypothesis is in line with the model developed by Paganetto and Scandizzo (2000), based on the assumption that the economy may choose to allocate its resources to two alternative uses: the 'traditional' sector and the 'new economy', that is a set of higher risk, innovative industries, whose performance is largely unpredictable and whose value depends on the outcome of a large number of independent stochastic variables. These industries are linked to the traditional ones by a positive externality, so that the apparent 'over-investment' in the 'new economy' that occurs because of lack of information has the beneficial effect of fostering the increase in productivity of the traditional economy.

We assume that the utility function is separable in the two control variables, so that the market solution is equivalent to the maximization:

$$\max U_0 = \int_0^T e^{-\rho t}\big(U(c) - V(\sigma)\big)dt \tag{3}$$

subject to: $\dot{k} = Af(k) + g(\sigma) - \theta k - c$

Forming the Hamiltonian from (3), we obtain:

$$H = e^{-\rho t\backslash}\big[U(c) - V(\sigma) + \lambda\big(Af(k) + g(\sigma) - \theta k - c\big)\big] \tag{4}$$

The optimizing state and co-state conditions are:

$$U_c - \lambda = 0 \tag{5}$$

$$-V_\sigma + \lambda g_\sigma = 0 \tag{6}$$

$$\dot{\lambda} = (\rho - Af_k + \theta) \tag{7}$$

where $U_c = \frac{\partial u}{\partial c} > 0$, $V_\sigma = \frac{\partial V}{\partial \sigma} < 0$, $g_\sigma = \frac{\partial g}{\partial \sigma} > 0$

Differentiating again (5) and (6) and applying (7), assuming, for simplicity that $\theta = 0$ (i.e. zero population growth and no depreciation), we find the (private) optimizing growth rates of consumption and risk

$$\frac{\dot{c}}{c} = \frac{1}{\eta}(Af_k - \rho) \tag{8}$$

$$\frac{\dot{\sigma}}{\sigma} = \frac{1}{\varepsilon}(Af_k - \rho) \tag{9}$$

where $\eta = -\frac{U_{cc}}{U_c}c$, $U_{cc} = \frac{\partial^2 U}{\partial c^2} < 0$ and

$\varepsilon = -\left(\frac{V_{\sigma\sigma}}{|V_\sigma|} + \frac{g_{\sigma\sigma}}{g_\sigma}\right)\sigma$, $V_{\sigma\sigma} \frac{\partial^2 V}{\partial \sigma^2} >\leq 0$ and

$$g_{\sigma\sigma} = \frac{\partial^2 g}{\partial \sigma^2} < 0$$

Note that η and ε are local measures of curvature that synthesize the diseconomies of scale embedded in the utility and the production function.

As expressions (8) and (9) show, the growth rate of consumption and the growth rate of risk are a direct function of the excess of the marginal productivity of capital over the discount rate. This result is expected for consumption, and coincides with the result of neoclassical growth theory. It is less expected for risk, but it can be explained recalling that firms as an alternative to traditional investment may undertake risky innovation. The opportunity cost of the increased production for both is the value of consumption foregone. The growth rates of consumption and risk are also a function of the utility and the production function, but only indirectly through their convexity parameters. In other words, the *extent* of growth is determined by the net gain from postponing consumption, while the *intensity* of growth is determined by how weak are the diseconomies of scale in utility or production. The two growth rates are related through the expression:

$$\frac{\dot{c}}{c} = \frac{\eta}{\varepsilon}\frac{\dot{\sigma}}{\sigma} \tag{10}$$

This implies that, along the optimal path, a higher rate of growth of consumption may be matched by a negative or positive rate of growth of risk. The rate of growth will be negative under increasing relative risk aversion and decreasing returns to risk sufficiently severe on its impact on productivity. It will be positive if, on the contrary, risk aversion will be decreasing with risk and the diseconomies of scale in risk taking are sufficiently weak. Both these characteristics, in fact, may be the consequence of institutional factors: on one hand, increasing relative risk aversion, which appears natural at the individual level, may be reduced by risk sharing, while it may be increased by adverse selection and moral hazard. On the other hand, diseconomies of scale in risk taking may be attenuated by the efficient selection of projects and entrepreneurs (Phelps, 1999), by a contestable market for managerial skills, and by other arrangements of good corporate governance.

Assuming that the production function is homogeneous of degree α $(0 < \alpha \leq 1)$, and using the expression (8), we can re-write equation (2) as follows:

$$\frac{c}{k} = \frac{1}{\alpha}\left[\rho + |\eta|\frac{\dot{c}}{c}\right] + \frac{g(\sigma)}{k} - \frac{\dot{k}}{k} \tag{11}$$

Thus, along the optimal path, the ratio between consumption and capital is higher, *ceteris paribus*, the higher is the growth rate of consumption, the lower the growth rate of capital and the higher the level of risk taking, net of its effect on capital growth.

Substituting expression (9) into equation (2), on the other hand we obtain:

$$\frac{c}{k} = \frac{1}{\alpha}\left[\rho + \varepsilon\frac{\dot{\sigma}}{\sigma}\right] + \frac{g(\sigma)}{k} - \frac{\dot{k}}{k}, \text{ where } \varepsilon \text{ may be positive or negative.} \tag{12}$$

Expressions (11) and (12) show that the ratio between consumption and capital may be interpreted as depending either on the growth rate of consumption or on risk, but that these two alternative determinants are, in a sense, the two sides of the same coin. The consumption rate of growth and the rate of growth of risk taking, in fact, are determined by the same difference between the marginal productivity of capital, enhanced by the external effect of risk taking, and the rate of discount.

Consider again expressions (8) and (9). Assume that we start in an economy where a high degree of risk taking is made possible by the institutional arrangements, the existence of a well-organized capital market and the possibility of efficient risk sharing deriving from both these conditions. In this case capital accumulation will proceed at full speed and so will consumption and risk taking growth. If the fall in the marginal productivity of capital is more than countered by neutral technological progress engendered by risk taking, the increase in capital growth will proceed unabated until risk has reached its upper bound. Endogenous growth may thus go on both for capital (the productive base) and consumption. This happy occurrence, however, may not necessarily happen. Because the marginal productivity of capital falls toward zero, the multiplicative nature of neutral technological progress is such that it may be easily countered by a sufficiently rapid decrease in the marginal product of capital. A more vigorous initial uprising of risk and capital build up, in fact, may engender a more rapid fall in the rate of return to capital.

This vulnerability of the growth path to sudden decreases of productivity and possible reversals of growth suggests that a high risk environment, together with more ample opportunities for progress, presents several dangers. On one hand, in fact, not only the growth of risk cannot go on forever, but also a very high level of risk is difficult to sustain except for limited and possibly short periods of time. This may imply a certain endogeneity of the parameters of the utility function as well as of the productivity of risk to engender real innovations. These parameters will probably be unstable, and fluctuate partly in response to circumstances, exogenous technological progress and the famous 'sentiment' of the market. Secondly, even if agents were willing to undertake increasing amounts of risks, these would imply a parallel rise in the turbulence of the environment that would itself not be sustainable for long. Third, the rise of the capital stock versus consumption would also be a factor of fragility of the equilibrium, since capacity accumulation would continually run the danger of being confronted with a fall in effective demand. As capacity turns larger and larger, in other words, we should expect agents to become preoccupied with the potentially devastating effects of demand shocks. This would also, presumably, favor a change in the sentiment of the market, perhaps switching from a regime of decreasing risk aversion to one of increasing risk aversion.

If the institutional environment is not such, on the other hand, to ensure that risk taking may increase, without being forced down by increasing risk aversion and diseconomies of scale, an alternative sequence of events may materialize. In this case capital accumulation may cause the marginal productivity of capital to fall more than proportionally with respect to the increase in technological progress allowed by risk taking. This will cause risk taking and capital growth to fall. As capital starts de-cumulating, however, the difference between capital productivity and the discount rate will turn positive again, thereby starting another cycle of accumulation. Thus, in an economy where institutions allow high risk taking, decreasing risk aversion and low diseconomies of scale, the transitional dynamics of the model on hand are certainly positive at first, but they may turn out negative in a second phase. In an economy where the institutions are not so virtuous, on the other hand, things may look bad in the beginning, but may turn out to be better than predicted later on. In spite of the fact that risk taking is the engine of technological progress, in other words, its working on the economy may be more complex than it may appear at first sight. By favoring too much accumulation, in fact, risky innovations may turn out to concur in reducing the rate of return to capital below the discount rate, thereby stifling consumption growth and reducing the incentives to innovative enterprises.

5. The 'Steady State'

In order to solve some of the questions raised by the ambiguous characteristics of the optimal path, we now want to investigate the existence of a 'steady state', i.e. of a condition in which the growth rate of consumption, risk and capital are constant. We start with consumption and risk growth, which, in order to be constant, have to satisfy the condition that their derivative of (8) and (9) with relation to time be zero:

$$\dot{A}f_k + Af_{kk}\dot{k} = 0 \tag{13}$$

Which, in view of expression (3) and of the fact that $f_{kk} < 0$, may be written as:

$$\dot{k} = \frac{f_k}{|f_{kk}|} b\sigma \quad or \quad \frac{\dot{k}}{k} = \frac{b\sigma}{|\eta_k|} \tag{14}$$

where $|\eta_k| = \dfrac{|f_{kk}|}{f_k} k$ is the elasticity of the marginal utility of capital, i.e. a local measure of the convexity of the production function (or the severity of its decreasing returns to scale). Thus, a steady state requires that their local measure is constant, and this is so for all homogenous function of degree α and, in particular, for the so called Cobb-Douglas function:

$$q = Ak^{\alpha} \tag{15}$$

In this case, we can write:

$$\frac{\dot{k}}{k} = \frac{b\sigma}{1-\alpha} \tag{16}$$

Assume now that the utility and the production function exhibit constant elasticities. In this case, we can write the expressions for the private optimal growth rates as follows:

$$\frac{\dot{c}}{c} = \frac{1}{\eta}\left(\alpha Ak^{\alpha-1} - \rho\right) \tag{17}$$

$$\frac{\dot{\sigma}}{\sigma} = \frac{1}{\varepsilon}\left(\alpha Ak^{\alpha-1} - \rho\right) \tag{18}$$

where

$$U(c) = \frac{c^{1-\eta}}{1-\eta} \text{ and } - V(\sigma) = -\frac{\sigma^{1-\gamma}}{1-\gamma}, g(\sigma) = B\sigma^{\beta} \text{ and } \varepsilon = \gamma + \beta - 1.$$

In view of (16), if consumption and risk are characterized by constant growth, the marginal productivity of capital can be expressed as follows:

$$\alpha A k^{\alpha-1} = \alpha A(0) \exp\left(b \int_0^t \sigma(\tau) d\tau \right) \left[k(0) \exp\left(\frac{b}{1-\alpha}\right) \left(\int_0^t \sigma(\tau) d\tau \right) \right]^{\alpha-1} = \alpha A(0) k(0)^{\alpha-1} \quad (19)$$

The marginal productivity of capital thus converges to a constant that depends on initial conditions. As a consequence, consumption and risk may evolve at the constant rates given by:

$$\frac{\dot{c}}{c} = \frac{1}{\eta}\left(\alpha A(0) k(0)^{\alpha-1} - \rho\right) \quad (20)$$

$$\frac{\dot{\sigma}}{\sigma} = \frac{1}{\varepsilon}\left(\alpha A(0) k(0)^{\alpha-1} - \rho\right) \quad (21)$$

Consumption will thus grow at a constant rate, provided that the marginal productivity of capital defined by the initial conditions is greater than the rate of discount. Risk and capital, however, will follow a different course, according to whether the scale parameter ε is positive or negative. If it is positive, as it will presumably occur in a healthy environment, where managers are efficient and risks may be appropriately shared, risk taking will increase until it reaches its upper bound. Capital, on its part, will accumulate firstly at an increasing rate and then at a constant rate, according to expression (16). With capital and consumption growing at a constant rate, the marginal productivity of capital will be constant at the level indicated by (19). In this case the ratio between consumption and capital will be given by the expression:

$$\frac{c}{k} = A(0) k(0)^{\alpha-1} + \frac{B\bar{\sigma}^{\beta}}{k(0) e^{\frac{b}{1-\alpha}\bar{\sigma} t}} - \frac{b\bar{\sigma}}{1-\alpha} \quad (22)$$

where $\bar{\sigma}$ is the maximum bearable degree of risk.

The second term of the RHS of expression (22) will tend to zero as time tends to infinity, so that the ratio between consumption and capital will converge to a constant. The rates of growth of the two variables will thus be identical in the steady state. We can use this equality to obtain the initial level of capital consistent with the steady state:

$$k(0) = [\frac{1}{\alpha A(0)}(\eta \frac{b\bar{\sigma}}{1-\alpha} + \rho)]^{\frac{1}{\alpha-1}} \tag{23}$$

Expression (23) shows that, given an arbitrary initial level of total factor productivity *A(0)*, the corresponding level of capital consistent with the steady state is smaller, the larger the maximum bearable degree of risk. Thus, an economy that can bear a higher amount of risk can afford to access steady growth (of the endogenous variety) with a smaller stock of capital.

What happens if, on the other hand, the risk aversion scale parameter ε is negative? In this case, which may be construed to represent an economy with ineffective risk sharing arrangements and inefficient methods of selecting managers and projects, risk taking will go more or less gradually to zero. Capital growth will stop and, as a consequence, the only pattern of growth consistent with the steady state will be zero growth throughout. In spite of the possibility of endogenous growth, the economy will return on the path of neoclassical growth, with consumption given by:

$$c = \frac{\rho}{\alpha}k(0) \tag{24}$$

and capital by:

$$k(0) = \left(\frac{\rho}{\alpha A(0)}\right)^{\frac{1}{\alpha-1}} \tag{25}$$

In sum, the model may exhibit two alternative steady states: one of sustained growth and one of zero growth of the neoclassical type. In principle, both states can be reached from arbitrary initial conditions, regardless of risk aversion and technology parameters. An economy characterized by sufficiently decreasing risk aversion and not too large diseconomies of scale in risk taking on the production side, however, is more likely to converge to the sustained growth state, while an economy with lower propensity to assume risks is more likely to converge and stay on the zero growth path.

Table 6.1 Simulation of the Model under Endogenous Risk Taking (values after 2000 iterations)

M. Prod. Capital	Risk Level	Technical Progress	Innovation Increase	Capital Level	Capital Increase	% Capital Increase	Consump. Level	Consump. Increase	% Consump. Increase
0.02	2.310649	1.69E+36	7.795E+34	2.71E+53	1.80711E+52	0.066666667	0.190136	-6E-17	-3.2E-16g
0.089258	10	5E+153	1E+153	2.1E+220	6.2688E+219	0.29752599	3.7E+37	0.046172	0,29
0.043759	5	9.92E+81	9.92E+80	2.1E+118	3.1347E+117	0.145862238	2.69E+13	0.015839	0,15
0.026041	3	5.5E+50	3.302E+49	1.01E+74	8.74116E+72	0.08680402	4305.554	0.004027	0,09

Table 6.1 reports the main results of a simulation exercise, where the model has been run for a period of 2000 years, starting from a unit level of capital and technical progress. The model is based on the assumption of a Cobb-Douglas (separable) production function and an iso-elastic separable utility function, with parameter values: $\alpha = 0{,}3\beta = 0{,}3; \quad \eta = 1{,}5$. $\varepsilon = -2$ in the first experiment and +2 in the others.

6. Conclusions

Financing technology poses a special challenge to economic institutions for two main reasons. First, the uncertainty surrounding all the investment decisions is particularly acute and pervasive in the case of R&D, as well as developing and testing process and product innovation. Greater uncertainty spurs more highly asymmetric information on both sides of the financial deal, thus rendering contracts more difficult to negotiate, enforce and take successfully to completion. Further problems arise from lack of credit history for innovators, weak property rights and difficulty of supervising and monitoring increasingly intangible technologies (Scandizzo, 2001).

Second, technology ventures appear to face a basic trade-off between profit and growth, which may be exacerbated by a difficult relationship with credit institutions. For this reason, combined with the harder rationing of credit on the part of the bank, innovators generally prefer to invert the traditional order of financing sources. They thus favor resorting to equity over debt financing, even though this may involve loss of control or, at the very least, heavy interference in managing the firm on the part of outside financiers. It is indicative, in this respect, that most new capital in the US equity market has come in recent years in technology stocks. In this framework, the financing of Internet firms, at least in the first, most euphoric phase of growth of the NASDAQ, has been accomplished with risk capital and only a minimum resort to debt.

While the banks appear to have an important role to play, for many types of innovative businesses, they cannot be the sole source of financing. Indeed, in all advanced countries, regardless of the prevalence of the banking or the equity markets in their tradition, several operators have evolved that specialize in providing risk capital, combined with management skills and financial advice, to start-ups and high tech ventures. Among these operators venture capitalists and business angels figure prominently and, unlike banks, do not approach financing with their 'hands off', but rather with 'hands on' and 'gloves off'. They appear to be a critical element of success in the difficult and risky enterprise of recovering and providing fresh resources to finance innovation.

The prevalence of debt financing has a long history in the countries of continental Europe, while in the countries of the Anglo-Saxon tradition their presence is tempered, if not more than balanced by large and vital equity markets. These institutions appear to be capable of sustaining a higher degree of risk taking in the economy and this seems particularly important for innovation and the so-called 'new economy'. Is the extent of equity financing so important a systemic factor that it may be able to determine a form of self-sustained, endogenous growth? The answer to this question is necessarily problematic for several reasons. On one hand, Anglo-Saxon countries do give the impression of more flexible markets, where new and possibly risky ideas more easily flower and prosper. On the other hand, if the willingness to undertake risky enterprises may be rooted in the efficiency of the institutions and in the 'sentiment' of the agents, increasing risks cannot be borne out without ultimately rising costs. Thus, the very fact that the system is risk prone suggests that it may be subject to 'boom and burst' patterns, with risk aversion declining into elation during the 'booms', and increasing into self-fulfilling demise during the 'bursts'. Furthermore, a sustained growth based on increasing risks implies a more turbulent environment, with a higher rate of bankruptcies and higher social costs. These negative externalities will presumably be increasing and may catch up, eventually, with the positive ones even if 'sentiment' and 'animal spirits' remain favorably disposed. Finally, a high risk equilibrium is necessarily more fragile, in the sense that it may more easily be disrupted by external shocks. Higher propensities to take risks are generally associated with higher 'nervousness' and herd behavior, as any casual observer of the stock markets has abundantly noticed. Switching from 'bull' to 'bear' attitudes has been known to occur without credible warnings and, once established, bearish behavior may be particularly hard to reverse.

The above considerations do not deny the main thrust of the model result demonstrating the sharp difference between the characteristics of a 'high risk' versus a 'low risk' regime. They do however suggest that reality may in fact present a mix of the two and that this may be specially relevant for the equity driven economies. The more efficient systems of financing, in other words, because they are more firmly based on the willingness to share risks by a plurality of agents, would be, at the same time, more apt to take increasing risks and more vulnerable to sudden decreases of confidence in the economy. They would thus match more dynamic and higher risk performances with periods of crisis where preferences would turn against risk taking. In these periods perhaps the economic variables could follow evolutionary paths as conservative as those of the 'low risk' regime that are instead more typical of the economies dominated by banking and debt financing.

References

Aghion, P. and Howitt, P. (1992), 'A Model of Growth through Creative Destruction', *Econometrica*, March, 60(2), pp. 323-51.

Anton, J.J. and Yao, D.A. (1994), 'Expropriation and Inventions: Appropriable Rents in the Absence of Property Rights', *The American Economic Review*, 84(1), pp. 190-209.

Arrow, K.J. (1962), 'Economic Welfare and the Allocation of Resources for Invention', in R.R. Nelson (ed.), *The Rate and Direction of Inventive Activity: Economic and Social Factors*, Princeton University Press, Princeton.

Berger, A.N. and Udell, G. (1998), 'The Economics of Small Business Finance: The Roles of Private Equity and Debt Markets in the Financial Growth Cycle', *Journal of Banking and Finance*, 22(6-8), pp. 613-73.

Berkovitch, E. and Kim, E.H. (1990), 'Financial Contracting and Leverage Induced Over- and Under-Investment Incentives', *Journal of Finance*, XLV (3), July, pp. 765-794.

Bhattacharya, S. and Ritter, J.R. (1983), 'Innovation and Communication: Signalling with Partial Disclosure', *The Review of Economic Studies*, 207, pp. 197-222.

Brouwer, M. and Hendrix, B. (1998), 'Two Worlds of Venture Capital: What Happened to US and Dutch Early Stage Investment?', *Small Business Economics*, 10, pp. 333-48, Fall.

Brown, W. (1997), 'R&D Intensity and Finance: Are Innovative Firms Financially Constrained?', *Financial Markets Group Discussion Papers* 271, London School of Economics.

Brynjolfsson, E. and Hitt, L. (2000), 'Beyond Computation: Information Technology, Organizational Transformation and Business Performance', *Journal of Economic Perspectives*, 14(4), pp. 23-48.

Carpenter, R.E., Fazzari, S.M. and Petersen, B.C. (1995), 'Three Financing Constraint Hypotheses and Inventory Investment: New Tests with Time and Sectoral Heterogeneity', *Economics Working Paper Archive*, University of Washington [reference no. ewp-mac/9510001].

Cobham, A. (1999), 'The Financing and Technology Decisions of SMEs: 1. Finance as a Determinant of Investment', *Working Paper*, 24, Finance and Trade Policy Research Centre, University of Oxford, Oxford.

Gordon, R.J., (2000), 'Does the "New Economy" Measure up to the Great Inventions of the Past?', NBER Working Paper No. W7833, August.

Greenwald, B., Salinger M. and Stiglitz J.E. (1990), 'Imperfect Capital Market and Productivity Growth', mimeo, Stanford University.

Guiso, L. (1997), 'High-Tech Firms, Asymmetric Information and Credit Rationing', in Bagella, M. (ed.), *Finance, Investment and Innovation: Theory and Empirical Evidence*, Ashgate, Aldershot, England, pp. 275-307.

Hall, B. (1992), 'Investment and Research and Development at the Firm Level: Does the Source of Financing Matter?', *Brooking Papers on Economic Activity*, 1, pp. 85-136.

Hamburg, D. (1966), *Essays on the Economics of Research and Development*, Random House, New York.

Hao, K.Y. and Jaffe, A.B. (1993), 'Effect of Liquidity on Firm's R&D Spending', *Economic Innovation and New Technology*, 2, pp. 275-282.

Hicks, J.R. (1969), *A Theory of Economic History*, Clarendon Press, Oxford.

Himmelberg, C.P. and Petersen, B.C. (1994), 'R&D and Internal Finance: A Panel Study of Small Firms in High-Tech Industries', *Review of Economics and Statistics*, LXXVI(1), pp. 38-51.

Jensen, M.C. and Meckling, W.H. (1976), 'Theory of the Firm: Managerial Behaviour, Agency Costs and Ownership Structure', *Journal of Financial Economics*, 3, pp. 305-360.

Jorgenson, D. (2001), 'Information Technology and the US Economy', *American Economic Review* 91, 1 (March): pp. 1-32.

Kortum, S. and Lerner, J. (1998), 'Does Venture Capital Spur Innovation?', *Working Paper*, 6846, National Bureau of Economic Research, Cambridge (MA).

Levine, R. (1997), 'Financial Development and Economic Growth: Views and Agenda', *Journal of Economic Literature*, Vol. 35(2), pp. 688-726.

Levine, R. and Zervos, S. (1995), *Stock Markets, Banks, and Economic Growth*, World Bank, processed.

Lucas, R.E. Jr. (1988), 'On the Mechanisms of Economic Development', *Journal of Monetary Economics*, 22(1), pp. 3-42.

Muller, D.C. (1967), 'The Firm Decision Process: an Econometric Investigation', *The Quarterly Journal of Economics*, 2, pp. 395-442.

Myers, S.C. (1977), 'Determinants of Corporate Borrowing', *Journal of Financial Economics*, 5, pp. 147-175.

Paganetto, L. and Scandizzo, P.L. (2000), 'Post-Fordism, New Economy and the Case of the Italian "Mezzogiorno"', *Villa Mondragone Paper*, June.

Paganetto, L. and Scandizzo, P.L. (2001), *Crescita Endogena ed Economia Aperta*, Il Mulino, Bologna.

Phelps, E. (1999), 'Creating the Institutions for Capitalism in Italy and Wage Setting Plans for the "Mezzogiorno"', *5th Semi-annual Advisor's Report, November, CNR Strategic Project: Italy in Europe*.

Reekie, W.D. and Crook, J.N. (1995), *Managerial Economics*, Prentice Hall, London.

Romer, P.M. (1986), 'Increasing Returns and Long-run Growth', *Journal of Political Economy*, 94(5), pp. 1002-37.

Scandizzo, P.L. (1997), 'The Structure of Financing and Intellectual Property Rights', in Bagella, M. (ed.), *Finance, Investment and Innovation: Theory and Empirical Evidence*, Ashgate, Aldershot, England, pp. 393-407.

Scandizzo, P.L. (2001), 'Financing Technology: An Assessment of Theory And Practice', Global Forum on Technology Management with Focus on the Arab Region, UNIDO, Vienna, 29-30 May.

Scherer, F.M. (1965), 'Firm Size, Market Structure, Opportunity and the Output of Patented Inventions', *American Economic Review*, 55, pp. 1097-1125.

Stiglitz, J. (1993), 'Endogenous Growth and Cycles', *Working Paper*, 4286, National Bureau of Economic Research, Cambridge (MA).

Temple, J. (1999), 'The New Growth Evidence', *Journal of Economic Literature*, 37(1), pp. 112-156.

Chapter 7

Capital Market Imperfections, High-Tech Investment and New Equity Financing

Robert E. Carpenter and Bruce C. Petersen

1. Introduction

Standard neoclassical models of investment typically assume that capital markets are perfect. In recent years, however, a body of theoretical work has challenged the key assumptions required for perfect capital markets. If the firm has better information about its investment returns than potential investors, external finance may be expensive, if available at all, because of adverse selection and moral hazard problems. These problems are accentuated when assets have low collateral value. In addition to this theoretical work, a large number of recent empirical studies report evidence that investment for some firms appears to depend on their financial condition.[1] There are, however, potential weaknesses in the empirical methodologies used to test for the presence of financing constraints, and some of the key evidence in the financing constraint literature has recently been challenged.[2] The nature of the imperfections in capital markets, how to detect their presence, and how to measure their quantitative impact on firm investment remains controversial.

This chapter examines how capital market imperfections may affect firms in high-tech industries. There are three reasons why high-tech investment is particularly likely to be affected by capital market imperfections. First, the returns to high-tech investment are skewed and highly uncertain, in part because R&D projects have a low probability of financial success.[3] Second, substantial information asymmetries are likely to exist between firms and potential investors. Because high-tech investments are difficult to evaluate and frequently embody new

---

1 For reviews of the literature, see Schiantarelli (1995) and Hubbard (1998). For an extended discussion of the financing problems facing small high-tech firms in the UK, see the Bank of England, 1996.

2 A criticism of some studies is that investment demand is difficult to measure with precision and cash flow, a proxy for access to internal finance, may be positively correlated with demand, rather than reflecting the relative severity of financing constraints. Kaplan and Zingales (1997) challenge much of the empirical financing constraint literature. Fazzari, Hubbard and Petersen (2000) dispute most of Kaplan and Zingales's criticisms.

3 Mansfield et al. (1977) report a probability of financial success for R&D projects of only 27 per cent. Harhoff, Narin, Scherer and Vopel (1999) report evidence on the high degree of skewness of the returns of German patents.

knowledge, insiders will have much better information than outsiders about the prospects of the firm's investments.[4] Even if firms could educate outsiders, appropriability problems may induce firms to limit the amount of information they are willing to provide to suppliers of funds. Firms in many US industries appear to view patents as an ineffective method of appropriating returns to R&D and often prefer secrecy (Levin, Klevoric, Nelson and Winter, 1987). Finally, high-tech investments often have limited collateral value. R&D investment, which is predominantly salary payments, has little salvage value in the event of failure. Furthermore, physical investments designed to embody R&D results are likely to be firm-specific, and therefore may have little collateral value.

Surprisingly, high-tech investment has received very little attention in the empirical literature on financing constraints.[5] Research has not focused on particular sectors of the economy, but has instead examined such issues as the role of firm size and the importance of access to publicly traded debt.[6] One theme of our chapter is that financing constraints arising from imperfections in capital markets may have a much greater impact on some sectors, in particular high-tech, than in other sectors, such as retail and wholesale trade. An important reason to examine the high-tech sector is because it supplies much of the new knowledge required for economic development. If financing constraints are widespread in the high-tech sector they could potentially inhibit economic growth. Finally, the high-tech sector provides an excellent example for discussing key ideas in the literature on capital market imperfections.

The second dimension of our chapter is an examination of the role new equity finance (i.e. issues of new shares) may play in partially relaxing financing constraints. We consider equity finance for several reasons. First, most of the literature on capital market imperfections has focused on debt finance, often assuming that new equity finance is prohibitively expensive or unavailable. Second, new equity has many advantages over debt for financing high-tech investment. Equity financing does not require collateral or increase the probability of financial distress, and investors' upside returns are not bounded. Third, in recent years the use of equity finance and the number of initial public offerings appear to have risen sharply in a number of countries, including the US, UK, and Japan. Given the problems with debt financing, countries with relatively well-developed markets for

---

[4] Cornell and Shapiro (1988, p. 14) provide a succinct statement of the problem: 'The credibility gap between management and investors is likely to be most pronounced in the case of growth companies because management in such cases will often have far better information about future profitability of undeveloped products and untapped niches. This greater possibility for important information increases the amount by which investors will discount the price of new corporate securities to compensate for information disadvantages.'

[5] One exception is Himmelberg and Petersen (1994), who examine R&D investment for a comparatively small set of firms in the high-tech sector. They find evidence of financing constraints for both R&D and physical investment. See also Harhoff (1998).

[6] Some examples include Gilchrist and Himmelberg (1995), who consider both size and access to public debt, and Calomiris, Himmelberg and Wachtel (1995). Carpenter, Fazzari and Petersen (1994) use firm size as proxy for access to external finance and examine whether inventory cycles can be explained by fluctuations in internal finance.

venture capital and new equity may have a comparative advantage in the production of high-tech goods.

We examine an unbalanced panel of over 2400 publicly traded US high-tech companies over the period 1981 to 1998. Most of these firms become publicly traded firms ('go public') during the sample period. We find that most small and medium-sized high-tech firms make little use of debt finance. For small firms, virtually all long-term debt is secured debt. New equity financing, however, plays a critical role at the time the firm makes its initial public offering (IPO). The IPO is typically very large relative to the size of the firm and it often leads to a dramatic change in the firm's size. This increase in size could be difficult to achieve if the firm's only source of external finance was debt. We find that most firms do not continue to make heavy use of external equity finance after they go public. Rather, the typical firm finances most of its growth with internal finance. These financing patterns suggest that many publicly traded high-tech firms, especially small firms, face financing constraints on investment and that new equity finance may be key to their growth.

Policy makers in Europe have recognized the importance of promoting markets for risk capital and liquid equity markets for the development of small, high-technology companies. The US is frequently used as a benchmark for comparison for other countries' high-tech sectors and risk capital markets (e.g., HM Treasury, 1998, p. 13). Consequently, our results may be informative for the conduct of public policy in Europe.

The next section of the chapter summarizes the reasons why the extensive use of debt finance is likely to be prohibitively costly or unavailable for firms in high-tech industries. Section 3 describes the potential advantages and disadvantages of external equity finance. The discussion in sections 2 and 3 helps explain the financing choices of high-tech firms. Section 4 examines the financing patterns of high-tech firms and presents new empirical evidence on the lack of debt finance and the role of new equity financing for high-tech firms. The last section briefly discusses the critical role of venture capital in bringing high-tech firms to the stage where they can conduct an IPO. We also discuss how the relative lack of venture and equity capital in Europe may impede the development of the European high-technology sector.

2. Problems With Debt

Most of the modern literature on capital market imperfections and financing constraints has ignored external equity financing, focusing instead on the firm's access to debt. This focus is due in part to the literature's emphasis on macroeconomic issues, particularly the role played by credit market frictions in propagating cyclical fluctuations (e.g., Greenwald and Stiglitz, 1993; Bernanke, Gertler and Gilchrist, 1998). In Hubbard's (1998) review of the empirical literature, his discussion of financing constraints is motivated by the link between collateral net worth and the cost of debt. Schiantarelli's (1995) summary of the international evidence and the empirical methodologies, particularly the modeling of debt in the

Euler equation for the capital stock of the firm, highlights the literature's focus on debt finance.

There are several reasons why the extensive use of debt finance may be inappropriate for high-tech firms and why their shadow cost of debt finance may increase rapidly with greater leverage. First, the very nature of the debt contract is not well suited for high-tech investment. Creditors do not share in firms' returns in good states of nature, and thus 'lenders are only concerned with the bottom part of the tail of the distribution of returns' (Stiglitz, 1985, p. 146). When borrowers' returns are highly uncertain, as they are in the high-tech sector, extensive use of debt may provide negative expected returns to lenders.

Second, adverse selection problems in debt markets are likely to be most pronounced for high-tech investment. High-tech investment involves much greater uncertainty about returns than typical investments. It is also likely that firms have better knowledge than lenders about the inherent riskiness of projects. In such an environment, lenders may choose to ration credit, rather than raise interest rates, in the hopes of not exacerbating adverse selection problems (e.g., Jaffee and Russell, 1976; Stiglitz and Weiss, 1981). Credit rationing could cause the debt supply schedule to become vertical.

Third, debt financing can lead to *ex post* changes in behavior (moral hazard). High-tech firms are likely to have the greatest scope for substituting high-risk projects for relatively low-risk projects. When creditors anticipate this behavior, they may ration credit or insist that covenants be attached to debt that restrict the firm's behavior. Since moral hazard problems increase with the degree of leverage, the restrictions placed on the firm should become more severe as leverage increases.

Fourth, much of high-tech investment is intangible or firm-specific and therefore provides little or no *inside* collateral value.[7] A large body of research points to the importance of collateral for debt finance. Bester (1985, 1987) shows that collateral can be used as a signaling device to separate high-risk from low-risk borrowers and as an incentive device to confront problems of moral hazard. Boot, Thakor and Udell (1991) provide a theoretical model, together with empirical evidence, showing that collateral can be a powerful instrument for dealing with moral hazard. Berger and Udell (1990) state: 'Collateral plays an important role in U.S. domestic bank lending, as evidenced by the fact that nearly 70 per cent of all commercial and industrial loans are currently made on a secured basis.'[8] Berger and Udell (1998) summarize the empirical findings on collateral and conclude that

---

7 Berger and Udell (1998, pp. 639-642) provide an overview of the literature on inside and outside collateral. Outside collateral involves assets outside of the firm (e.g., the owner's personal assets). While outside collateral is important for very small firms, inside collateral is presumably the critical form of collateral for firms of some size (e.g., corporations with multiple shareholders). Berger and Udell (1998) note that the practitioner literature has focused on inside collateral and usually predicts that lenders will more often require riskier borrowers to secure their loans.

8 Cressy and Toivanen (1998) provide similar evidence on the proportion of loans that are collateralized in Europe.

riskier firms are more likely to pledge collateral. Empirical evidence suggests that there is a negative relationship between a firm's leverage and its intangible assets.[9] The lack of collateral assets held by high-tech firms should limit their access to debt financing.

Finally, the expected marginal costs of financial distress are likely to rise rapidly with greater leverage. Brealey and Myers (2000, pp. 510-523) review the many types of costs associated with financial distress, including enhanced conflict of interest problems between stockholders and lenders. They single out high-tech firms – because of their high degree of intangible and firm-specific assets – as an example where the costs of distress will be important. In particular, financial distress can lead to the loss of key employees and the abandonment of critical projects. Much of the market value for young high-tech firms is based on future options that rapidly depreciate when firms face financial distress (Cornell and Shapiro, 1988).

Berger and Udell (2002) emphasize 'one of the most powerful technologies available to reduce information problems in small firm finance is relationship lending'. They explain that, under relationship lending, 'banks acquire information over time through contacts with the firm, its owner and its local community on a variety of dimensions ...' They point out that small businesses tend to have long relationships with their banks. Relationship lending, however, may not work well in all sectors of the economy. In particular, young high-tech firms, because they operate in a rapidly changing environment, may have to make major investments in a time frame that is too brief to develop a close relationship with a lender. Evidence in Gompers and Lerner (1999) and Ritter (1991) shows that high-tech firms receive external equity financing at a very young age.[10]

De Meza and Webb (1987, 1990) and de Meza (2002) present provocative models of asymmetric information in debt markets where the equilibrium outcome is characterized by overlending as opposed to the underlending that we emphasize in this chapter. While their models may be insightful for some sectors of the economy, we believe that it is unlikely for the high-tech sector to be characterized by too much lending. Their models do not capture all of the reasons (e.g., financial distress) why the shadow cost of debt finance may increase rapidly with greater leverage for high-tech firms. In particular, their models do not capture the fact that inside collateral may be a critical determinant of the size of loans.[11] As discussed

---

9 See Gompers and Lerner (1999, pp. 143-144) for a brief review of the literature.

10 Berger and Udell (2002, Table 7.2) report that the average length of the relationship between the sample firms and their banks is 9.37 years, indicating a lengthy relationship. In contrast, Gompers and Lerner (1999, Table 7.4) indicate that the first private equity financing typically occurs when firms are only a few years old. Ritter (1991) presents evidence that shows the high-tech firms in his sample go public when they are very young. (In the industries that correspond approximately to those in our sample, the weighted average of the firms' age at the IPO was 5.4 years.)

11 In de Meza and Webb (1987), entrepreneurs invest their personal wealth in the project. de Meza (2002) refers to the personal wealth as collateral. The entrepreneur's wealth, however, is not part of the bank's return in the event of bankruptcy. That is, the loan is not secured in the sense that, in the event of bankruptcy, inside or outside assets go to the bank.

above, the evidence indicates that when uncertainty is great, banks will likely insist that loans be secured by collateral, and inside collateral is severely limited for high-tech firms. Finally, we will present findings indicating very low debt usage, both prior to and after the IPO, for the high-tech firms in our sample.

In summary, for high-tech firms, the limited collateral value of assets, together with adverse selection, moral hazard, and financial distress should cause the marginal cost of debt to increase rapidly with leverage. These factors can cause a large difference between the intersection of supply and demand under perfect capital markets and the intersection of supply and demand when the marginal cost of debt is upward sloping.

3. Is New Equity Financing a Solution?

Most theoretical models of financing constraints assume that financing with new share issues is impossible or prohibitively expensive.[12] However, the rapidly growing number of publicly traded companies in many developed economies, together with the creation of equity markets in many developing nations, suggests the role of new equity financing should be given more consideration in models of imperfect capital markets. One recent effort is Bolton and Freixas (2000, p. 325) who 'provide the first synthesis of capital structure choice theories and financial market equilibrium based on information and incentive considerations'. In their capital market equilibrium, the riskiest firms (e.g., start-ups) do not receive debt financing but they may obtain equity financing.

For firms in the high-tech sector, new equity has a number of advantages over debt. Equity finance does not require the firm to post collateral, investors' upside returns are not bounded, and additional equity financing does not increase the probability of financial distress. In addition, equity financing does not create incentives for managers to substitute towards excessively risky projects.[13]

There are, however, capital market imperfections for new equity that can lead to a substantial wedge between the costs of internal and external equity financing. Lee, Lockhead, Ritter and Zhao (1996) report average issue costs (i.e. underwriter spreads and administrative costs) of over 13 per cent for issues of

---

[12] The reviews of the literature by Hubbard (1998) and Schiantarelli (1995) indicate that little attention has been given to new equity financing. Most studies do not mention equity as a possible source of finance. Many studies (e.g., Greenwald and Stigliz, 1993, p. 79) explicitly assume that external equity financing is prohibitively expensive.

[13] As discussed in Jensen and Meckling (1976), issuing external equity may have agency costs. When the owner-manager owns a smaller fraction of the firm, there may be a reduction in effort. We note, however, that for young start-up firms, owner-managers typically have most of their wealth and compensation tied up in the fate of the firm. This suggests that owner-managers will have very powerful incentives to put forth maximum effort.

seasoned equity of less than $10 million and costs of nearly 10 per cent for issues between $10 and $20 million. Their estimates for IPOs are larger still.[14]

A second source of the wedge is the lemons premium caused by adverse selection problems arising from asymmetric information. Myers and Majluf (1984) build on Akerlof's (1970) 'market-for-lemons' paper to explain why asymmetric information may force firms to sell equity at a sharp discount, if they can sell it at all. Himmelberg and Petersen (1994) argue that adverse selection problems may be pronounced in high-tech industries because firms may have to actively maintain information asymmetries to appropriate returns on innovation. Empirical evidence indicates that the lemons premium can be large. For example, Asquith and Mullins (1986, p. 85) report that the drop in the value of outstanding shares when primary new equity issues are announced averages 31 per cent of the planned proceeds of the issue.[15] Brealey and Myers (2000, p. 423) state: 'Most financial economists now interpret the stock price drop on equity issue announcements as an information effect and not a result of the additional supply.'

We now turn to an examination of the financing patterns of high-tech firms. The arguments in section 2 suggest that small, high-tech firms should use little debt both prior to and after going public. The arguments in section 3 (summarized in Table 7.2) indicate that the size of the IPO may be very large relative to the size of the firm. We therefore examine both the absolute and relative magnitudes of the IPO. We also consider the role of internal versus external equity financing after the IPO. If new equity issues after the IPO send strong negative signals to investors, it may cause firms to rely predominantly on internal equity financing after they go public.[16]

4. The Financing of High-Tech Firms

The Data and Sample of Firms

We use the most recent version of the Compustat tapes to construct the sample. To permit identification of changes in financial patterns over time, we divide the sample period into three six-year sub-periods: 1981-1986, 1987-1992, and 1993-

---

[14] Jenkinson (1990) provides a comparison of the regulations governing the IPO process in the US and UK. He reports slightly smaller direct costs of making an IPO in the UK, but like the US, direct costs are larger for smaller issues.

[15] This evidence is consistent with Loughran and Ritter (1997), who find that firms appear to take advantage of information asymmetries in their choice of the timing of new share issues. There is also a substantial body of evidence supporting a lemons premium for IPOs. See, for example, the review of the literature in Gompers and Lerner (1999, Chapter 10).

[16] In the model developed by Myers and Majluf (1984), assets in place are critical to the size of the lemons premium and whether good firms choose to issue stock. For start-up companies, assets in place are typically very small. After the IPO, however, assets in place are larger, and therefore asymmetric information may cause more serious adverse selection problems in the market for follow-up equity issues.

1998. We select the set of high-technology industries based on the US Department of Commerce's classification of high technology.[17] The list of industries in the sample consists of: drugs and medicinals (SIC 283), office and computing equipment (SIC 357), communications equipment (SIC 366), electronics components (SIC 367), industrial measuring instruments (SIC 382) and surgical instruments (SIC 384). All of these industries are very R&D intensive, particularly when they are compared to the rest of the US manufacturing sector.[18]

One advantage of our data is that we have not only data for existing publicly traded companies, but also financial information for firms just before they go public. Standard and Poor's, which maintains the data, informed us that Compustat typically contains one or two years of data (from the company's prospectus) prior to the year in which the firm goes public. Standard and Poor's also informed us that the first incidence of a non-missing stock price indicates the year in which the firm goes public.[19]

Table 7.1 reports the number of firms that are already public at the beginning of our sample period as well as the number of firms that go public over each of the three sub-periods of the data. The first column of Table 7.1 indicates that the data contain 630 publicly traded firms in 1981. Drug and medicinals has the fewest number of firms (72) and office and computing equipment has the largest (127). The next three columns report the number of new public firms, by period, in each of the six high-tech industries. There are 605 new public firms in the first period, 500 in the second, and 703 in the last period. The industry with the largest number of new public firms is computing equipment in the first period, surgical instruments in the second period, and drugs and medicinals in the last period.

---

[17] US Department of Commerce, 'An Assessment of US Competitiveness in High-Technology Industries', February 1983. We exclude industries from the Department of Commerce's list that have only a small number of firms (SIC 361, 362, 366, 386, and 387). We also exclude the aerospace industries because the US government supplies much of the financing for R&D.

[18] The ratio of R&D spending to total assets for all manufacturing industries not included in our definition of high-tech was less than two per cent at the median, far smaller than the R&D intensity we find in the firms in our sample.

[19] In approximately 85 per cent of the cases, Compustat reports information for a new firm one or two years prior to it becoming a public firm. We checked the company histories of a large fraction of the new firms to determine if the initial public offering occurs in the year the stock price appears. We found no exceptions. We excluded a small number of new firms with missing values for new equity from the sample.

Table 7.1 Sample Composition: Number of Existing and New Public Firms

	Industry	1981 # Existing Firms	1981-1986 Entry	1987-1992 Entry	1993-1998 Entry
1.	283 Drugs and Medicinals	72	103	131	204
2.	357 Office and Computing Equipment	127	145	94	130
3.	366 Communications Equipment	93	94	47	92
4.	367 Electronics Components	118	68	50	92
5.	382 Industrial Measuring Instruments	129	77	44	68
6.	384 Surgical Instruments	91	118	134	117
7.	Column Total	630	605	500	703

The Absolute and Relative Size of the IPO

Table 7.2 reports information on the size of firms and the absolute and relative magnitude of equity issues for the year that the firm goes public. Since the cross-industry variation is not substantial and to economize on space, we have not reported the results for individual industries. We report information at both the median and the 90th percentiles of the distribution. Most firms are small at the time they go public. The median firm had 89 employees in the first period, 70 in the second, and 75 in the last period. Employment at the 90th percentile is close to 500 employees in each of the periods. In terms of total assets, which consist primarily of physical investment and working capital, but not R&D investment, the median firm had slightly more than $5 million in the first two periods and approximately $9 million in the last period. Overall, the size distribution of firms is similar across the three time periods. Total assets are commonly used as a measure of firm size, and we use it as the scale factor in subsequent tables.

Table 7.2 Sample Statistics for Firms in the Year of their IPO

		1981-1986		1987-1992		1993-1998	
		50th	90th	50th	90th	50th	90th
1.	Employment	89	468	70	500	75	483
2.	Total Assets (millions of $)	5.22	30.92	5.25	39.26	9.14	40.56
3.	Ratio of Long-Term Debt to Total Assets	0.08	0.41	0.05	0.50	0.05	0.50
4.	Ratio of New Long-Term Debt to Total Assets (flow)	-0.002	0.22	-0.004	0.18	-0.01	0.10
5.	New Equity Issues (Millions of $)	5.27	31.51	8.99	44.29	17.67	51.36
6.	Ratio of New Equity to Total Assets	1.36	7.86	1.73	10.31	2.10	12.38

Note: Dollar figures are expressed in real terms (1992=100). Total assets and the ratio of long-term debt to total assets (stock) are calculated using their beginning-of-year values.

Rows 3 and 4 show the firms' use of debt finance in the year of the IPO. Row 3 shows the beginning-of-year stock of long-term debt scaled by total assets. The median debt-asset ratio is 0.080 in the first period and 0.050 in the next two periods, indicating low debt use just prior to the IPO. Row 4 shows the flow of debt finance in the year of the IPO. The median firm retires a small amount of debt while firms at the 90th percentile have positive debt flows. The small debt stocks are consistent with the theoretical prediction that high-tech firms do not use debt finance extensively. As we now show, the stock and flow of debt ratios are very small when compared to the new equity raised by firms in the year of the IPO.

Rows 5 and 6 provide information on the absolute and relative size of new equity issues. Median new equity issues (in 1992 dollars) have risen from $5.27 million in the first period to $17.67 million in the last period. At the 90th percentile, the figures are much larger, ranging from $31.51 million to $51.36 million. Median values of new equity issues relative to beginning-of-year assets is 1.36 in the first period and 2.10 in the last period. At the 90th percentile, they range from 7.86 in the first period to 12.38 in the last period. The results show the importance of the

IPO for increasing the size of the firm. The median new public firm doubles, or even triples, its assets. Firms in the tail of the distribution increase their asset size by ten-fold or more with their IPO. Over time, there has been a sharp rise in both the absolute and the relative size of the IPO.

Table 7.3 Use of Equity by New Public Firms: Post-IPO

	Median	*t+0*	*t+1*	*t+2*	*t+3*	*t+4*	*t+5*
1.	New Equity Issues (Millions of $)	10.15	0.29	0.53	0.62	0.54	0.46
2.	Ratio of New Equity to Total Assets	1.76	0.01	0.02	0.02	0.02	0.01
	90th Percentile	*t+0*	*t+1*	*t+2*	*t+3*	*t+4*	*t+5*
3.	New Equity Issues (Millions of $)	44.45	15.60	16.71	13.35	15.39	12.62
4.	Ratio of New Equity to Total Assets	10.48	0.89	0.92	0.93	0.83	0.70

Note: the year of the IPO has the time index *t*+0. Dollar figures are expressed in real terms (1992=100).

Table 7.3 reports information on the absolute and relative size of equity issues by new public firms in the year of the IPO and for the five years following it. Reading across the top of the table, the year the firm goes public is denoted *t+0*. Rows 1 and 2 report the median value of new equity issues and the size of the issue scaled by the firm's beginning-of-year assets. In the year of the IPO, median new equity, combining the data for all three sub-periods of the sample, is approximately $10 million and the median ratio of new equity to total assets is 1.76. In year *t+1*, new equity financing plummets, falling to $0.29 million. The equity finance-total asset ratio falls to 0.011. The median values for both statistics in years *t+2* through *t+5* are only slightly larger than those for *t+1*.

Rows 3 and 4 report the absolute and relative size of equity issues at the 90th percentile. In the year of the IPO, the value of the equity issue is $44.45 million, and the relative size of the issue is 10.48. These figures fall within the range of results (for the corresponding statistics) reported for the three sub-periods in Table 7.2. Like the medians, the value of equity issues at the 90th percentile, as well as the relative size of the issue, drops off sharply in year *t+1*. Funds raised by issuing new shares fall to $15.60 million and size of the equity issue relative to the firm's total assets is 0.89. The values in *t+2* to *t+5* are similar to those in *t+1*. The results in Table 7.3 indicate that after the IPO, equity issues drop off dramatically for most firms.[20] Some firms, however, continue to use equity after the IPO in quantities large enough to substantially increase their size.

We also computed the size of the median firm for the years immediately following the IPO. Firms experience a very sharp increase in size. At *t+0*, the median firm has assets of $6.9 million and 85 employees. By *t+5*, the median firm has assets of $23.37 million and 144 employees, or more than a three-fold increase in assets and a 70 per cent increase in employees. The IPO appears to bring about a very large increase in firm size.

After the IPO: The Financing Behavior of Established Firms

Table 7.4 reports information on the sources and uses of finance for established firms. Established firms are defined as those who have been publicly traded for at least two years. Thus, two years after going public, the firms examined in Table 7.2 are allowed to enter the data used to construct Table 7.4. Because the literature on financing constraints has argued that small firms are more likely to face substantial financing constraints, we break the established firms into three size classes. Small firms are defined as those with asset sizes between $1 and $50 million; medium firms have assets between $50 and $250 million; and large firms have assets greater than $250 million. For each of these three size categories, we calculated the financial statistics for each of the three sub-periods reported in Tables 7.2 and 7.3. With only a few exceptions noted below, the results are stable over time. Therefore, to simplify the presentation, we report Table 7.4 for the entire sample period. Because the sample period spans 17 years, we allow firms to move between size categories.

To construct the results in Table 7.4, we calculate the financial ratios for each year for each firm. We use beginning-of-year assets as the scale factor. For each size category, we use the firm's average (while it is in a size category) as a data point when we compute the distribution of the ratios. An alternative approach would be to use each observation for each firm as a data point. This approach, however, would understate the importance of external finance if it is 'lumpy' because of fixed issue costs. We report the median and 90th percentile of each variable. Rows 2 through 4 report information on uses of finance while rows 5 through 10 provide information on sources of finance.

---

[20] The results are similar for other points in the distribution. In all years after the IPO, equity issues at the 10th percentile are zero and are very small at the 25th percentile. At the 75th percentile, for t+0 through t+5, issue sizes are: $24.78, $2.50, $3.64, $3.65, $4.19 and $3.43. The corresponding relative issue sizes are: 4.34, 0.190, 0.285, 0.234, 0.187 and 0.113.

Table 7.4 Summary Statistics: Established Firms

		Small Firms		Medium Firms		Large Firms	
		50th	90th	50th	90th	50th	90th
1.	Number of Firms	1030		582		268	
2.	Ratio of Investment to Total Assets	0.05	0.12	0.07	0.15	0.08	0.18
3.	Ratio of R&D Spending to Total Assets	0.11	0.39	0.11	0.29	0.09	0.21
4.	Ratio of Dividends to Total Assets	0	0.02	0	0.02	0	0.03
5.	Ratio of Gross Cash Flow to Total Assets	0.20	0.51	0.30	0.60	0.31	0.54
6.	Ratio of (Gross Cash Flow, Investment, R&D) to Total Assets	0.03	0.21	0.10	0.28	0.12	0.27
7.	Ratio of New Long-Term Debt to Total Assets (flow)	0	0.09	0	0.12	0.02	0.18
8.	Ratio of Long-Term Debt to Total Assets (stock)	0.08	0.32	0.08	0.42	0.15	0.42
9.	Ratio of Secured Debt to Total Long-Term Debt	0.96	1.22	0.70	1.10	0.13	1.00
10.	Ratio of Equity Finance to Total Assets	0.05	0.62	0.02	0.39	0.01	0.12

Note: gross cash flow (row 5) is defined as cash flow plus research and development expenses.

The ratio of physical investment to assets and the ratio of R&D expenditures to assets are listed in rows 2 and 3. The median values for the physical investment ratio range from 0.05 for small firms to 0.08 for large firms. The median values for the R&D ratio are large, and range from 0.11 for small firms to 0.09 for large firms. At the 90th percentile, R&D expenditures are extremely high, especially for small firms. These results indicate that for many high-tech firms, R&D investment is often much greater than physical investment. The results also underscore the fact that a large fraction of a high-tech firm's investment is intangible, particularly for small firms. Row 4 reports the ratio of dividends to assets. The median value is zero for all size classes. Even at the 90th percentile, dividend payouts are small, indicating that most firms retain essentially all of their internal funds, as would be expected if there are financing constraints.

The remainder of Table 7.4 reports information on the firms' sources of finance. Following Hall (1992) and Himmelberg and Petersen (1994), we define gross cash flow as cash flow plus R&D expenses. We add R&D back to cash flow because R&D is treated as an expense for accounting purposes, not as an investment. Gross cash flow scaled by assets provides a measure of the internal finance of the firm available for total investment, including R&D. Since we wish to compare the size of cash flow relative to investment, we also construct the ratio of gross cash flow net of physical investment and R&D to total assets.

In row 5, the median value of the gross cash flow to asset ratio ranges from 0.20 for small firms to 0.31 for large firms. For all size classes, internal finance typically exceeds the sum of physical plus R&D investment. The gross cash flow to asset ratio exceeds the sum of the median values of the investment to asset ratio plus the R&D to asset ratio at both the median and the 90th percentile. Row 6, which reports gross cash flow net of physical investment and R&D, divided by assets, confirms this fact. At the median, this ratio is 0.03 for small firms and it is larger for the other two size classes. Since the sample firms do not typically pay dividends, one may wonder where the residual cash flow is going. Part of the residual cash flow is used for working capital investment, which includes inventories and accounts receivable (see Fazzari and Petersen, 1993 and Carpenter, Fazzari and Petersen, 1994). In addition, firms can also use cash flow to acquire the assets of other firms.[21]

Row 7 reports that the ratio of the median flow of new long-term debt relative to assets is zero, or close to zero, in all size classes. At the 90th percentile, the use of debt is modest, and it is only about 50 per cent of the size of *median* gross cash flow. Row 8 reports the ratio of the stock of long-term debt to assets. For small and medium firms, the median value is 0.08, similar to the value reported in Table 7.2 for firms at the time of the IPO. The median value is 0.15 for large firms. These debt-stock ratios are small, particularly when one considers that the stock of assets in the denominator of the ratio does not include R&D investment.[22]

Row 9 reports the ratio of secured debt to total long-term debt. Presumably, even high-tech firms have some assets (e.g., buildings) that can be pledged as security for loans. For small firms the median value of the ratio is near one. For medium firms the median is 0.70. These high ratios suggest that most loans must be secured, consistent with the evidence in Berger and Udell (1990) and Berger and Udell (2002). These ratios, together with the limited collateral value of high-tech investment, help to explain firms' low use of debt (indicated in rows 7 and 8). In contrast, for large firms the ratio of secured debt to total long-term debt is only

---

21 Compustat's measure of investment, capital spending, explicitly excludes the property, plant, and equipment of acquired companies.

22 The ratio of the stock of total debt (which includes short-term liabilities such as accounts payable in addition to long-term debt) to assets was also small. It was 0.16, 0.12, and 0.18 for small, medium, and large firms at their respective medians. The median flow of total debt, scaled by assets, was 0, 0.002, and 0.02 for small, medium, and large firms, respectively.

0.131. The sharp drop and low value of this ratio suggests that the problems associated with debt finance for high-tech investment is much smaller for large, established firms.

The final row shows that the median value of the flow of equity financing to assets is small for all size classes, ranging from 0.05 for small firms to 0.01 for large firms. Even for small firms, external equity financing is only approximately 25 per cent the size of gross cash flow.[23] At the 90th percentile, however, the ratio of equity financing to assets is 0.62 for small firms and 0.39 for medium firms. These ratios are sizable, especially for small firms, where the 90th percentile of equity financing is larger than the 90th percentile of gross cash flow. While the use of new equity by existing firms is nowhere near as large as equity issues at the time of the IPO (see the last row in Table 7.2), Table 7.4 suggests that some small firms do obtain large amounts of follow-up equity financing.[24]

In contrast to our results, Berger and Udell (2002) report that debt constitutes approximately 50 per cent of total financing for the sample of small firms discussed in his study. Their sample (and an identical sample they use in their 1998 paper) comes from the 1993 National Survey of Small Business Finances. The majority of the firms (68.4 per cent) are in business services, professional services, retail trade, and wholesale trade. Only a very small proportion of the surveyed firms are in the high-technology sector.[25] In general, information problems in service industries and in retail and wholesale trade are likely to be much less important than they are in the high-tech sector. In addition, assets in these sectors are likely to have substantially higher collateral values than the assets of a high-tech firm. The importance of collateral for small firms is apparent from the results presented by Berger and Udell (1998, Table 7.2, Section D), who report that approximately 90 per cent of debt is secured, similar to our findings in Table 7.4. Thus, a likely explanation for the low debt figures in our sample compared with Berger and Udell's is that the composition of the two samples is very different, and that high-tech firms have relatively little collateral to secure their loans.

---

[23] This result is consistent with Lerner and Merges, 1998, Table 1, who report that follow-up public equity offerings in the biotechnology industry are small in most years.

[24] We examined the new equity figures by time period (as defined in the text). There is a sharp trend in the data, with much larger figures for new equity financing in the most recent time period. This is consistent with the sharp increase over time in the size of IPOs reported in Table 7.2.

[25] Source: 1993 National Survey of Small Business Finances: Public Use Data Base Frequency Distributions (26 May 1999). The National Survey of Small Business Finances contains information about the two-digit SIC classification of sample firms. Only 3.2 per cent of the firms in the survey are in the four, two-digit SIC categories that contain the three-digit SIC categories that we use to define high-tech firms. Therefore, the number of high-tech firms in the sample must be less than 3.2 per cent of the total, and is probably substantially so.

5. Conclusions and Implications

Because of asymmetric information problems and a lack of collateral, many high-tech firms, especially small firms, are likely to face financing constraints. Adverse selection and moral hazard problems, together with financial distress, suggest that the marginal cost of debt finance may rise rapidly and potentially lead to large 'debt gaps'. For high-tech firms, new equity finance has several potential advantages over debt finance. In our panel of over 2400 US high-tech firms, we find that most small firms obtain little debt financing. The IPO, however, is typically very large relative to the existing assets of the firm and it often leads to a dramatic change in the firm's size. After going public, new equity financing remains important for some firms, but most firms appear to obtain the bulk of their financing from retained earnings. Overall, new equity finance appears to be very important to the rapid growth of high-technology firms.

The issues addressed in our research have several implications for public policy. It is likely that firms in many countries conduct too little investment in the high-tech sector compared to a benchmark model with perfect capital markets. Given the problems of debt finance outlined in section 2, together with our findings on its limited use, overlending (e.g., de Meza, 2002) is unlikely to be present in the high-tech sector. De Meza (2002) also discusses the possibility that asymmetric information can lead to too much equity financing. But as we note below, even developed countries often do not have well-developed markets for external equity finance. When there are relatively few publicly traded companies, it seems unlikely that there are socially excessive levels of external equity financing.

Venture capital, a form of external equity financing, is a market response that partially addresses the financing problems faced by new high-tech firms. The majority of venture capital in the United States is invested in the high-tech sector, where monitoring and information evaluation are important (Gompers and Lerner, 1999, Table 7.2). One role of venture capitalists is to provide start-up funding for new firms. Should a new firm reach a stage where it requires large amounts of funding, a second role of venture capitalists is to use their reputation to provide some assurance to public investors about the quality of the firm and the value of the IPO (Megginson and Weiss, 1991).[26] Given our findings on the relative size of IPOs, the certification role played by venture capitalists is likely to be important.

Lerner (2002) examines public venture capital programs as a possible public policy response to the shortage of finance faced by SMEs. An alternative policy would be for the government to supply funds to existing private venture capitalists. One advantage of this alternative is that the government would act as a limited partner and would not directly choose individual firms.[27] Other government policies rely to a greater extent on markets to efficiently allocate financial capital to firms. For example, governments can actively encourage the development of

---

26 Gompers and Lerner (1999) review the literature and provide new evidence that venture-backed firms outperform non-venture IPOs.

27 Venture capitalists who received a public subsidy might still, however, have to address the social objectives of their government partner when setting their investment strategy.

stock markets for small high-tech companies, and remove regulatory barriers to listing. In the US, low barriers to listing on the NASDAQ and the NASDAQ Small Cap increase the odds that a small high-tech firm can obtain external equity finance. The regional system of exchanges that form the recently developed Euro NM, as well as the EASDAQ and the AIM in the UK, are all examples of markets that are similar to NASDAQ in terms of their relatively low barriers to listing. These markets should aid in the development of the European high-tech sector.

Financial obstacles to entrepreneurship and to the growth of the high-tech sector have been the focus of much public policy discussion in Europe and have been identified as potential weaknesses of the EU (Bank of England, 1996; European Commission, 1998, 1999b). There is concern that a lack of venture capital (private equity) may be an important barrier to the development of the European high-tech sector. While venture capital in Europe has grown rapidly in the past few years, it is significantly smaller than in the US.[28] Venture capital in the US is also concentrated in the high-tech sector to a much larger degree than it is in Europe, and US venture capitalists focus more intensively on early-stage investments.[29] There is also continued concern that small high-technology firms in Europe have more difficulty than their US counterparts in gaining access to public equity capital. Despite efforts to lower barriers to listing, in 1997, for example, small firms raised more than seven times the amount of capital on the NASDAQ as was raised on the EASDAQ, Euro NM, and AIM combined (European Commission, 1998).

To promote the growth of small high-tech firms, we believe that European policy makers have correctly emphasized the development of markets for public equity finance and private venture capital. Debt is likely to be a poor substitute for equity. High-tech firms unable to obtain equity financing may face substantial financial barriers to entry and mobility. Our results suggest that institutional factors that affect the availability and cost of equity financing may be an important determinant of the comparative advantage of nations in the production of high-tech goods.

---

28 For example, European venture capital investment totaled 7 billion Euros in 1998 compared to 12 billion Euros in the US. (European Commission, 1999b, p. 4).

29 Over 80 per cent of US venture capital investments are directed toward information technology, biotechnology, and healthcare. These sectors account for less than 28 per cent of European private equity investment (European Commission, 1999a). Only 1.6 billion Euros were invested in early stage financing in the EU in 1998, compared to 4.5 billion Euros in the US. Early stage venture capital investment in the UK, one of Europe's leading sources for venture capital, was only six per cent as large as in the US in 1997 (HM Treasury, 1998). And although early stage investments are growing rapidly, the largest portion of venture capital investment in Europe is still devoted toward later stage investments, and in particular, management buyouts and buy-ins. For evidence on composition of UK venture capital investments, see the Bank of England (2000, p. 39) and for Europe see the European Commission (2000, pp. 4 and 5).

References

Akerlof, G.A. (1970), 'The Market for "Lemons": Quality and Uncertainly and the Market Mechanism', *Quarterly Journal of Economics*, 84, 488-500.

Asquith, P. and Mullins, D.W. (1986), 'Equity Issues and Offering Dilution', *Journal of Financial Economics*, 15, 61-89.

Bank of England (1996), *The Financing of Technology-Based Small Firms*, October.

Bank of England (2000), *Finance for Small Firms: A Seventh Report*, January.

Berger, A.N. and Udell, G.F. (1990), 'Collateral, Loan Quality, and Bank Risk', *Journal of Monetary Economics*, 25, 21-42.

Berger, A.N. and Udell, G.F. (1998), 'The Economies of Small Business Finance: The Roles of Private Equity and Debt Markets in the Financial Growth Cycle', *Journal of Banking and Finance*, 22, 613-673.

Berger, A.N. and Udell, G.F. (2002), 'Small Business Credit Availability and Relationship Lending: The Importance of Bank Organizational Structure', *The Economic Journal*, 112, F32-53.

Bernanke, B.S., Gertler, M. and Gilchrist, S. (1998), 'The Financial Accelerator in a Quantitative Business Cycle Framework', *Handbook of Macroeconomics*.

Bester, H. (1985), 'Screening vs. Rationing in Credit Markets with Imperfect Information', *American Economic Review*, 75, 850-855.

Bester, H. (1987), 'The Role of Collateral in Credit Markets with Imperfect Information', *European Economic Review*, 31, 887-899.

Bolton, P. and Freixas, X. (2000), 'Equity, Bonds and Bank Debt: Capital Structure and Financial Market Equilibrium under Asymmetric Information', *Journal of Political Economy*, 108, 324-351.

Bond, S. and Meghir, C. (1994), 'Dynamic Investment Models and the Firm's Financial Policy', *Review of Economic Studies*, 61, 197-222.

Boot, A.W.A., Thakor, A.V. and Udell, G.F. (1991), 'Secured Lending and Default Risk: Equilibrium Analysis, Policy Implications and Empirical Results', *The Economic Journal*, 101, 458-472.

Brealey, R.A. and Myers, S.C. (2000), *Principles of Corporate Finance*, Irwin/McGraw-Hill.

Calomiris, C.W., Himmelberg, C.P. and Wachtel, P. (1995), 'Commercial Paper and Corporate Finance: A Microeconomic Perspective', *Carnegie-Rochester Conference on Public Policy*, 42, 203-250.

Carpenter, R.E. and Petersen, B.C. (2000), 'Is the Growth of Small Firms Constrained by Internal Finance?', *Review of Economics and Statistics*, forthcoming.

Carpenter, R.E., Fazzari, S.M. and Petersen, B.C. (1994), 'Inventory Investment, Internal-Finance Fluctuations, and the Business Cycle', *Brookings Papers on Economic Activity*, 2:1994, 75-138.

Cornell, B. and Shapiro, A.C. (1988), 'Financing Corporate Growth', *Journal of Applied Corporate Finance*, 1, 6-22.

Cressy, R. (1995), 'Business Borrowing and Control: A Theory of Entrepreneurial Types', *Small Business Economics*, 7, 291-300.

Cressy, R. and Olofsson, C. (1997), 'European SME Financing: An Overview', *Small Business Economics*, 9, 87-96.

Cressy, R. and Toivanen, O. (1998), 'Is There Adverse Selection in the Credit Market', CSME Working Paper, University of Warwick.

de Meza, D. (2002), 'Overlending', *The Economic Journal*, 112, F17-31.

de Meza, D. and Webb, D. (1987), 'Too Much Investment: A Problem of Asymmetric Information', *Quarterly Journal of Economics*, 102, 281-292.

de Meza, D. and Webb, D. (1990), 'Risk, Adverse Selection and Capital Market Failure', *The Economic Journal*, 100, 206-14.

European Commission (1998), *Risk Capital: A Key to Job Creation in the European Union*, April.

European Commission (1999a), *Risk Capital: Implementation of the Action Plan: Proposals for Moving Forward*, October.

European Commission (1999b), *Risk Capital: A Key to Job Creation: Implementation of the Action Plan*, December.

European Commission (2000), 'Communication from the Commission to the Council and the European Parliament: Progress Report on the Risk Capital Action Plan', Brussels, 18.10.2000 COM(2000)658 final.

Fazzari, S.M. and Petersen, B.C. (1993), 'Working Capital and Fixed Investment: New Evidence on Financing Constraints', *Rand Journal of Economics*, 24, 328-342.

Fazzari, S.M., Hubbard, R.G. and Petersen, B.C. (1988), 'Financing Constraints and Corporate Investment', *Brookings Papers on Economic Activity*, 2:1988, 141-206.

Fazzari, S.M., Hubbard, R.G. and Petersen, B.C. (2000), 'Investment-Cash Flow Sensitivities are Useful: A Comment on Kaplan and Zingales', *Quarterly Journal of Economics*, 115, 695-705.

Gilchrist, S. and Himmelberg, C.P. (1995), 'Evidence on the Role of Cash Flow for Investment', *Journal of Monetary Economics*, 36, 541-572.

Gompers, P. and Lerner, J. (1999), *The Venture Capital Cycle*, The MIT Press, Cambridge, MA.

Greenwald, B.C. and Stiglitz, J.E. (1993), 'Financial Market Imperfections and Business Cycles', *Quarterly Journal of Economics*, 108, 77-114.

HM Treasury (1998), *Financing of High Technology Businesses: A Report to the Paymaster General*, November 1998.

Hall, B. (1992), 'Investment and R&D at the Firm Level: Does the Source of Financing Matter?', Department of Economics Working Paper #92-194, University of California at Berkeley.

Harhoff, D. (1998), 'Are There Financing Constraints for Innovation and Investment in German Manufacturing Firms?', *Annales d'Economie et de Statistique*, 49/50, 421-456.

Harhoff, D., Narin, F., Scherer, F.M. and Vopel, K. (1999), 'Citation Frequency and the Value of Patented Inventions', *Review of Economics and Statistics*, 511-515.

Himmelberg, C.P. and Petersen, B.C. (1994), 'R&D and Internal Finance: A Panel Study of Small Firms in High-Tech Industries', *Review of Economics and Statistics*, 38-51.

Hubbard, R. (1998), 'Capital Market Imperfections and Investment', *Journal of Economic Literature*, 36, 193-225.

Jaffee, D.M. and Russell, T. (1976), 'Imperfect Information, Uncertainty, and Credit Rationing', *Quarterly Journal of Economics*, 651-666.

Kaplan, S.N. and Zingales, L. (1997), 'Do Investment-Cash Flow Sensitivities Provide Useful Measures of Financing Constraints?', *Quarterly Journal of Economics*, 112, 169-215.

Jenkinson, T.J. (1990), 'Initial Public Offerings in the United Kingdom, the United States, and Japan', *Journal of the Japanese and International Economies*, 4, 428-499.

Jensen, M.C. and Meckling, W.H., 'Theory of the Firm: Managerial Behavior, Agency Costs and Ownership Structure', *Journal of Financial Economics*, 3, 305-360.

Lee, I., Lockhead, S., Ritter, J.R. and Zhao, Q. (1996), 'The Costs of Raising Capital', *Journal of Financial Research*, 19.

Lerner, J. (2002), 'When Bureaucrats Meet Entrepreneurs: The Design of Effective "Public Venture Capital" Programs', *The Economic Journal*, 112, F73-84.

Lerner, J. and Merges, R. (1998), 'The Control of Technology Alliances: An Empirical Analysis of the Biotechnology Industry', *Journal of Industrial Economics*, 46, 125-156.

Levin, R.C., Klevoric, A.K., Nelson, R.R. and Winter, S.G. (1987), 'Appropriating the Returns from Industrial Research and Development', *Brookings Papers on Economic Activity*, 3, 783-831.

Loughran, T. and Ritter, J.R. (1997), 'The Operating Performance of Firms Conducting Seasoned Equity Offerings', *Journal of Finance*, 52, 1823-1850.

Megginson, W.C. and Weiss, K.A. (1991), 'Venture Capital Certification in Initial Public Offerings', *Journal of Finance*, 46, 879-893.

Mansfield, E. and Wagner, S., et al. (1977), *The Production and Application of New Industrial Technology*, Norton, York.

Myers, S.C. and Majluf, N.S. (1984), 'Corporate Financing and Investment Decisions When Firms Have Information that Investors Do Not', *Journal of Financial Economics*, 13, 187-221.

Ritter, J. (1991), 'The Long-Run Performance of Initial Public Offerings', *Journal of Finance*, 46, 3-27.

Schiantarelli, F. (1995), 'Financial Constraints and Investment: A Critical Review of Methodological Issues and International Evidence', in *Is Bank Lending Important for the Transmission of Monetary Policy*, J. Peek and E. Rosengren (eds), Federal Reserve Bank of Boston, 177-214.

Stiglitz, J.E. (1985), 'Credit Markets and Capital Control', *Journal of Money, Credit and Banking*, 17, 133-152.

Stiglitz, J.E. and Weiss, A. (1981), 'Credit Rationing in Markets with Imperfect Information', *American Economic Review*, 71, 393-410.

Chapter 8

Inside the 'Magic Box': The Internet and the Growth of Small and Medium-Sized Enterprises

Giovanni Ferri, Marzio Galeotti and Ottavio Ricchi

1. Introduction

The information and communication technology (ICT) revolution is transforming both developed and emerging economies, providing a significant boost to growth. While this effect is clear for ICT specialized countries, it is not obvious through which channels ICT investment might favor growth in the other economies. The question becomes even more murky if we focus specifically on small and medium-sized enterprises (SMEs) operating in 'old economy' sectors. This is certainly the situation we face by looking at Italian SMEs.

In this chapter we make an effort to identify the channels through which access to the Internet might benefit sales growth in a sample of Italian SMEs. Specifically, we contemplate two possible avenues through which SMEs could reap such benefits. First, we consider the possibility that there is a direct positive impact on sales growth for firms that gain access to the Internet, possibly stemming from the enlargement of their market. Second, we take into account the possibility that access to the Internet exerts an indirect effect by loosening the numerous constraints to SME growth. In particular, we consider the following list: financial constraints; infrastructure bottlenecks; the intensity of R&D expenditure; constraints in the labor market.

The rest of the paper is organized as follows. Section 2 takes a snapshot of the debate on the impact of the New Economy on growth. Section 3 casts the discussion within the specific situation of the Italian economy and describes the main features and results of our sample survey to 450 Italian SMEs. Our regression analysis is presented in Section 4, while Section 5 provides some conclusions.

2. 'New Economy', Aggregate Economic Growth and the Growth of Small Firms

Innovation and information and communication technology (ICT) are playing an increasingly important role in the process of economic growth. While GDP in the

OECD countries has grown more slowly in the 1990s than in the 1980s, a few countries – including the U.S., Australia, Denmark, Ireland, the Netherlands and Norway – have experienced higher growth. In most of them total factor productivity seems to have accelerated (OECD, 2000a).

Particularly in the U.S. this acceleration in productivity has taken place in the second half of the 1990s and has been accompanied by a rapid increase in the capital stock, led by ICT investment. Moreover, while ICT producing sectors have mostly enjoyed an increase in total factor productivity (disembodied technical change), the sectors outside the computer industry have mostly experienced capital deepening (embodied technical change). Actually, most of the acceleration in productivity has taken place outside the ICT industry.

Whether or not the acceleration in productivity growth can be attributed to a technological revolution brought about by ICT has been the subject of a recent heated debate. The implications for growth without inflation, for the business cycle, for employment and for all the other relevant aspects of this 'New Economy' have been discussed by several authors, including Gordon (2000), Oliner and Sichel (2000), and Jorgenson and Stiroh (2000). The debate is still going on (Stiroh, 2001; Bailey and Lawrence, 2001).

The notion of the 'New Economy' is related to the effect that ICT has on technical progress. Enthusiasts of the New Economy observe that new technologies are bringing about a revolution with far-reaching implications for all economic activities, from production to consumption and to the exchange of goods and services. Organizational change and efficiency benefits are seen as the main aspects related to the network aspects of ICT, particularly as far as the explosive access to the Internet and the rise of electronic commerce especially among business firms. According to Mariotti (1997) key features of the 'ICT revolution' are: (i) compression of time and space. This drastically reduces the costs of transaction and of co-ordination and control of organizations; (ii) codification of knowledge. This allows transportability of knowledge at low cost, reduction in learning costs, in catching-up time, easier imitation; (iii) increased flexibility; (iv) shift toward more intangible capital; (v) transformation of big infrastructures. All big networks, transport, energy, communications, are affected by ICT; (vi) product and process innovation. In summary, the efficiency gains accruing from the use of ICT originate from the reduction in management costs, from increased possibility of delegation and from the more intense use of idiosyncratic knowledge generated in the production place (Schivardi and Trento, 2000).

It is apparent that the above aspects are especially relevant for small and medium-sized enterprises (SMEs). The developments in ICT are likely to provide new opportunities allowing the combination of the advantages of small size with network externalities.

Despite the considerations made so far, there is little evidence in other OECD countries that the use of ICT is boosting economic growth or that ICT production is having a major influence. One important reason has to do with the need of suitable data on ICT investment and appropriate quality-adjusted prices. In addition, different accounting methods complicate any attempt at international comparisons. Nevertheless, an attempt has been made by Bassanini, Scarpetta and

Visco (2000) and Daveri (2000). The first study shows a decrease in productivity growth for the main European economies; the second study documents for these countries a modest contribution to overall growth of the increase in ICT capital. These remarks apply to Italy as well.

Although better data might deliver a more encouraging picture, two aspects distinguish the U.S. experience relative to other developed countries. The first one is that there is a lag in the diffusion of ICT in continental Europe, and more markedly in Italy. The second reason is that the ICT sector is relatively small in European economies relative to the U.S. It follows that the most significant contribution to growth is to be expected from capital deepening and from improvements in sectors outside ICT. These aspects are necessarily intertwined with the size structure of enterprises in European economies. Indeed, the contribution of SMEs to employment, innovation and the overall dynamism of growing service sectors underlies trends now being characterized as part of a New Economy. SMEs play a key role in the economies of all OECD countries, especially in terms of employment. According to the OECD (2000c), these firms make up over 95 per cent of OECD enterprises and account for 60-70 per cent of total employment in most countries. Although the distribution varies across countries, the bulk of employment today is found not in manufacturing but in services, where the overwhelming majority of businesses are small firms. In fact, SMEs currently account for close to 100 per cent of firms in many service activities, such as wholesale and retail trade, hotels and restaurants. SMEs are increasingly present in technology-intensive industries such as ICT and biotechnology. At the same time, SMEs predominate in strategic business services such as computer software and information processing or human resource development. Thus, not only does ICT appear to be critical for overall economic growth, but it is also likely to affect the growth of businesses in which it is especially lively.

Understanding how firms grow, especially small firms, is an important issue which has been studied for quite some time (Brock and Evans, 1989; Acs, 1996; Sutton, 1997). The study of the determinants of firms' growth can provide important insights into the dynamics of the competitive process, strategic behavior, evolution of market structure, and even aggregate economic growth. Smaller firms have the advantage of being more flexible than larger enterprises and are often innovative in new and different ways, for example, in their approaches to management or marketing. They can be characterized as innovative in areas relating to commercialization of existing technologies, in creating or re-engineering products or services, and introducing flexible work practices. Smaller firms tend to be incremental innovators and have the ability of adapting and customizing products more to consumer needs and market demand.

The advantages of being small notwithstanding, a typical issue tackled by the literature on firm growth has been the factors that constrain firms striving to grow bigger. Several factors have been mentioned: a non-competitive environment making entry in new markets difficult; an inefficient labor market in which labor is not easily reallocated and regulation is heavy; administrative burdens and red tape; excessive and distortive taxation; relatively inefficient financial systems. The extreme difficulty or even the impossibility of raising outside capital on reasonably favorable terms has been especially a subject of much empirical analysis (see Carpenter and Petersen, 2001).

It could be argued that many of the aforementioned problems confronting SMEs – lack of financing, difficulties in accessing and exploiting technology, regulatory burdens – become more acute in a globalized, technology-driven environment, which also brings in its wake new problems such as accessing information networks and making the best use of electronic commerce. However, the New Economy is also a big opportunity for SMEs. In fact, ICT allows the advantages of small scale to be combined with economies of scale and scope through networking among firms and with other actors such as universities, research institutions, etc. The advent of Internet-based electronic commerce allows smaller firms to expand their customer base, enter new product markets and rationalize their businesses. The Internet provides the ability to overcome obstacles in infrastructure or, more generally, structural obstacles. Companies that access the Internet make use of a privileged channel for trading with other companies (B2B) and for approaching customers (B2C); at the same time they also benefit from a reduction of the fixed costs represented by compliance with bureaucracy requirements (G2B). The Internet allows the removal, at least partially, of entry barriers to foreign markets. It represents an outstanding means for promoting sales abroad and a very cheap vector of publicity – indeed, that is true for internal markets as well. The opportunity to enter more easily into the markets of different countries allows the diversification of risks and makes firms less vulnerable to economic downturns.

As argued before, one limit to firm growth is often represented by labor constraints. In this case access to more flexible forms of employment and outsourcing of some functions related to the Internet can provide companies with an efficient way of expanding their production potential without complicating excessively their working organization. Finally, an argument applies to the well-known financing constraints story. These are likely to become less stringent. Indeed, one of the most apparent aspects of the New Economy has been the increased use of the stock market as a source of financing by quoted companies; at the same time, the performance of the market has attracted more firms and freed resources for non-quoted, often medium and small-sized firms. The success of venture capital in nurturing the growth of U.S. ICT businesses have led to efforts in other countries to stimulate venture finance. The Internet and the New Economy often go hand in hand with a new management more open to innovation and more inclined to open the firms to external hands. Companies that access the Internet are also likely to find themselves in a better position by becoming more appealing to prospective investors.

All in all, despite the fact that the literature on the impact of ICT on SMEs is still scant, the arguments just offered point to the important role that the New Economy can potentially play: that of significantly lessening most of the obstacles to their growth.

3. The 'New Economy' and SMEs in Italy

3.1 The New Economy in a Productive System Specialized in the Old Economy

Three overarching aspects affect the diffusion and impact of ICT investment in Italy. First, the country does not enjoy a productive specialization in the ICT sector itself.[1] This is an important aspect since, as described above, while the positive impact of ICT investment is clear for firms operating in the ICT sector itself, the situation is not as straightforward for firms belonging to other sectors. Second, the specialization of the Italian economy is in high-quality consumer goods whose production largely depends on (often locally) specialized labor, which might potentially pose specific requirements for the application of ICT investment different than in other sectors. Third, Italy's productive system relies on small and medium-sized enterprises (SMEs) to the largest extent among G7 countries and these SMEs are often clustered in industrial districts.[2] Again, as argued above, the application of ICT investment for SMEs raises issues certainly different than for large companies.

Schivardi and Trento (2000) have recently addressed the above issues for the Italian economy. As regards the high reliance on SMEs, they remark that we can expect two different effects. On one hand, the small size of firms may limit the pace of ICT adoption. On the other hand, however, the ICT revolution lowers the incentives to vertical integration in the business sector and allows greater flexibility in the organization of production across separate units, thus potentially favoring SMEs' competitiveness. In addition, Schivardi and Trento (2000) argue that Italy's specialization in specific high-quality consumer good sectors limits the productivity gains that can be obtained through ICT investment. More generally, they observe that Italy's specialization has two drawbacks. First, it achieves a low score in terms of the factors that (according to Helpman and Trajtenberg, 1998) should promote the ICT revolution. Second, the lack of vicinity between ICT producing firms (outside of Italy) and ICT adopting firms (in Italy) may limit the extent of complementary innovation. On the opposite side, to the extent that the diffusion of ICT reduces transaction costs (Williamson, 1975) and facilitates the working of firms' networks, the competitiveness of industrial districts would be promoted. Finally, the availability of ICT-specific human capital, infrastructure (Freeman, 1982) and finance (Rajan and Zingales, 1998) could also be binding to reap productivity gains in Italy.

Beside these arguments, however, our view is that an additional ICT effect for SMEs should not be downplayed: namely, the fact that access to the Internet and e-commerce may be an effective way for SMEs to expand their market. Indeed, the cost of gaining access to foreign retail markets may be incommensurably lowered for SMEs essentially thanks to the ICT revolution. Cursory evidence tells

---

[1] For instance, OECD (2001) shows that the share of computer sales over total merchandise exports is approximately two per cent for Italy, by far the smallest among G7 countries.

[2] See, for instance, Pagano and Schivardi (2000) on the first issue and Brusco and Paba (2001) on the second.

us that this is happening in practice. Furthermore, the avenue we will take below is to ascertain whether ICT use also achieves an indirect effect on SMEs' potential by helping relax some of the numerous constraints on their growth. Should our conjecture turn out to be true, then the impact of ICT could not be assessed simply in terms of productivity. Just to give an example, in their study on French firm level data Greenan, Mairesse and Topiol-Bensaid (2001) reach the main time series finding that the intensity of ICT investment is negatively related to the share of blue-collar workers. In cases where it was difficult for SMEs to hire blue-collar workers, this means that the reorganization of production implied by ICT investment has relaxed that constraint.

All in all, in view of the above, the expectation is that the ICT revolution might be lagging in Italy. But what is the actual situation as to the adoption of ICT in Italy *vis-à-vis* other European countries? According to OECD (2000b), the percentage of employees using e-commerce-enabling technologies is below 35 per cent in Italy, the minimum value among G7 countries and just above half of what is recorded in the USA, Canada, the UK and Japan. Coppel (2000) reports for Italy very low values for two internationally comparable indicators of the diffusion of e-commerce. Italy counts eleven secure servers per million inhabitants and nine Internet hosts per thousand inhabitants, *vis-à-vis* 60 and 54 respectively for the OECD average and *vis-à-vis* 56 and 47 respectively for the G7 countries' average.

And what is the specific situation for SMEs? Eurostat (2000) reports that some 35 per cent of Italian SMEs have access to the Internet, which compares with an average of 42 per cent throughout the entire EU. Percentages are higher for Nordic countries: Denmark, Finland, Norway and Sweden all approach 60 per cent or reach higher than that. Thus, we do have some confirmation that the ICT revolution is lagging in Italy's SMEs.

In any event, Italy being laggard or not, now we want to try to examine whether the adoption of ICT has an impact on individual SMEs' growth. We will accomplish this with the database that we gathered via a sample survey questionnaire that it is now time to describe.

3.2 Description of the Sample and of the Main Survey Results

In the summer of 2000, we interviewed 450 Italian SMEs with between 5 and 50 employees. In addition, our sample has the following characteristics. First, half of the firms have less than 16 employees while the other half have more than 15 employees. This was chosen in order to have an adequate representation for firms both below and above the threshold for application of the Laborer Statute (*Statuto dei lavoratori*), raising the extent of labor protection. Second, half of the firms in the sample are incorporated as limited liability companies (*Società a responsabilità limitata*) while the other half are joint stock companies (*Società per azioni*). Third, 80 per cent of the firms belong to the manufacturing sector, while the rest are in the service sector. Fourth, the sample shares are more or less equally distributed between the four geographic areas into which Italy may be subdivided (Northwest, Northeast, Centre, South Islands).

Average growth of sales over the three-year period (1997-99) is 17.4 per cent. As a ratio to sales our firms export a significant share (19.2 per cent) and spend non-negligible amounts on R&D (5.4 per cent). 18.9 per cent of our firms have education agreements with schools and/or universities; 29.1 per cent belong to industrial districts and 24.4 per cent participate in a *Consorzio fidi*, business consortia offering joint insurance to facilitate member firms' access to bank credit. The paramount role of family control on our firms is testified by the fact that only in 23.1 per cent of the cases are managers not also members of the family who owns the firm.

In the first part of the questionnaire[3] we directly asked SMEs which ones among the possible constraints to firm growth they perceived as most binding. In particular, we listed the following possible constraints: (i) access and cost of external financial resources; (ii) labor market regulation and ability to hire skilled employees; (iii) the tax system; (iv) relationship with local and central Public Administrations; (v) infrastructure quality.

The area where SMEs in our sample find the most binding constraints to growth is the labor market. 30.5 per cent of the firms find relevant non-price constraints there: 14.9 per cent lament the inadequate flexibility of the labor market (in particular the difficulty to fire); 9.8 per cent deplore the insufficient supply of skilled workers and only 5.8 per cent point out that the labor cost is too high. The second most binding constraint is the tax system (28.8 per cent), be it because of excessive tax rates or because of too high social contributions on labor. The third most binding constraint to growth (20.4 per cent of the firms) is bureaucracy of local and central Public Administrations. The next constraint is the availability of adequate external financial resources (19.6 per cent), stemming from difficulties in obtaining financing, lack of flexibility by banks, the high cost of bank loans: reportedly, the main problem comes from the high cost of bank loans and the large collateral required by banks. Finally, 6.0 per cent of the SMEs in our sample lament the lack of adequate infrastructure and/or supply of business services as the chief constraint to growth.

Even before we venture into our regression analysis, we can show descriptively that those SMEs with higher sales growth tend to have special features with respect to potential constraints. First, more often than the others, these firms either lament problems in securing skilled workers or else try to circumvent labor market rigidity via short-term hiring (*lavoro interinale*). Second, more often than the others, these firms have moved to reduce financial outlays opening up to capital injections (e.g. through venture capital). Third, more often than the others, these firms point out inadequate infrastructure. Fourth, these firms tend to have higher R&D expenses than the others. Figure 8.1 looks at these indicators separately for high-growth firms (the top quartile in terms of sales growth) and for low-growth firms (the bottom quartile in terms of sales growth).

3 The questionnaire is available upon request to the authors.

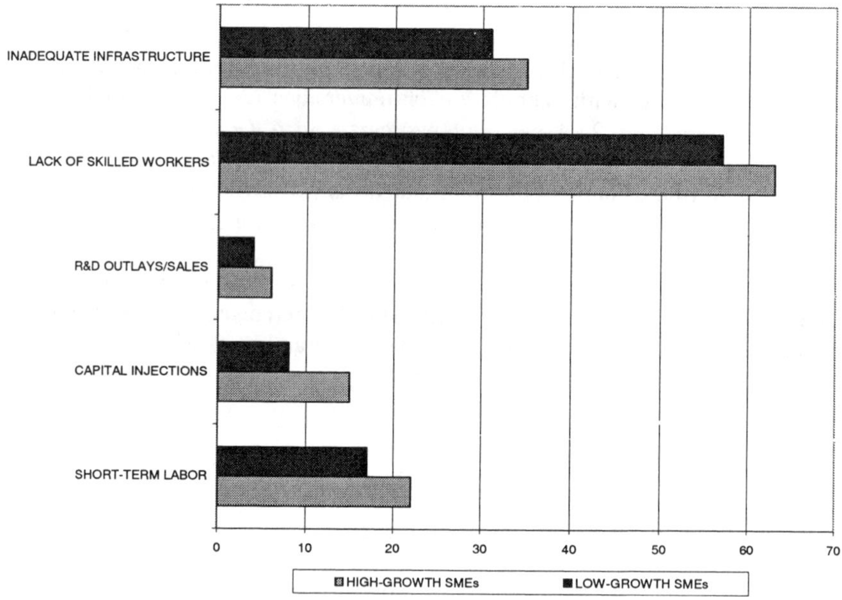

Figure 8.1 Features of High-Growth and Low-Growth Firms (percentages)

In the second part of the questionnaire we guided firms to reveal where they stood in terms of the adoption of ICT, namely whether and how: (i) they operate their own Internet site; (ii) they effectively run e-commerce business.

Our first remark is that, in spite of the small firm-size in our sample (less than 50 employees), the use of Internet and e-commerce is quite widespread. Sixty per cent of our SMEs already have their own Internet website and 70 per cent of the remaining state they intend to open up their website very soon.[4] As to the resources employed by our SMEs to set up their website, the sample is split in half between those firms that use internal resources and those that go for outsourcing. Furthermore, some 24 per cent of the entire sample (not just of the 60 per cent that already have their own Internet website) already run e-commerce business and 47 per cent of the remaining firms intend to start such an operation in the near future. Finally, consistently with our *a priori* that SMEs find the Internet most attractive to gain access to larger/further away markets, we find that some 60 per cent of those

---

4 Our figures appear consistent with those obtained by the Italian Industrialists Association (Centro Studi Confindustria-Doxa, 2001) in another survey questionnaire to Italian SMEs run in February 2001. Specifically, referring to a sample of SMEs larger-sized on average (their sample includes firms up to 250 employees) they find that 79 per cent of the firms already have their own Internet website. On the other hand, our figures are higher than those reported for Italy in Eurostat (2000), likely as a result of the passage of more than two years between their survey and our survey.

SMEs already running e-commerce use this business to sell their output and claim the largest benefit from lower trading cost. All of this can be grasped from Figure 8.2. In Figure 8.2 the percentages of firms 'have website', 'will have website', 'do e-commerce' and 'will do e-commerce' are calculated over the total sample; the percentages of firms 'sell own output' and 'lower trading cost' are calculated over the sub-sample of firms 'do e-commerce' that were asked to report, respectively, the main use of e-commerce and the main benefit they reap from it.

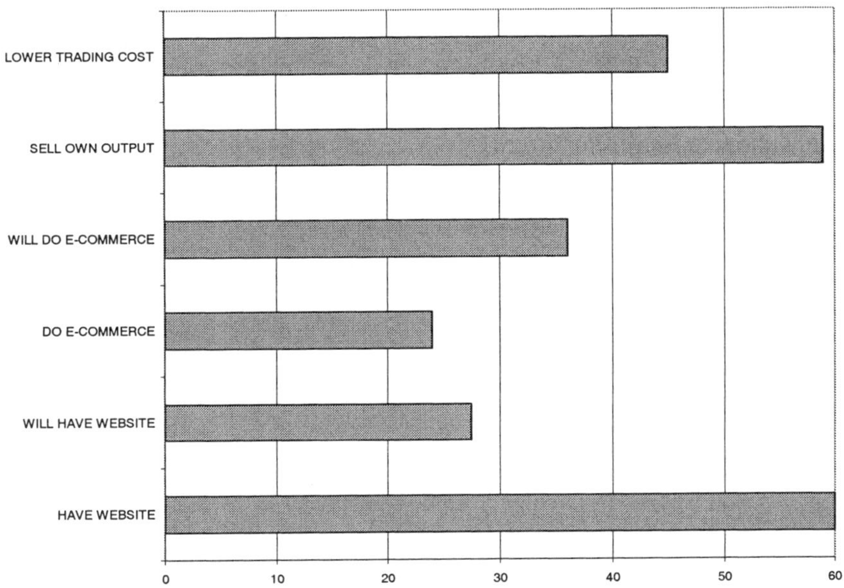

Figure 8.2 Firms' Features as to Internet and E-commerce (percentages)

4. The Empirical Analysis

In the econometric analysis we follow a two-step approach. The first set of regressions intends to ascertain to what extent the constraints that were highlighted in the theoretical sections are related to firms' sales growth. In the second set of regressions we test whether the intensity of the constraints is affected by access to the Internet/e-commerce. We proceed in two ways: (i) to start with, the sales growth analysis is enhanced by allowing for the impact of e-commerce and the Internet; (ii) secondly, we turn our attention to the constraints that affect growth and consider them as dependent variables; in this case the coefficients related to Internet can be interpreted as the impact on the constraints (i.e. the ability to loosen them). By looking separately at point (i) and point (ii) we provide, respectively, a measure of the direct and indirect impact of the New Economy on SME performance.

Table 8.1 Sales Growth Regressions *Without* Internet/E-commerce

	ALL	LT16	MT15	SRL	SPA
C	7.840	11.006	3.558	8.464	6.813
	(1.070)	(0.838)	(0.575)	(0.571)	(1.358)
RUQ	9.353	12.969	2.465	15.124	1.547
	(2.655)	(2.135)	(0.741)	(2.261)	(0.577)
LAVINT	8.564	19.948	0.941	17.155	3.705
	(2.096)	(2.409)	(0.275)	(1.883)	(1.358)
INFR	1.497	-2.999	6.330	4.978	-5.091
	(0.388)	(-0.43)	(1.767)	(0.685)	(-1.65)
VENTURE_CAPITAL	9.290	10.111	9.892	16.204	-2.462
	(2.058)	(1.317)	(2.334)	(1.926)	(-0.68)
TASSI	-5.734	-13.193	2.157	-10.468	-1.233
	(-1.53)	(-2.01)	(0.619)	(-1.46)	(-0.44)
CESSIONE_QUOTE	15.322	22.455	1.096	25.057	9.986
	(2.603)	(2.239)	(0.192)	(2.097)	(2.324)
CONGIUNTURALE	-3.536	-3.039	-7.196	-7.041	-4.922
	(-0.70)	(-0.34)	(-1.62)	(-0.61)	(-1.52)
RES	0.343	-0.422	0.946	-0.162	0.894
	(1.349)	(-0.93)	(3.937)	(-0.33)	(4.631)
EXPORT	-0.086	-0.115	-0.064	-0.072	-0.099
	(-1.34)	(-0.92)	(-1.19)	(-0.56)	(-2.14)
A_COMUNE	2.067	2.366	1.776	2.430	0.134
	(1.540)	(1.066)	(1.337)	(1.012)	(0.125)
FUNFIN	3.906	-0.872	4.702	6.351	-0.881
	(1.082)	(-0.13)	(1.318)	(0.910)	(-0.31)
TIPO_SPA	-6.617	-5.463	-6.020		
	(-1.56)	(-0.76)	(-1.47)		
DIP01	-1.951			-1.802	-1.392
	(-0.50)			(-0.23)	(-0.49)
SUD+ISOLE	12.390	20.042	-0.010	7.795	20.583
	(2.357)	(2.222)	(-0.00)	(0.723)	(4.945)
CENTRO	3.164	8.863	0.770	-2.640	4.431
	(0.588)	(0.928)	(0.157)	(-0.24)	(0.993)
NORD_EST	-1.347	-3.849	0.512	-8.736	0.682
	(-0.28)	(-0.40)	(0.135)	(-0.64)	(0.239)
SERV	11.044	12.293	8.196	16.717	5.383
	(2.328)	(1.695)	(1.484)	(2.147)	(1.210)
PEM	-5.209	-5.953	-3.346	-4.382	-0.521
	(-1.33)	(-0.82)	(-0.96)	(-0.58)	(-0.17)
DISTRETTI	-7.832	-13.694	-1.018	-15.646	-1.614
	(-2.05)	(-1.93)	(-0.30)	(-2.04)	(-0.57)
CONFIDI	-7.871	-14.955	-2.595	-16.369	-1.358
	(-1.88)	(-1.73)	(-0.75)	(-1.96)	(-0.44)
R-squared	0.208	0.269	0.244	0.232	0.340
F-statistic	3.863	2.711	2.306	2.109	3.886
Prob(F-statistic)	0.000	0.000	0.003	0.008	0.000

The output regressions relate the sales growth of the companies (more precisely the average growth of the period 1997-1999) to a number of explanatory variables divided into two main groups: a group that includes the constraints to growth for the firms and a set of control variables bound to capture the growth performance irrespectively of the acting constraints.

The same independent variables specification is applied to a general equation, that includes all the companies surveyed, as well as to two pairs of additional restricted samples. The two breakdowns refer to the company size (up to 15 workers and more than 15 workers) and to the company title (limited liability or joint-stock). The equations are estimated using ordinary least squares and are reported in Table 8.1.

The regressions results show that most of the constraints identified in section 3.2 have a significant coefficient and, in general, a sign in line with our *a priori*. Concerning the labor market constraints, we find that the variables that signal difficulties in securing skilled labor (RUQ) and the utilization of short-term hiring (LAVINT) are generally significant across all equations and characterized by a positive sign. This finding confirms that high-growth companies will generally face labor market constraints more than low-growth companies. Interestingly, when the sample is broken down by company size, the temporary hiring variable is significant only for companies up to 15 workers. This provides indirect evidence that small companies, when in need of increasing the labor input, are reluctant to overtake the 15 workers threshold, implying a higher degree of employment protection legislation in Italy.

The conveyance of control stakes to third parties (CESSIONE_QUOTE) and the venture capital variable are, as expected, associated to dynamic companies, i.e. they have a positive sign. Venture capital is not significant for the less-than-16 (LT16) restricted sample. This is compatible with the notion that venture capital is generally not involved with very small companies. Financial constraints are represented by the variable (TASSI), a binary variable that takes the value 1 for companies stating that their main financial problem is represented by the loan rate level. This variable takes a negative value, confirming that high-growth companies will face less severe credit constraints. The variable is significant in particular in the LT16 sample; also this result is not surprising as financial constraints are often found to decrease with the size of the company. Lack of adequate infrastructure (INFR) is generally found not to be significant.

The dimensional issue becomes very relevant in the case of R&D expenditure (RES). R&D as a proportion of companies gross sales is associated with high growth in the MT15 sample.

Amongst the control variables we find that companies from the South have enjoyed a higher growth in the last three years. Finally, the variables DISTRETTI and CONFIDI often have a negative sign. It is quite difficult to interpret these findings. It might perhaps be argued that our data suggest in recent years the most dynamic companies are developing outside the areas that 'traditionally' represented the core of the 'made in Italy', where DISTRETTI and CONFIDI run high.

The second part of the empirical analysis has the aim of ascertaining the impact of the New Economy on companies' performance.

Table 8.2 Sales Growth Regressions *With* Internet/E-commerce

	ALL	LT16	MT15	SRL	SPA
C	6.406	7.478	7.378	4.059	6.601
	(0.871)	(0.568)	(1.149)	(0.267)	(1.307)
RUQ	9.482	12.291	3.264	15.289	1.204
	(2.669)	(2.027)	(0.972)	(2.245)	(0.438)
LAVINT	7.854	19.314	2.103	17.030	3.193
	(1.911)	(2.351)	(0.605)	(1.824)	(1.121)
INFR	2.209	-1.788	6.356	6.817	-5.125
	(0.571)	(-0.25)	(1.769)	(0.915)	(-1.62)
VENTURE_CAPITAL	8.793	9.487	10.784	14.061	-2.522
	(1.944)	(1.245)	(2.529)	(1.633)	(-0.69)
TASSI	-5.752	-12.063	2.118	-9.391	-1.476
	(-1.53)	(-1.85)	(0.602)	(-1.28)	(-0.53)
CESSIONE_QUOTE	14.187	17.012	0.809	19.902	10.364
	(2.405)	(1.664)	(0.142)	(1.594)	(2.393)
CONGIUNTURALE	-3.469	-4.590	-6.938	-7.301	-5.104
	(-0.69)	(-0.52)	(-1.56)	(-0.63)	(-1.57)
RES	0.265	-0.521	0.959	-0.187	0.836
	(1.029)	(-1.16)	(3.862)	(-0.38)	(4.113)
EXPORT	-0.097	-0.166	-0.055	-0.082	-0.107
	(-1.49)	(-1.32)	(-1.01)	(-0.63)	(-2.26)
A_COMUNE	1.842	1.720	1.853	2.240	0.047
	(1.368)	(0.777)	(1.401)	(0.923)	(0.044)
FUNFIN	4.520	-0.299	4.201	6.845	-0.772
	(1.248)	(-0.04)	(1.175)	(0.969)	(-0.27)
TIPO_SPA	-6.595	-5.544	-6.090		
	(-1.55)	(-0.77)	(-1.49)		
DIP01	-2.475			-3.516	-1.735
	(-0.63)			(-0.43)	(-0.60)
SUD+ISOLE	13.158	20.599	0.558	9.577	20.632
	(2.500)	(2.307)	(0.108)	(0.880)	(4.930)
CENTRO	3.097	8.231	1.266	-1.959	4.182
	(0.575)	(0.871)	(0.259)	(-0.17)	(0.932)
NORD_EST	-1.205	-3.206	1.282	-7.209	0.754
	(-0.25)	(-0.33)	(0.337)	(-0.52)	(0.262)
SERV	10.641	11.917	9.194	15.966	4.960
	(2.235)	(1.656)	(1.643)	(2.030)	(1.101)
PEM	-5.112	-5.931	-3.122	-5.480	-0.465
	(-1.31)	(-0.82)	(-0.90)	(-0.72)	(-0.15)
DISTRETTI	-7.700	-13.811	-1.071	-14.781	-1.564
	(-2.02)	(-1.97)	(-0.32)	(-1.91)	(-0.55)
CONFIDI	-6.979	-14.620	-2.621	-15.760	-1.028
	(-1.65)	(-1.69)	(-0.76)	(-1.85)	(-0.33)
INTERNET	-0.104	8.202	-7.491	4.594	1.037
	(-0.02)	(1.260)	(-2.02)	(0.607)	(0.336)
E_COMMERCE	8.436	10.574	0.584	9.164	2.458
	(2.030)	(1.342)	(0.160)	(1.082)	(0.787)
R-squared	0.219	0.295	0.268	0.244	0.345
F-statistic	3.729	2.750	2.318	1.994	3.537
Prob (F-statistic)	0.000	0.000	0.002	0.010	0.000

Table 8.2 reports the results of a re-run of the previous regression with the addition of two variables indicating, respectively, that the firm has an Internet website and that it does e-commerce. Previously found results do not undergo qualitative/sizable changes. Concerning the newly introduced variables, E-COMMERCE and INTERNET, they are significant respectively in the general specification with a positive sign and the MT15 sub-sample (with a negative coefficient). In all, it is difficult to identify a direct correlation between the New Economy variables and sales growth.

The previous set of regressions led to quite ambiguous and indecisive results; therefore we also look for possible indirect effects of INTERNET/E-COMMERCE.

This is achieved by running regressions that have the most relevant constraints (EXPORT RES LAVINT RUQ and TASSI) as, in turn, dependent variables (see Table 8.3). The set of regressors includes a number of Internet-related variables; namely we add to INTERNET and E-COMMERCE the intention to do e-commerce (INTENZ_E_COMMERCE), and the use of Internet for B2B and B2C. The New Economy variables can act in two directions: we expect them mostly to loosen constraints; however, it is conceivable that in some circumstances constraints will be made more binding.

Additional variables that can interact with constraints are also added. FINANZIAMENTI takes the value 1 for companies that in the last three years got access to government-based financing programs; SCORP_INC is also binomial and indicates the companies that recently underwent the process of M&A; finally COLLEG_AZ indicates companies that have shareholding links with other companies.

The infrastructure constraint, which was not found to be significant in the sales growth regressions, is dropped, but is replaced in the set of explanatory variables by the modality which most frequently associated with infrastructure constraints, namely the transport system.

We find that the New Economy plays a relevant role in determining the export performance; the regression coefficient tell us, for instance, that companies with an Internet site have a higher export share (as a percentage of their gross output) of approximately seven per cent. B2C is found to have some impact on the R&D expenditure; it is possible that companies that sell their product via the Internet have a higher innovation content. B2C also seems to reduce the likelihood that companies meet financial constraints; however, e-commerce has a positive (even if less significant) sign. Again the Internet variables' impact on financial constraints, in this case, seems to pass mainly through overall effects on cash-flows.

The evidence of the impact of the Internet on labor constraints is mixed. Whilst the use of temporary work is seemingly not affected, in the lack of skilled labor regressions (these regressions are no longer OLS but probit) several Internet variables are triggered. In the latter the combined effect of the Internet and e-commerce leads to a reduction of the probability of facing a skilled labor shortage; however, at the same time the choice of going B2C brings about – on average – a tightening of the constraint.

The labor shortage equation is probably the one that offers a better story if read jointly with the initial set of regressions. If we look at the complete sample, there is some evidence that the New Economy boosts company growth. Considering that high output growth goes hand in hand with a shortage of skilled labor it is possible that at times the New Economy tightens this constraint.

Table 8.3 Regressions Estimating the Impact of Internet/E-commerce on the Constraints

	EXPORT	RES	LAVINT probit	RUQ probit	TASSI probit
C	10.420	6.199	-1.154	-0.113	-0.038
	(1.583)	(3.487)	(-3.12)	(-0.35)	(-0.11)
FATTURATO	-0.056	0.015	0.006	0.006	-0.005
	(-1.18)	(1.154)	(2.181)	(2.344)	(-1.65)
INFR_TRASPORTI	-5.476	-1.580	0.333	0.081	-0.223
	(-1.59)	(-1.66)	(1.657)	(0.465)	(-1.25)
CONGIUNTURALE	-1.587	-0.283	-0.105	0.023	0.262
	(-0.36)	(-0.24)	(-0.43)	(0.109)	(1.260)
A_COMUNE	0.576	-0.231	0.030	-0.017	0.002
	(0.514)	(-0.77)	(0.457)	(-0.31)	(0.029)
FUNFIN	3.235	-0.161	-0.153	0.000	-0.009
	(1.069)	(-0.19)	(-0.89)	(0.001)	(-0.05)
TIPO_SPA	0.708	-0.182	0.116	-0.035	-0.161
	(0.194)	(-0.18)	(0.554)	(-0.19)	(-0.84)
SUD+ISOLE	-1.433	-0.436	-1.087	-0.379	0.147
	(-0.32)	(-0.36)	(-4.03)	(-1.73)	(0.656)
CENTRO	7.858	-0.396	-0.400	-0.252	-0.046
	(1.734)	(-0.32)	(-1.59)	(-1.10)	(-0.19)
NORD_EST	3.285	-0.831	0.031	0.128	0.003
	(0.822)	(-0.77)	(0.152)	(0.617)	(0.012)
PEM	-2.718	0.245	-0.074	0.002	-0.062
	(-0.83)	(0.276)	(-0.39)	(0.010)	(-0.37)
DISTRETTI	-1.108	0.596	0.177	0.306	-0.219
	(-0.35)	(0.697)	(1.005)	(1.893)	(-1.32)
CONFIDI	-1.762	2.011	0.045	0.085	0.050
	(-0.50)	(2.191)	(0.238)	(0.490)	(0.283)
NUM_DIP	0.146	-0.048	0.006	0.009	0.018
	(0.707)	(-0.86)	(0.590)	(0.871)	(1.678)
DIP01	3.315	-0.043	-0.002	-0.232	-0.314
	(0.678)	(-0.03)	(-0.00)	(-0.93)	(-1.19)
SERV	-5.356	-0.331	-0.669	-0.471	0.040
	(-1.29)	(0.30)	(-2.30)	(-2.34)	(0.194)
INTERNET	7.750	0.860	0.137	0.360	-0.155
	(2.409)	(0.991)	(0.732)	(2.282)	(-0.94)
E_COMMERCE	-2.156	-0.261	-0.548	-1.140	0.655
	(-0.26)	(-0.12)	(-1.23)	(-2.81)	(1.680)
INTENZ_E_COMM	5.624	0.002	-0.078	0.129	-0.245
	(1.689)	(0.002)	(-0.40)	(0.785)	(-1.44)
B2B	-2.392	0.572	0.336	0.151	0.009
	(-0.35)	(0.311)	(0.956)	(0.452)	(0.026)
B2C	12.438	3.400	0.551	1.261	-0.786
	(1.665)	(1.719)	(1.360)	(3.391)	(-2.21)

FINANZIAMENTI	-3.044	-0.739	0.436	0.160	-0.321
	(-0.95)	(-0.86)	(2.472)	(1.001)	(-1.93)
SCORP_INC	2.749	2.053	0.029	0.324	-0.835
	(0.450)	(1.218)	(0.082)	(0.978)	(-2.00)
COLLEG_AZ	4.395	0.366	0.431	0.194	-0.220
	(0.918)	(0.295)	(1.760)	(0.786)	(-0.84)
R-squared/McFadden R2	0.136	0.088	0.160	0.102	0.065
F-statistic/LR statistic	2.213	1.264	64.448	51.191	29.941
Prob(F-statistic) (LR – stat)	0.001	0.190	0.000	0.000	0.151

5. Conclusions

In this chapter we gave a contribution to the understanding of how the 'magic' of the Internet may affect sales growth at small and medium-sized enterprises (SMEs). Specifically, we considered two possible avenues for such an effect. First, we could have a direct effect on sales growth. Second, we conjectured that access to the Internet may also exert an indirect positive effect on SME growth by relaxing some of the numerous constraints affecting SMEs. In particular, we focused on the following direct or indirect indicators of constraints to SME growth: (i) financial constraints; (ii) infrastructure bottlenecks; (iii) intensity of R&D expenditure; (iv) constraints in the labor market.

The empirical part of the paper used a database appropriately constructed via a sample survey of 450 Italian SMEs. We took two steps. First, we searched for direct effects of the Internet/e-commerce on firms' sales growth, alongside identifying indirect indicators of constraints also affecting growth. Second, we tested whether the intensity of these constraints is affected by firms' access to the the Internet/e-commerce. Our overall findings are as follows: (i) it is difficult to identify a direct impact of the Internet/e-commerce on firms' sales growth; (ii) generally, our indirect indicators of constraints limit growth; (iii) constraints to SME growth are weaker for those firms active on the Internet/e-commerce. In all, our evidence supports the commonly held view that ICT investment favors SME growth, but this is achieved through an indirect rather than a direct route.

References

Acs, Z. (1996), *Small Firms and Economic Growth*, Vermont: Edward Elgar.

Bailey, M.N. and Lawrence, R.Z. (2001), 'Do We Have a New E-Conomy?', National Bureau of Economic Research Working Paper No. 8243.

Bassanini, A., Scarpetta, S. and Visco, I. (2000), 'Knowledge, Technology and Economic Growth: Recent Evidence from OECD Countries', *OECD Economics Department Working Paper*, 259.

Brock, W.A. and Evans, D.S. (1989), 'Small Business Economics', *Small Business Economics*, 1, 7-20.

Brusco, S. and Paba, S. (2001), 'Towards a History of Italian Industrial Districts from the End of World War II to the Nineties', University of Modena, mimeo.

Carpenter, R.E. and Petersen, B.C. (2001), 'Is the Growth of Small Firms Constrained by Internal Finance?', forthcoming *Review of Economics and Statistics*.

Centro Studi Confindustria (2001), 'Indagine sulle piccole imprese italiane', Rome.

Coppel, J. (2000), 'E-Commerce: Impacts and Policy Challenges', OECD Economics Department Working Paper No. 252.

Daveri, F. (2000), 'Is Growth an Information Techology Story in Europe too?, mimeo università di Parma.

Eurostat (2000), *The European Observatory for SMEs – Sixth Report*, Brussels: European Commission.

Freeman, C. (1982), *The Economics of Industrial Innovation*, 2nd rev. ed., London: Pinter.

Gordon, R.J. (2000), 'Does the "New Economy" Measure Up to the Great Inventions of the Past?', *Journal of Economic Perspectives*, 14, 49-74.

Greenan, N., Mairesse, J. and Topiol-Bensaid, A. (2001), 'Information Technology and R&D Impacts on Productivity and Skills: Looking for Correlations on French Firm Level Data', National Bureau of Economic Research Working Paper No. 8075.

Helpman, E. and Trajtenberg, M. (1998), 'Diffusion of General Purpose Technologies', in Helpman, E. (ed.), *General Purpose Technologies and Economic Growth*, Cambridge: MIT Press.

Jorgenson, D.W. and Stiroh, K.J. (2000), 'Raising the Speed Limit: U.S. Economic Growth in the Information Age', *Brookings Papers on Economic Activity*, 1, 125-211.

Mariotti, S. (1997), 'Il paradigma tecnologico emergente', in P. Ciocca (ed.), *Disoccupazione di fine secolo. Studi e proposte per l'Europa*, Torino: Boringhieri.

OECD (2000a), *A New Economy? The Changing Role of Innovation and Information Technology in Growth*, Paris.

OECD (2000b), *Information Technology Outlook 2000. ICTs, E-commerce and the Information Economy*, Paris.

OECD (2000c), *Small and Medium Enterprise Outlook*, Paris.

OECD (2001), *Economic Outlook 2001*, Paris.

Oliner, S.D. and Sichel, D.E. (2000), 'The Resurgence of Growth in the Late 1990s: Is Information Technology the Story?', *Journal of Economic Perspectives*, 14, 3-22.

Pagano, P. and Schivardi, F. (2000), 'Firm Size Distribution and Growth', Working Paper, Bank of Italy.

Rajan, R. and Zingales, L. (1998), 'Financial Dependence and Growth', *American Economic Review*, 88, 559-86.

Schivardi, F. and Trento, S. (2000), 'La *nuova economia*: alcune implicazioni di politica economica', paper presented at the XLI Annual Meeting of the Italian Economist Society, Cagliari, 26-28 October.

Stiroh, K.J. (2001), 'What Drives Productivity Growth?', Federal Reserve Bank of New York Economic Policy Review, March.

Sutton, J. (1997), 'Gibrat's Legacy', *Journal of Economic Literature*, 35, 20-49.

Williamson, O.E. (1975), *Markets and Hierarchies: Analysis and Anti-trust Implications*, New York: The Free Press.

Index